Hiking the

SOUTHWEST'S
CANYON COUNTRY

Hiking the
SOUTHWEST'S
CANYON COUNTRY

Sandra Hinchman

The Mountaineers/Seattle

The Mountaineers: Organized 1906 ". . . to explore, study, preserve, and enjoy the natural beauty of the outdoors."

4 3 2 1 0
5 4 3 2 1

Published by The Mountaineers
306 Second Avenue West, Seattle, Washington 98119

Published simultaneously in Canada by Douglas & McIntyre,
Ltd., 1615 Venables Street, Vancouver, B.C. V5L 2H1

Manufactured in the United States of America

Edited by Joan C. Gregory
Maps by Hannah Hinchman
Cover photograph by Sandra Hinchman
All other photographs by the author
Cover design by Betty Watson
Book design and layout by Barbara Bash
Frontispiece: The North Fork of the Virgin River, Utah, above the Narrows.
Page 5: Tukuhnikiyats Arch frames the La Sal Mountains, Utah.

Library of Congress Cataloging-in-Publication Data

Hinchman, Sandra, 1950–
    Hiking the southwest's canyon country / Sandra Hinchman.
        p. cm.
    Includes bibliographical references and index.
    ISBN 0-89886-208-6
    1. Hiking—Southwest, New—Guide-books. 2. Southwest, New—
Description and travel—1981—Guide-books. I. Mountaineers
(Society) II. Title.
GV199.42.S68H56   1990   90-42929
917.9—dc20   CIP

To Lew, my first and favorite hiking partner,
and our little "goblin," Bryce

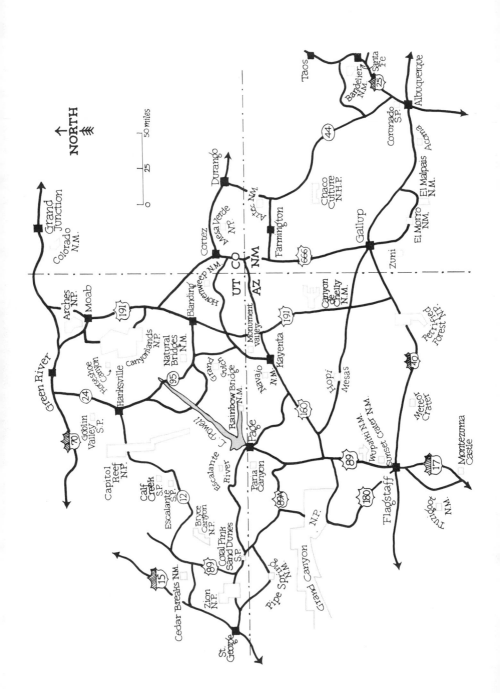

CONTENTS

PREFACE

When my husband and I began traveling in the Southwest in 1974, we were long on enthusiasm but short on experience. Although Lew had hiked and camped in California's Sierra Nevada range, I was new not only to backpacking but to exercise as well; being "in shape" was not even a concept for me. We had little sense of what equipment to buy, how to select a trail equal to our abilities, or how much ground we could cover each day. For our first trip in the desert, we hiked to the bottom of the Grand Canyon on a sweltering summer afternoon wearing stiff new boots and carrying everything we could squeeze into our packs. By the time we returned to the rim the next morning, I was suffering from sunburn, blisters, heat exhaustion, and muscle cramps. This fiasco convinced me that backpacking was sheer lunacy. But the irresistible lure of the desert, combined with my husband's dogged refusal to give up on me, convinced me to try again—on a more realistic scale. Eventually, the desert insinuated itself into my soul, becoming a vital part of the way I define myself. Although I have lived in the East all my life, it is the desert that feels most like home.

Over a decade later, I set out to write this guide to Southwestern camping, hiking, and exploring in the hope that others might profit from both our mistakes and our successes. We completed nearly every trip in this book during our summer vacations. Although desert travel is easier and more enjoyable in the spring or fall, when temperatures are not so extreme, summer is the season when most people can take time off. Therefore I have written this book with summer travelers in mind—those willing to brave the heat for two or three weeks in order to explore the Southwest's unforgettable canyon country.

In writing a guidebook, one risks bringing to an area people who will love that area to death, transforming it from the pristine and wondrous world one knew into the kind of crowded, littered, trampled-down place one had hoped to escape. But I am gambling that people who appreciate the Southwest will work in its behalf: writing letters to government personnel, joining organizations that protect wild places, or simply encouraging friends to experience nature's beauty and majesty. In recent years, the high desert has been beleaguered by proposals for constructing dams, power plants and incinerators, nuclear waste dumps, and other assorted horrors. If increased tourism can create a larger constituency in opposition to such proposals, then I think encouraging new visitors is worth any adverse side effects.

As a gesture toward maintaining the desert's ecological health, I pledge to donate at least twenty-five percent of my royalties to organizations such as the Southern Utah Wilderness Alliance (15 South 300 West, Box 518, Cedar City, UT 84720), the Utah chapter of the Sierra Club (177 East 900 South, Suite 102, Salt Lake City, UT 84111), and the Utah Wilderness Association (455 East 400 South, B 40, Salt Lake City,

UT-84111). These groups have struggled tirelessly and sometimes heroically to preserve and enlarge designated wilderness areas; our world would be a much poorer place without their efforts.

Inevitably in a guidebook such as this (and especially its first edition) mistakes will occur. Readers who detect errors or egregious omissions are urged to send corrections to me in care of my publisher, The Mountaineers, 306 Second Avenue West, Seattle, WA 98119.

ACKNOWLEDGMENTS

Among the people I've hiked with over the years, veteran desert rats Doug Dempster and Kath Anderson merit special mention, not only for all the places they've shown me but more importantly for their unfailing enthusiasm and good humor on the trail. My editors, Margaret Foster-Finan, Joan Gregory, and Marge Mueller, have spoiled me forever with their painstaking attention to my manuscript. My sister-in-law, Hannah Hinchman, an award-winning artist/writer/naturalist, lavished her time and considerable talent on the book's maps and illustrations. Christine Beekman, from the Canyonlands Natural History Association, volunteered to read the manuscript with a critical eye, and helped me find others who did the same. They also deserve special thanks.

I have saved the most important person for last: my husband, Lew, who hiked with me every mile of the way, printed up my computer files despite his intense Luddite proclivities, proofread my drafts for accuracy, helped call to mind many imperfectly remembered outings, served as my consultant on geology, and baby-sat while I finished the manuscript in a white heat. Although Lew probably wishes I had taken up needlepoint instead, this book simply would not exist in the absence of his companionship, encouragement, and generosity. In this, as in all aspects of my life, he has been my *sine qua non*.

Chapter 1

INTRODUCING THE DESERT

NATURAL AND HUMAN HISTORY

Most of the hikes described between these covers are within a day's drive of each other. With some notable exceptions, they are concentrated on the Colorado Plateau, near the so-called Four Corners, where Utah, Arizona, Colorado, and New Mexico meet. This is redrock country, a breathtaking landscape of canyons, fins, arches, hogbacks, and spires carved from stone. Ruins of buildings constructed by the prehistoric tribes that once inhabited the region are still amply in evidence. The rivers that helped shape the high desert's topography—most notably the Colorado, Green, Rio Grande, and San Juan—provide access to remote points of interest and offer what is arguably the most scenic floating and the most thrilling whitewater rafting in the United States. And the towering, geologically unusual mountains that frame this arid region add an extra dimension to its splendor and enchantment. Even a rudimentary grasp of the desert Southwest's natural and human history will greatly enhance the visitor's experience.

Geology

Forces at Work. The Colorado Plateau is an exciting and accessible geologic schoolroom. Domes, spires, cliffs, goblins, arches, and alcoves stand forth starkly, usually without cover of dense vegetation and topsoil. The neophyte geologist need not search for road cuts to see the earth layered here; the geologic past is everywhere on display.

Simplifying the task of understanding Southwestern geology is the dominance of sedimentary rocks. The component materials of these rocks were deposited layer cake-style, so that deeper-lying strata are almost always older than upper strata. Even an amateur geologist can distinguish the different kinds of sedimentary rock, recognizing the colorful badlands of the Morrison formation, the weirdly eroded Entrada sandstone goblins, the massive domes of Navajo sandstone, and the severe, vertically fractured Wingate cliffs. And each stratum offers clues about what kind of environment prevailed when the rock's component materials were laid down. For

Stonehenge-like Druid Arch, Canyonlands National Park, Utah

instance, the Coconino sandstone in the Grand Canyon is composed of rounded sand grains of more or less equal size, arranged in layers that often lie at angles to one another (a phenomenon known as "cross-bedding"). This formation suggests that the present-day Grand Canyon was covered by vast dunes when the Coconino was deposited, since we can observe shifting winds arranging desert sands in exactly such patterns today.

Yet high desert geology is not as simple as rock-layer diagrams make it appear; close inspection reveals unimagined complexities. First, sedimentary rocks are never deposited in layers of uniform thickness. Ancient ecosystems of relatively limited extent—river estuaries, beaches, dunes—determined the depth and size of each stratum. Consequently, formations characteristic of some sections of the Colorado Plateau may thin out or even vanish elsewhere. For example, the Elephant Canyon formation so prominent in the Needles District of Canyonlands National Park is entirely absent, both above and below the surface, in nearby Arches.

Second, because sediments can be laid down only in basins, whenever sections were uplifted, they stopped receiving sediments and instead began eroding away themselves. The result is an "unconformity"—two layers of rock with no geologic trace of an intervening time period between them. Thus, sedimentary rocks in the Southwest offer a fragmentary and incomplete guide to the region's geologic history. Whole pages, even chapters, of that history are missing (though a "grand tour" makes it possible to reconstruct much of it).

Third, faulting and uplifting have disturbed many of the strata that elsewhere form unbroken beds, pushing one part of the bed above, or dropping it below, another part. The Moab fault, near Arches National Park, provides a vivid illustration. Wingate sandstone cliffs, capped by Navajo sandstone, tower above the west side of the valley. On the east side, however, the Wingate layer is buried beneath the earth, while the Navajo and Entrada form the backdrop for the Arches Visitor Center. The offset of strata along this fault reaches 1000 to 1500 feet.

Finally, ancient vulcanism and mountain-building have played dramatic roles. Areas on the periphery of the Colorado Plateau, such as Bandelier National Monument, owe their peculiar geology to vast amounts of ash and/or lava from ancient volcanoes. Elsewhere, the region is crossed by long "folds" or "reefs," such as Utah's Waterpocket Fold and San Rafael Reef, caused when subterranean forces lifted up the overlying rock strata and tilted them at crazy angles—sometimes to a nearly vertical plane. Often, the uplifting occurred so slowly that pre-existing streams cut into the rock as fast as it was being raised up around them, creating deep, narrow "slot" canyons that run perpendicular to the axis of the reef.

In addition to such folds, the canyon and mesa country boasts several mountain ranges that rise 10,000 feet or more above sea level. Many—including the La Sals, Abajos (or Blues), and Henrys, and isolated, turtle-shaped humps like Sleeping Ute and Navajo Mountains—are "laccoliths":

roughly, failed volcanoes that created large bulges in the earth but never actually erupted. The rocks in and around them are mostly igneous types, such as granite. Deep canyons, similar to the slot canyons that cut through folds and reefs, formed on the flanks of laccoliths as meltwater rushed through soft, sedimentary rock. Navajo Mountain's Bridge Canyon, the site of Rainbow Bridge, offers a choice example.

The Rock Strata. Clear and simple on a grand scale, the geology of the high desert is complex and unique for each specific area. Following are descriptions of the region's more commonly seen and easily recognized rock strata.

Some of the region's oldest rocks are displayed in the Grand Canyon. Indeed, the youngest rocks laid down there, the Kaibab limestone formation, date back to the late Permian age (roughly 250 to 230 million years ago). Look especially for the bands of buff-colored Coconino sandstone near the top of the Grand Canyon and the red-tinted Redwall limestone, somewhat lower, that form sheer cliffs for miles.

In Utah, you will find some very ancient Paleozoic strata. The Needles of Canyonlands Park are composed of grayish-white Cedar Mesa sandstone, as are the cliffs of Grand Gulch and Natural Bridges National Monument. Cedar Mesa sandstone is actually a "member" of the Cutler formation, which includes other, quite different strata. Some Cutler rock is dark red and weathers into spires, gargoyles, and "standing rocks," visible in Canyonlands Park's Maze District and at Fisher Towers north of Moab. In Capitol Reef National Park, look for Chimney Rock and other monoliths around the park's western boundary. These towers resemble the Cutler but are composed of the newer, Triassic-era Moenkopi formation. A harder cap of Shinarump conglomerate retards the erosion of the mud and sandstone Moenkopi beneath.

The most spectacular formations in the region belong to the Glen Canyon Group of the Triassic and early Jurassic ages, the heyday of the great dinosaurs. Notable among these is Navajo sandstone, the classic tan to white "slickrock" of the high desert. This stratum, over 1500 feet thick in some places, may be appreciated well in the muscular domes of Capitol Reef and in Zion National Park, where it forms features such as the Great White Throne. The Navajo layer also produces nearly vertical cliffs in places like the Escalante River and the slot canyons of the San Rafael Reef.

Below Navajo sandstone, you will usually see the reddish, easily weathered rocks of the Kayenta stratum. The Kayenta forms ledges, "Swiss cheese" rock walls, and also arches, most notably in Capitol Reef's Upper Muley Twist Canyon. Some remarkable narrows cut through the Kayenta formation, too, such as those in parts of Crack Canyon near Goblin Valley State Park in central Utah.

Wingate sandstone, a fairly hard rock that often yields long vertical

Common Rock Strata of the Colorado Plateau

LAYER	Typical Maximum Thickness	WHERE FOUND:	Age
Claron formation	600'	Bryce Canyon	TERTIARY — up to 65 million years ago
Mancos Shale	3500'	Capitol Reef, Book Cliffs	CRETACEOUS — 136-65 million years ago
Dakota sandstone	350'	Capitol Reef	
Morrison formation	400'	Arches, Capitol Reef	JURASSIC — 195-136 million years ago
Summerville formation	300'	Goblin Valley, Arches	
Curtis formation	225'	Goblin Valley	
Entrada sandstone	800'	Arches, Goblin Valley, Cathedral Valley	
Carmel formation	650'	Capitol Reef, San Rafael Reef	
Navajo sandstone	1000'	Zion, Escalante, Arches, Rainbow Br., Capitol Reef	
Kayenta formation	350'	Muley Twist, Arches, Island in the Sky	TRIASSIC — 230-195 million years ago
Wingate sandstone	375'	Dead Horse Point, Capitol Reef, Colorado Nat. Mon.	
Chinle formation	650'	Island in the Sky, Capitol Reef	
Moenkopi formation	1000'	Natural Bridges, Capitol Reef, Fisher Towers	
Kaibab limestone	300'	Grand Canyon, Capitol Reef	PERMIAN — 285-230 million years ago
White Rim sandstone	250'	Island in the Sky	
Cedar Mesa sandstone	1200'	Grand Gulch, Natural Bridges, Needles, Maze	
Cutler formation	1400'	Monument Valley, Fisher Towers	
Honaker Trail formation	3000'	San Juan R. Gorge, Shafer Trail, Colo./green confluence	PENNSYLVANIAN — 320-285 million years ago
Paradox salt	5000'	Fisher Valley, Salt Valley (Arches)	

fractures, is the final member of the Glen Canyon group. Sometimes it erodes into towering, golden cliffs such as those of the Castle in Capitol Reef or along parts of the Colorado River north of Moab. Elsewhere, it weathers into isolated buttes and spires, of which the Six-Shooter Peaks of the Canyonlands Needles District offer a prime example. Usually, the base of the Wingate layer is formed by the sloping, rubble-strewn Chinle formation, a bearer of uranium.

Two other formations deserve mention because of the manner in which they erode. Above the Navajo in places lies Entrada sandstone. In Arches National Park, it is a reddish or gold-colored, fairly hard rock out of which most of the arches and fins were hewn. But at Goblin Valley, it is much softer, more crumbly, and mudlike. So here, it has eroded into grotesque and comical knobs, hoodoos, and pillars.

Farther west, at Bryce Canyon National Park, Navajo sandstone is the oldest rock that has been found, and that only by drilling. The rest of the formations go up to the Cenozoic period (after sixty-five million years ago), capped by the brilliant pastel and white Claron formation, a combination of limestone, shale, and sandstone. The Claron has weathered into the ethereal, dreamlike world of Bryce's Pink Cliffs.

Thus, if you traveled from the Grand Canyon through Capitol Reef and Zion and then on to Bryce, you would see the "grand staircase," a series of rock strata that displays geologic history from Precambrian times to the demise of the dinosaur and the emergence of early mammals. Each formation is unique and different, and each has its special qualities that contribute to the experience of hiking the Southwest.

Topographic Glossary

Alcoves (*overhangs, amphitheaters*) are shallow caves in cliffs or fins that result from flaking or falling rock.

Anticlines are domes or ridges formed when rock layers are pushed upward and bowed by subterranean forces. They often erode in the center, leaving—as their surface trace—valleys bounded on either side by upward-tilting strata.

Arches are natural openings formed when water percolates into porous rock, such as sandstone, and gradually breaks it down either by dissolving its chemical "cement" or by freezing and thawing. **Potty** (or *pothole*) **arches** form when the resultant rock openings occur at the tops of alcoves.

Badlands are dry, barren, clay hills, often multihued, that have been fluted by physical and chemical weathering.

Balanced rocks develop as the pedestal on which a caprock sits erodes rapidly, becoming ever-thinner.

Buttes are formed when water, frost, or wind action causes mesas to weather drastically and unevenly, until only tall remnants exist. These remnants are capped with hard, resistant rock that helps protect softer layers beneath.

Canyons (*gorges, gulches*) are carved into plateaus by streams, sometimes aided by simultaneous uplifting caused by underground forces. **Arroyos** occur when streams gouge out channels that are deeper than the level prevailing on the canyon floor; this can result from flash-flooding, especially when the landscape is denuded of vegetation, as happens sometimes with overgrazing.

Fins and **domes** occur when parallel vertical joints in solid rock are widened by erosional agents, eventually yielding freestanding formations. **Needles** are standing rocks that result when such joints also run perpendicular to each other.

Grabens are sunken fault blocks that show on the surface as narrow valleys or trenches bound by steep walls. Good illustrations are provided by Cyclone and Red Lake canyons in the Needles District of Canyonlands National Park, which formed when underlying beds of salt slowly leached away, allowing fault blocks to drop.

Hanging canyons are caused when a tributary does not cut into its bed at the same rate as the main stream; it becomes suspended above the stream, joining it in a waterfall.

Hoodoos (*goblins*) are standing rocks, sometimes found along the base of cliffs, that have eroded into improbable shapes.

Laccoliths are isolated mountains that form when subterranean molten materials force their way up without breaking through the earth's crust. The magma travels horizontally between thick beds of sedimentary rock, warping those layers.

Mesas (meaning "table" in Spanish) are high, flat plateaus with sloping or cliff-bounded sides.

Monoclines appear as sudden tilts or jogs in the plane of sedimentary rock strata. The term may designate the structure of one side of an anticline; Utah's San Rafael Reef provides a classic example.

Narrows occur when canyon walls pinch very close together, for a tunnellike effect.

Natural bridges, though they resemble arches, are created by the surge of water against a rock wall; for example, when a stream cuts off an old meander by breaking through a slender fin and slowly enlarging the opening, making a new course for itself.

Oxbows or **goosenecks** are places where a canyon stream has meandered enough to form a loop, in effect turning back on itself. **Entrenched streams** form when a meandering watercourse cuts into its bed as the land around it is uplifted.

Pour-offs (*dryfalls*) are found when canyon floors take sudden steep plunges, creating obstacles for hikers.

Reef is a colloquial term given by early settlers to any barrier to travel. Within the Southwest region, the term refers to drastically uptilted ridges.

Rincons are abandoned meanders that occur as the stream cuts through a narrow neck between loops to create a new channel. Where this happens, natural bridges sometimes develop.

Slickrock is a colloquial term referring to expanses of bare, undulating sandstone. It is generally not slick at all, except after rainstorms. Of all strata, Navajo sandstone is the most typical slickrock.

Spires (*pillars, towers*) usually originate when relatively soft rock strata are gradually thinned out by weathering, or when erosion breaks off vertical slabs of harder rock from isolated buttes, reducing them to free-standing pinnacles.

Synclines are downward slumpings of the earth's surface, the opposite of anticlines.

Climate

What makes the Four Corners region a desert is not simply the small amount of precipitation it receives (under 10 inches annually), but that most of this precipitation occurs in storms during late July and August, instead of falling evenly throughout the year. The parched, sparsely vegetated ground cannot absorb the moisture from these torrential rains, so much of it simply runs off, contributing to rapid erosion. Snowfall is generally light in the winter, though temperatures can fall below 20 degrees Fahrenheit. Summers can be intensely hot—90 degrees and up—at least before the brief but sometimes severe afternoon and evening thundershowers cool things off. These storms can cause flash floods and quicksand in previously dry "washes," or gullies. They also moderate temperatures and replenish the supply of drinking water in streams and potholes, and kill off much of the insect population. Summer visitors to the desert can expect hot, buggy, dry conditions during the first half of the season and wetter, cooler, relatively bugless conditions during the second half. April, May, September, and October are the ideal months for most high desert travel.

Flora and Fauna

The distribution of plant and animal species in the Southwest can be explained by the "life zone" concept formulated a century ago by botanist Clinton Hart Merriam. Merriam observed that the climate and latitude of an area help determine what flora and fauna will flourish there. "Communities" of plants and animals develop as the species residing in an area grow interdependent over millennia of evolutionary changes.

However, climate and latitude don't tell the whole story. Altitude

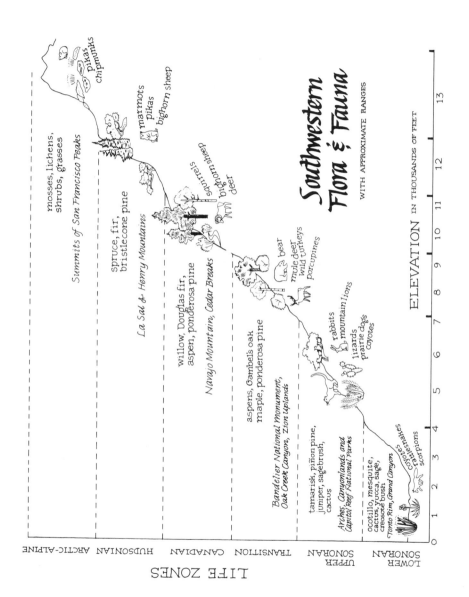

Southwestern Flora & Fauna

WITH APPROXIMATE RANGES

LIFE ZONES

ARCTIC-ALPINE | HUDSONIAN | CANADIAN | TRANSITION | UPPER SONORAN | LOWER SONORAN

mosses, lichens, shrubs, grasses

Summits of San Francisco Peaks

spruce, fir, bristlecone pine

La Sal & Henry Mountains

willow, Douglas fir, aspen, ponderosa pine

Navajo Mountain, Cedar Breaks

aspens, Gambel's oak maple, ponderosa pine

Bandelier National Monument, Oak Creek Canyon, Zion Uplands

tamarisk, piñon pine, juniper, sagebrush, cactus

Arches, Canyonlands and Capitol Reef National Parks

ocotillo, mesquite, cactus, yucca, sage, creosote bush

Toroto Rim, Grand Canyon

pikas chipmunks

marmots pikas bighorn sheep

squirrels bighorn sheep deer

bear mule deer wild turkeys porcupines

rabbits mountain lions lizards prairie dogs coyotes

coyotes rattlesnakes scorpions

ELEVATION IN THOUSANDS OF FEET

1 2 3 4 5 6 7 8 9 10 11 12 13

Top left: *Cholla in bloom, Bandelier National Monument, New Mexico.* Top right: *Tan lizard camouflaged against a rock.* Bottom left: *A curious coyote in Salt Valley, Arches Park, Utah.* Bottom right: *A plant makes its home in sandstone crevice.*

must also be factored into the equation. Air temperature decreases and precipitation increases with altitude, producing a new environment that can support different types of plants and animals. Every 1000 feet of elevation gain is equivalent to about 300 miles of latitudinal movement toward the pole.

Merriam postulated the existence of seven life zones, from the Tropical to the Arctic-alpine. Several zones prevail in the high desert. These zones, and their residents, overlap considerably, and the vegetation and wildlife found where water is relatively ample (lakeshores, riverbanks, intermittent streams, springs, and even potholes) may be anomalous.

The Lower Sonoran Zone. Reaching about 4000 feet in elevation, this zone is at the bottom of the Grand Canyon, along the Rio Grande River, and in the extreme southwestern corner of Utah. Cactus, mesquite, yucca, agave, creosote bush, blackbrush, rabbitbrush, and snakeweed are the dominant flora. The zone's animals include rattlesnakes, coyotes, scorpions, lizards, kangaroo rats, bats, skunks, deer, cactus wrens, and various hummingbird species.

The Upper Sonoran Zone. From 3500 to 7000 feet in elevation, this zone occupies by far the largest portion of the Four Corners region. Most typical of the Upper Sonoran is the so-called pygmy forest of pinyon pines and Utah junipers—"pygmy" because these trees are dwarfed by the region's scant rainfall. Locally, junipers are often termed "cedars." Other common trees here include oak, box elder, and cottonwood, which grow where the water table is high. But the zone's bushes and shrubs are even more diverse: sagebrush, blackbrush, bottlebrush, Mormon (or Brigham's) tea, rabbitbrush, tamarisk (an "exotic" riparian bush), willow (another riparian inhabitant), canyon grape, mock orange, cliffrose, buffaloberry, snakeweed, and greasewood, in addition to various grasses. Less welcome to most high desert visitors are poison oak and ivy. Floral displays in late spring and early summer can be extravagant, especially in years with high precipitation. Among the flowering plants prevalent in the Upper Sonoran zone are prince's plume, mule ears, bee plant, jimson weed (sacred *Datura*), sego lily, penstemon (or beardtongue), prickle poppy, geranium, globe mallow, phlox, four o'clock, evening primrose, scarlet gilia, Indian paintbrush, sunflower, and monkeyflower. Wildlife here includes coyotes, bats, rattlesnakes, scorpions, lizards, prairie dogs, kangaroo rats, mice, rabbits, squirrels, skunks, gray foxes, pronghorn antelopes, and mule deer. Among bird species, look for canyon wrens, hawks, swallows, kinglets, owls, vultures, scrub and pinyon jays, ravens, vireos, magpies, nighthawks, horned larks, finches, western tanagers, hummingbirds, towhees, and occasional golden and bald eagles.

The Transition Zone. A buffer between deserts and mountains (from 6500 to 9500 feet), this zone is a belt with two distinct associations of plants and animals. At lower altitudes, you will discover Gambel's oak, maple, Ponderosa pine, Rocky Mountain juniper, serviceberry, chokecherry, mountain mahogany, and manzanita. Higher up, Douglas and white fir, aspen, common juniper, and mountain ash predominate. Occasional stands of bristlecone pine trees—the earth's oldest living things—can also be found here. You may see wild turkeys, deer, porcupines, bears, squirrels, chipmunks, foxes, marmots, skunks, bobcats, and mountain lions. Common bird species include swallows, swifts, nuthatches, robins, flickers, jays, ravens, and chickadees.

Archaeology

Centuries before Europeans arrived in the New World, three early native American cultures flourished in the high desert: the Anasazi (a word that means something like "alien ancestors" in Navajo); the Sinagua (meaning "without water" in Spanish); and the Fremont, named after the explorer of a river valley that they earlier inhabited. All three cultural groups descended from the central Asian peoples who migrated across the land bridge that once connected Siberia with Alaska, and then gradually moved south- and eastward to populate two continents. The many relics of their respective ways of life are still scattered throughout the Southwest, offering valuable clues to their cultures. The Anasazi, believed to be ancestors of the modern-day Hopi and Pueblo tribes, dominated the Four Corners region, with the Fremont culture generally occupying lands to the north and west of the Green River, and the Sinagua residing farther south in Arizona.

Members of two of these Neolithic societies, the Anasazi and Sinagua, eventually lived in masonry homes and villages, some built ingeniously into deep alcoves high in south-facing cliffs for protection from the elements or from rival tribes. In addition to hunting small game and gathering nuts and berries, these peoples grew squash, beans, and corn in irrigated fields. To some degree, they may have been influenced culturally and technologically by societies from central and southern Mexico, with whom they traded for turquoise, shells, feathers, and other commodities. Like other aborigines, they had a thorough knowledge of indigenous plants, extracting dyes, medicines, and seasonings, and making sandals and ropes.

The Anasazi. Because their artifacts are abundant in this region, the Anasazi are particularly interesting to visitors to the Four Corners. Anthropologists sometimes divide the history of this Neolithic people into two broad periods—Basket Maker and Pueblo. During the late Basket Maker era, lasting until about A.D. 750, the Anasazi lived in underground pit houses in settled communities, developed bows and arrows for hunting, and began making pottery as a supplement to the fine woven baskets they had traditionally employed for storage and cooking purposes.

In the subsequent Pueblo phase, the Anasazi moved to surface houses and ultimately to masonry cliff dwellings, often grouped together in small villages or even in great cities accommodating hundreds of people. Increasingly they depended on irrigated agriculture for their sustenance. Also during the Pueblo phase, the pit house of yesteryear evolved into the

Mano and metate, ancient grinding tools

"kiva," the Hopi word for a subterranean ceremonial chamber used for religious, social, economic, and educational functions. The usual entrance into the kiva was from the top, by ladder.

Many of the cliff dwellings, typically erected in the twelfth and thirteenth centuries, were accessible only by toe and hand holds laboriously pecked out of solid rock. These stairways were specially coded: a person had to know whether to begin climbing with the right or left foot, or risk dangerous midcliff corrective maneuvering. Rural Mormons, anglicizing the Spanish word for Hopi, called these primitive ladders "Moki" steps. They assumed that because the doors of Anasazi houses have extremely low clearance, a Munchkin-sized race they called Mokis had built them. In fact, the Anasazi, like the Fremont and Sinagua peoples, were comparable in size to the Europeans of their day. The typical life span was comparable, too, at thirty to thirty-five years, with very high infant mortality (a fifty percent death rate for children under five).

Below the cliff dwellings were the "middens," a sort of dump where items such as broken pottery and old sandals were discarded. The dead were often buried in these middens, apparently not as a gesture of disrespect but because the digging was easiest there. Strangely, relatively few human corpses have been associated with the cliff dwellings. Some Hopi today maintain that the Anasazi, having perfected themselves in this life through harmonious dealings with nature and one another, ascended to the fifth level of creation, leaving our fourth level with its suffering and strife.

Many of the Southwest's most famous and breathtaking Anasazi sites were discovered by Richard and John Wetherill and their brothers in the late nineteenth and early twentieth centuries. These brothers were ranchers from Mancos, Colorado, who became amateur archaeologists after stumbling upon major ruins on nearby Mesa Verde. Excited by their early finds, the Wetherills spent years exploring the Southwest, searching for pottery and other ancient artifacts, which they sold to East Coast and European museums to finance their expeditions. Although by today's standards this practice would be considered looting, in the nineteenth century it was neither illegal nor even regarded as unethical. During his travels in Utah's canyons, Richard Wetherill formulated the distinction between the Basket Maker and Pueblo stages of Anasazi history that remains widely in use today.

The Fremont. Primarily hunters and gatherers, the Fremont peoples inhabited central Utah between 500 and 1200. Over time, they developed irrigation systems, probably as a cultural borrowing from the Anasazi. But their social organization remained relatively simple. They lived in small bands, building no towns to speak of and developing no elaborate division of labor. Although they were adept at masonry and left behind many small dwellings and granaries, they lived mainly in pit houses, which have not withstood the ravages of time. The Fremont, like other aboriginal cultures, decorated rock surfaces with shamanistic art, but it is hard to say with confidence exactly which panels are theirs. Art of the so-called Barrier Canyon style, once attributed by archaeologists to the Fremont peoples, is now believed to have been created centuries earlier by the Desert Archaic culture, from which the Fremont may have evolved. These remarkable drawings feature supernatural-looking, vase-shaped figures, sometimes horned, with geometric decorations on their bodies. The most striking examples of this style are panels in Horseshoe Canyon of Canyonlands National Park's Maze District.

The Sinagua. Having emigrated from southeastern Arizona in the seventh century, the Sinagua made their homes around modern-day Flagstaff in the shadow of the San Francisco Peaks. For hundreds of years they dry-farmed the land, living in one-room pit houses. Their tribal organization initially was loose, with isolated family groupings being the main social units, but eventually families gathered together to form villages. By the time they began erecting above-ground dwellings in the twelfth century, in places like Walnut Canyon, Tuzigoot, Montezuma Castle, and Wupatki national monuments, they had acquired irrigation techniques from the Hohokam culture (ancestors of the modern-day Papagos), whose members originally inhabited the Gila River basin. Few generalizations can be made about their preferred building styles, which varied greatly from place to place as a function of local conditions. But one noteworthy structure in the Wupatki complex is a masonry ball court, a cultural borrowing from Mesoamerica. It is generally agreed that the Sinagua learned how to build masonry dwellings from the Anasazi.

A replica of a kiva mural, Coronado State Park, New Mexico

The Demise of the Early American Cultures. After up to 2000 years of residence in canyon country, the three groups of indigenous peoples mysteriously abandoned their homes between A.D. 1100 and 1400. Some archaeologists argue that an unhappy coincidence of drought, global cooling, and resource depletion (of soil, game, and wood) made farming and hunting increasingly difficult, causing internal strife and placing an intolerable burden on the social structure. A different hypothesis stresses the impact of raiders on the tribes' welfare and security. Some speculate that the Fremont tribe evolved culturally into nomadic raiders, climatic changes having affected their way of life even more strongly and adversely than those of the other groups. The Anasazi and Sinagua probably moved to other parts of the region, such as the Little Colorado and Rio Grande drainages, where their modern descendants, the Hopi and Pueblo tribes, still live.

Whatever motivated their exodus, the aboriginal Americans left behind not only their homes but also artifacts such as pots, ropes, and sandals. They also left their rock art—mineral-dye paintings (pictographs) and etchings (petroglyphs). Specimens are typically found on smooth, flat sandstone cliff faces or boulders near ruins, monoliths, springs, or canyon mouths. Designs incorporate human, animal, and spirit figures, as well as hand prints, hunting implements, and geometric shapes. Attempts by modern-day descendants of the Southwest's Neolithic inhabitants to decipher the various symbols have proven fascinating, but inconclusive.

Unfortunately, an estimated eighty to ninety percent of the archaeological sites of the Southwest have been defaced or plundered. Some, however, remain in good condition. Of these, the sites at Mesa Verde National Park are the best known and generally the best preserved. But ruins of exceptional quality are also found in places like Navajo National Monument, Grand Gulch, Mule Canyon, and Chaco Canyon. Travelers interested in learning more about the prehistoric cultures of the Southwest and their artifacts should visit the Edge of the Cedars Museum just outside of Blanding, Utah, the Anasazi Heritage Center in Dolores, Colorado, north of Cortez, or the Museum of Northern Arizona in Flagstaff.

Native Cultures Today

The present-day Native Americans of the Four Corners region include the Utes, Navajo, Hopi, and Pueblo. Tribal members live suspended between two distinct worlds: the traditional world of ceremony, in which all the earth is seen as alive, and the larger society, with its technology and metaphysical religions. Please bear in mind, if you travel on any of their reservations, that you are a guest in another culture's homeland.

The Utes. Some anthropologists believe that the Utes descended from the Fremont peoples who once ranged across central Utah. Others think they descended from the Shoshone, who entered the region in the twelfth and thirteenth centuries. Before the Utes were vanquished by the U.S. Army, they lived as seminomadic hunters and warriors. Once pushed onto reservations, they were compelled to live in a more sedentary manner, dependent upon agriculture and rations from the Bureau of Indian Affairs. Currently, members of the tribe inhabit reservations in northern Utah and southwestern Colorado, adjacent to Mesa Verde National Park. Livestock-raising and agriculture, their economic mainstays, have been handicapped by the absence of reliable, good-quality water supplies. Visitors to the Ute Mountain Reservation in Colorado can tour Anasazi cliff dwellings located on Ute land.

The Navajo. Calling themselves "Dineh," which means simply "the people," the Navajo are ethnically unrelated to most pre-Columbian inhabitants of the Colorado Plateau, having descended, like the Apache, from nomadic hunters on the plains. Their common name comes from a Spanish corruption of other tribes' words for them, "Apache de Nebahu," meaning "enemies with cultivated fields." About 175,000 strong, the Navajo nation exceeds all other U.S. tribes both in number and in the extent of its territory, a reservation encompassing half of northern Arizona and spilling across the border into Utah and New Mexico. The Navajo previously were believed to have migrated into the region during the seventeenth century, but recent archaeological findings now suggest their presence in New Mexico as early as the 1200s A.D. Some anthropologists have even postulated a link between the coming of the Navajo and the exodus of the area's aboriginal peoples.

In many ways, the Navajo fared better than other Native American tribes in their nineteenth-century dealings with the federal government. Although they endured countless woes, including the destruction of their homes, livestock, and orchards, and the deaths of many kinsmen on a forced tribal march to eastern New Mexico in 1864, they ultimately were able to keep their land. And that land, which at first appeared worthless to Anglos, turned out to contain natural gas, oil, uranium, and coal, which is now mined extensively on Arizona's Black Mesa. The discovery of coal was a mixed blessing, however, since with it came the construction of lucrative (for some people) but polluting power plants, which supply energy to distant cities.

Some citizens of the Navajo nation are employed as energy workers. Others earn their living by selling high-quality wool rugs and turquoise and silver jewelry, while more traditional Navajo raise sheep and goats. Unemployment rates here, as on other Southwestern reservations, are high, and relatively few homes boast electricity and indoor plumbing. Although trailers and other prefabricated homes are common on the reservation, Navajo lands are also dotted with more traditional structures such as sweat lodges, ramadas, and hogans, one-room hexagonal or octagonal dwellings made of earth, logs, and modern materials, which traditionally face east toward the rising sun.

An excellent source of information about Navajo culture is Santa Fe's Wheelwright Museum of the American Indian.

The Hopi. A small tribe of under 10,000 members, the Hopi have been relatively successful in preserving their cultural traditions ever since the days of Spanish conquistadors and missionaries, who sought to convert them to Christianity. Their reservation is surrounded by Navajo land, which has caused great friction between these tribes over the years. Recently, it occasioned a bitter lawsuit over disputed joint-use territory that resulted in the displacement of many Navajo families. Unlike the Navajo, the Hopi are primarily farmers. They live on arms of Black Mesa in villages like Oraibi, the oldest, continuously occupied town in the United States. Although the tribe has its outspoken faction of "modernizers," many Hopi continue to observe their old customs, evidently derived in part from the practices of the Anasazi. Like the Navajo, the Hopi consider certain mountains in the area to be sacred, such as the San Francisco Peaks, where their nature gods, deified spirits of ancestors (or "kachinas"), supposedly reside.

The Pueblo. This population is scattered among nineteen independent villages, mainly in the Rio Grande Valley. Conquest by the Spanish in the seventeenth century led to pillaging, enslavement, and attempts at forced conversion to Christianity. Bloody revolts and equally bloody reprisals ensued. Somehow, the Pueblo managed to retain much of their cultural integrity in the face of both long-term Spanish dominion and subsequent waves of Mexican and Anglo immigration. Today some of their villages seem relatively prosperous, with economies based on agriculture and on crafts like pot- and jewelry-making. Kivas are still in use here, as on the Hopi Reservation, though many are now above-ground structures. Sacred dances are held in the villages several times a year, in keeping with ancient rituals. Visitors are generally welcome to tour the pueblos for a small fee; photographing and sketching privileges (not available during ceremonies) cost extra.

The Havasupai and Hualapai. Members of these tribes inhabit portions of the western Grand Canyon. Both very small in number, they farm terraces inside the canyon and graze stock in high meadows along the rim, earning extra money by selling permits for hiking and camping on their land. The Havasupai town of Supai, a shangri-la near the bottom of the canyon, is famed for its teal-blue travertine waterfalls. Reachable by an 8-mile foot trail, it is the last town in the United States to have its mail delivered on mule back.

HIKING AND DRIVING

Now that your appetite for the high desert has (I hope) been whetted, it is time to discuss the practicalities and mechanics of desert travel, so your trip will be safe and enjoyable.

Every desert traveler should be well informed about certain potential hazards and how to avoid them or at least remedy their effects. All problems included in the following list are exacerbated by remote locations and difficult terrain. A good first aid kit and manual are essential.

Hiking Safety

Water. During the summer months, plan on at least 1 gallon of water per person each day for drinking, washing, and cooking. This may seem excessive, but it is not, and you shouldn't be tempted to skimp on it. In most places, you can't count on finding groundwater, so you will usually have to carry all you need. At over 8 pounds per gallon, this can be a heavy proposition.

Sometimes water will be available from springs and perennial streams. Conditions change seasonally, even weekly. Map and guidebook information regarding possible water sources may be outdated; therefore, always confirm such information at local ranger stations or visitor centers.

Poor water quality presents an increasingly serious problem for hikers throughout the American wilderness, and the desert is no exception. Many water sources—even those that look absolutely pristine—have been contaminated by cattle, horses, and wild animals, not to mention careless campers. The main contaminant is *Giardia lamblia,* a bacterium released into water and soil as human and animal feces decompose. When ingested, this bacterium can cause severe diarrhea and dehydration. Sometimes the symptoms do not appear for several weeks, but they tend to persist until treated with drugs.

To avoid contracting giardiasis and other water-borne diseases, follow these recommendations religiously:

- Boil all drinking water for one minute.
- Or purify water chemically with a small amount of clorox bleach (one or two drops per quart) or commercially available tablets. Shake the container well and wait at least twenty minutes until drinking.
- Alternatively, buy a portable charcoal-based filtration system (several brands are on the market). Strain the water through cheesecloth or let it settle a while in a canteen before filtering it, since sediment will clog the filter and dramatically shorten its useful life. (Of course, don't drink from any canteen employed for this purpose.)
- Never drink from any water source that supports no life, since it may contain arsenic or some other toxic compound.

Flash Floods. Mid-July through early September is a time of frequent afternoon thunderstorms in the Southwest. These brief but heavy downpours (called "male rains" by the Navajo) sometimes cause flooding even in faraway streams. You can hear a flash flood coming—it sounds like a locomotive—but you may be inconvenienced, injured, or even killed by one unless you take certain precautions:

- Never camp in or near the bed of a dry wash, or in any narrow section of canyon lacking an easy and obvious escape route.
- Listen to weather reports and pay attention to natural phenomena that signal impending storms, such as sudden shifts in air temperature or wind direction. Avoid travel in remote areas when storms seem imminent.
- Never try to cross a wash on foot or by car during a flash flood.
- Should you be trapped in a canyon during a flash flood, find very high ground and wait for it to subside. Never try to beat a flood out of a canyon. Sometimes it takes twelve to twenty-four hours for flood waters to recede, though minor floods will not delay you for as long. Quicksand of-

ten develops in the aftermath of flash-flooding; this can make it difficult to complete a hike.

Quicksand. Sometimes encountered in or along streambeds, quicksand rarely presents a genuine hazard for desert travelers. People usually sink no farther than knee- or waist-deep, and the sinking is so gradual that you can pull yourself out, though you may need a helping hand or a rope from one of your companions. If you are hiking alone and this happens, bend at the waist as though you were going to swim through the muck. Stay calm and extricate yourself without making too many unnecessary movements. During the thunderstorm season, quicksand will form in conjunction with pools of water in normally dry canyons. If it poses enough of a problem, alter your plans.

Heat. Foot travel on hot desert days can result in dehydration, muscle cramps, heat exhaustion, and (in severe cases) sunstroke, a life-threatening condition. To avert such ailments, drink small amounts of water frequently—a cup or two every half hour—whether thirsty or not. Give yourself time to acclimatize to desert conditions before tackling strenuous trails in hot weather, and rest sodium-depleted muscles at the first sign of cramping. If heat is extreme, alter your plans.

Doctors agree that the best treatment for heat-related ailments is to

Sandstone and sky define slickrock hikers' world

find some shade, remain quiet, drink cool nonalcoholic beverages (to which you can add a small amount of salt), and immerse yourself in a pool of water if one is available. In the case of sunstroke (hyperthermia), emergency medical attention is an absolute necessity. Usually the onset of heat exhaustion and sunstroke is gradual. The initial symptoms of heat-related illness include dizziness, weakness, nausea, headache, and disorientation. Sunstroke can result if these early warning signs are ignored. It is characterized by rapid pulse-rate, high temperature, gooseflesh, loss of consciousness, chills, delirium, and dry (not clammy) skin.

Hazardous Terrain. To hikers in the Southwest, sheer drops pose a significant danger, since many of the desert's most appealing trails either descend into or wind along the rims of steep-walled canyons. Certain varieties of sandstone, the dominant kind of rock found in the region, are notoriously crumbly, and sand on slickrock can create slippery conditions. Since medical help may be hours or even days away, prudence dictates caution on steep trails, especially for those hiking with children. Knowledge of the basic principles of first aid is a must. Avoid unnecessary rock climbing unless you are an experienced, well-equipped climber. Don't cut switchbacks, and never throw or roll rocks.

Getting Lost. Particularly when they traverse talus fields or slickrock, desert trails can be difficult to follow. To avoid getting lost, never proceed far until you have located the next trail marker. As insurance, tell someone in advance about your hiking plans. If you do get lost, stay where you are, signal your position in some obvious way (such as laying out gear and clothes in an open area), and wait for help to arrive.

Poisonous Creatures. Although the Southwestern deserts are home to rattlesnakes, scorpions, and black widow spiders, you will almost never see these creatures. They are largely nocturnal, preferring to take shelter under rocks or in woodpiles or brush during the heat of the day. Rattlesnakes generally will give you fair warning of their presence. Their bites are not often fatal, and statistically about one in three snakes inject no venom when they bite, having spent their reserves on their prey. The bites of black widow spiders are likewise rarely fatal, for though their venom is more toxic than that of the rattlesnake, they inject a much smaller quantity. Among scorpions, only a 2-inch-long yellow species with a slender tail is deadly (especially to young children or unhealthy adults); of the areas covered in the book, this species normally resides only at the bottom of the Grand Canyon.

Common sense, however, does suggest certain precautions. Be careful when climbing rocks or turning them over, and try not to place your hands anywhere that you can't examine visually first. Always shake out your shoes before putting them on, and inspect the underside of your tent before rolling it up. Poisonous desert creatures are more common in wet areas, such as the micro-environment around perennial streams.

If someone is bitten by a venomous snake or poisonous spider or stung by a scorpion, consult a good first aid manual for the recommended immediate treatment and obtain medical assistance as soon as possible. In general, authorities recommend that the victim of a poisonous bite or sting be kept warm and quiet, to retard the spread of the poison through the bloodstream or nervous system. If medical assistance is far away, venom can be drawn from the wound by mouth or suction cup for a minimum of forty-five minutes, and the injured limb can then be placed in a sling. A *loose* tourniquet can be placed above the wound, to be moved gradually toward the heart as the affected area swells. The site of a scorpion sting or spider bite can be immersed in cold water—or, preferably, treated with an icepack—to make the victim more comfortable. (Cryotherapy is *not* recommended for snake bites.) Painkillers can also be administered, but the victim should ingest no sedatives or alcoholic beverages.

Dangerous Plants. One of the most common desert hiking injuries is getting pricked by cactus spines, which are mildly poisonous and become easily imbedded under the skin. Avoid contact with cacti by watching where you are stepping. If you do pick up some spines, scratch or dig them out, then douse the affected area with hydrogen peroxide or some other disinfectant. The sharp tips of yucca and agave leaves can also irritate skin, though to a lesser degree. Beware, too, of poison ivy and oak.

Insect Pests. Late spring and early summer, prior to the onset of the thunderstorm weather pattern, is prime bug season on the Colorado Plateau. Aside from mosquitoes, most common in watery canyons, there are four especially annoying species. Red ants can inflict a painful sting, best treated with cold-water immersion. Biting gnats, which favor pinyon and juniper vegetation, go after the tender eye and ear areas, causing itchy welts and even swollen glands to form. Like mosquitoes, gnats are most bothersome around dusk. Deerflies, concentrated in moist, reedy places where livestock have grazed, are attracted to motion and usually aim for the backs of the knees. Finally, blowflies—though they do not bite—make life unpleasant merely by their presence on the scene; they are drawn to open wounds, where they seek to lay eggs.

Deep woods-type repellents containing seventy-five to one hundred percent DEET are effective against many of these pests. Use only unscented beauty and hygiene products while camping and hiking. Wear hats with no-see-um netting, long-sleeved shirts, and long, lightweight pants. Choose breezy, exposed campsites and build smoky fires, if regulations allow. As a last resort when insects become intolerable, try another trail or even another park, since bugs are not uniformly distributed but vary with altitude, water supply, and other local conditions.

A Note about Safety

Travel in many parts of the desert entails unavoidable risks that every traveler assumes and must be aware of and respect. The fact that an area is described in this book is not a representation that it will be safe for you. Trips vary greatly in difficulty and in the amount and kind of preparation needed to enjoy them safely. Some routes may have changed, or conditions on them may have deteriorated since this book was written. Also, of course, conditions can change even from day to day, owing to weather and other factors. A trip that is safe in good weather or for a highly conditioned, properly equipped traveler may be completely unsafe for someone else or unsafe under adverse weather conditions.

You can minimize your risks by being knowledgeable, prepared, and alert. There is not space in this book for a general treatise on general wilderness safety and safety in the desert, but there are a number of good books and public courses on the subject, and you should take advantage of them to increase your knowledge. Just as important, you should always be aware of your own limitations and conditions existing when and where you are traveling. If conditions are dangerous, or if you are not prepared to deal with them safely, change your plans! It is better to have wasted a few days than to be the subject of a wilderness rescue. These warnings are not intended to keep you out of the desert and backcountry. Many people enjoy safe trips through the desert and backcountry every year. However, one element of the beauty, freedom, and excitement of these areas is the presence of risks that do not confront us at home. When you travel in these areas, you assume those risks. They can be met safely, but only if you exercise your own independent judgment and common sense.

The Mountaineers

Driving Safety

Desert driving is usually delightful and unchallenging: Vistas are grand, skies are clear, and traffic is light. Yet remote locations, extreme temperatures, and rough roads may pose unaccustomed hazards.

Because towns in the Four Corners region are few and far between, and because service stations tend to close early, it is important to keep plenty of gas in your tank and to check your car's fluid levels frequently. The low octane ratings of much of the regular unleaded gasoline sold in the area, coupled with above-average elevations, may adversely affect your car's performance; to prevent sluggishness, you might want to buy premium unleaded. Consider storing extra motor oil, coolant, battery water, hoses, belts, tools, and a shovel in the trunk, in addition to a spare tire. Turn off your air conditioner to deter engine overheating. Always have extra food and plenty of drinking water available in case your car breaks down miles from nowhere, and remember that small town service stations may have to mail-order any parts needed to repair your vehicle.

When hiking, lock up, bring along an extra set of keys, and try to leave nothing valuable in your car. Although car "clouting," or the practice of stealing items from vehicles, still remains relatively uncommon in the Southwest as a whole, it seems to be a growing problem, particularly at certain trailheads, and an incident can quickly ruin the victim's vacation.

Driving on Unpaved Roads. On gravel surfaces, slow down when approaching other vehicles to avoid sustaining a broken windshield. Sharp rocks on the road may also cause flat tires or blow-outs. Dirt roads can be rough when dry and impassable when wet, either because they cross wash bottoms or because they are composed of clay-type soil. On washboards, the closely spaced, parallel ridges that often characterize dirt roads, be sure to slow down when rounding curves so you won't lose control. Slower speeds are also advisable when the road is bumpy or twisty, or when it descends into gullies or crosses exposed rock. The absence of guard rails on many desert roads, both paved and unpaved, poses another danger, as does the presence of unfenced-in livestock. Try to avoid night driving on unpaved roads; otherwise, you may have a close encounter with a deer, a cow, or a frame-bending gully. Never drive off established roads, for this practice will harm the desert (and possibly your car).

Drivers should always familiarize themselves in advance with a road map of the area into which they are heading, particularly when they plan to travel off the main highways. Unfortunately, maps rarely show all of an area's unpaved roads; people using such roads should therefore seek precise directions and current road-quality information locally before starting out. The condition of an unpaved road can vary dramatically within short periods of time, mainly as a function of weather. If you will be driving on very poor or very remote roads, it is a good idea to inform someone of the route you intend to take in case you get lost or experience car trouble.

Ethics and Hygiene

The desert is a fragile ecosystem, easily harmed by thoughtless human practices. Decomposition is slow, erosion is rapid, and unsightly scars made by vehicles, fires, and even lugged soles often take decades to heal. It is therefore even more vital here than elsewhere to camp in a low-impact manner, as epitomized in the familiar motto, "Take nothing but pictures, leave nothing but footprints." In particular, visitors should abide by the following guidelines:

- Stay on trails or designated routes wherever possible. Do not cut across switchbacks to shorten your hike, for this practice hastens erosion.
- Do not drive off established roads.
- Bury human waste 6 inches to 12 inches deep and at least 300 feet from water sources. Pack out your toilet paper or carefully burn it if fires are allowed.
- Do not bring pets with you into the wilderness. They might harm, or be harmed by, wild animals, and they often frighten or annoy other hikers.
- Resist the temptation to make souvenirs of cacti and exotic plants, rocks, pottery fragments or arrowheads, or petrified wood from protected areas. These practices violate federal and state laws.
- Avoid trampling the black, crusty, microbiotic (formerly called "cryptogamic") soil that retards erosion throughout the Southwest. Composed of lichens, mosses, algae, and fungi, this substance stabilizes the sand, permitting larger plants to take root.
- Camp and wash dishes at least 100 feet away from all ground water. Never pollute pools or streams with dishwashing soap, even the biodegradable kind. As a conservation measure, clean dirty pots partially by abrading them with sand and tiny pebbles prior to washing.
- Use a backpacking stove instead of building a campfire, since fire rings scar the desert. Fires are prohibited in many places. If you do make a fire where they are permitted, observe these rules:
- Gather only dead wood that is lying on the ground; do not pull limbs from bushes and trees.
- Use already-established fire rings wherever they are available. Consider using a fire pan.
- Build your fire far away from vegetation.
- Pack out all trash, including cans, foil, plastic, and other non-burnable refuse.
- Drown your fire with water, stirring to make sure you have killed all the live coals, and double check it before leaving camp.
- Destroy your fire ring by throwing the rocks in different directions.

Antiquities

Appreciation for the Southwest's priceless archaeological heritage led federal and state governments to make laws designed to protect ancient ruins, drawings, and artifacts from vandalism, damage, and theft. Simply put, it is illegal to remove, deface, or destroy any Neolithic object found on public land. Violation of these laws carries stiff penalties, including fines and jail terms.

Most people who harm ruin sites probably do so in an innocent manner. They don't realize that even the tiniest potsherd taken from a ruin will complicate the task of scholars trying to reconstruct how prehistoric tribes lived. They don't stop to think that adding their initials to a petroglyph will detract from the enjoyment of others. Or they don't understand how fragile ancient artifacts are, so they touch wall plaster and rock art, camp inside ruins, walk on middens, or stand, climb, or lean on ruin walls—all practices to be strictly avoided.

Please respect all antiquities that you find and make sure that others do the same.

Equipment

Outfitting yourself for backcountry desert travel need not involve extraordinary effort or expense. If you are an experienced mountain hiker, most of the gear you already own will suffice. Major items needed, of course, include a backpack, daypack, tent with no-see-um netting, lightweight sleeping bag, ground pad, camp stove, cooking equipment, water bottles (at least a 2-gallon capacity per person), and water purification system.

Always carry with you the Ten Essentials recommended by The Mountaineers: extra clothing, extra food, sunglasses, knife, matches, firestarter, first aid kit, flashlight, map, and compass. In the desert, it is also essential to carry extra water and sunscreen. For a more complete list of recommended gear and supplies, consult any good manual on backpacking.

Summer travelers should pack clothing appropriate for warm to hot days and cool nights. Long-sleeved tops and long, loose-fitting pants offer protection from sun, bugs, and dangerous plants. Wide-brimmed hats are also advisable. For footwear, bring comfortable, high-top nylon and leather boots; rigid, heavy-duty mountain boots are needed only for the most rugged trails. Because some hikes demand a considerable amount of wading through shallow streams, pack a pair of old sneakers or boots, as well as several extra pairs of socks.

Maps

Some of the hikes outlined in this book can be completed easily, either with no map at all or with a very basic diagram of the sort found in national park and monument brochures. Others, however, require the use of topographic maps made and sold by the United States Geological Survey (USGS). The 7.5-minute series is generally preferable, but for many parts of the desert only the less detailed 15-minute maps are available. The maps cost a few dollars each and can be obtained either at outdoors stores in the region, or by writing to the following address: U.S. Geological Survey, Distribution Section, Denver Federal Center, Building 41, Denver, CO 80225.

Waterproof, tear-proof versions of the topo maps for many Southwestern parks, published by Trails Illustrated, are available locally. Also widely available is the AAA map *A Guide to Indian Country,* which shows all the major paved and unpaved roads of the area and gives accurate distances to 0.1 mile.

Trip Planning

An enjoyable camping trip requires a good deal of advance planning. Write away for topographic maps or national park literature and secure reservations months ahead for popular campsites and backcountry trails. (In our desert experience, we have found that this is necessary—sometimes—only in Grand Canyon National Park.)

Always inquire about weather, water, and insect conditions locally before beginning a major hike. Calculate carefully how long your chosen route will take so that you can provision and plan accordingly. If yours is not a loop or a round-trip hike, arrange for a car shuttle or hire someone to drive you to your trailhead. Rangers in national parks and employees in outdoors stores or other wilderness-related businesses can often help you make contact with local people eager to earn extra money in this manner.

Also consider the availability of showers, laundromats, and grocery stores in a given area. Showers pose a particular problem in the rural Southwest. Some state and national parks have shower facilities, and many RV parks will allow nonguests to take showers on the premises in exchange for a few dollars. Otherwise, unless you decide to stop at a motel, you may have to settle for a dip in a lake or river, or even a local YMCA or swimming pool.

Above all, consider the capability and experience of the members of your party. Plan to step up your exercise program weeks in advance of the trip. Novices should stick to short, well-established trails through terrain that is not too rugged or challenging. Even veteran backpackers need time to adjust to the heat and elevation of the Southwest desert. A "conditioning" hike or two will help you avoid problems.

Camping. Most national and state parks have modern camping facilities, though in some cases you will have to put up with pit toilets (outhouses) and the absence of running water. Some campgrounds are closed during the winter months; others remain open, offering fewer services. During the peak season, and especially on holiday weekends, try to arrive at campgrounds as early in the day as possible to avoid disappointment. If sites are full, bear in mind that much of the high desert (especially in Utah) is public land, administered by the Bureau of Land Management (BLM), and you are allowed to camp virtually anywhere on it. Basically, you just turn onto a dirt road, follow it for a mile or so, and find a comfortable, level spot, preferably one that was previously used. Be careful not to run over vegetation as you pull off the road. Don't be intimidated by fences and closed gates, since on public lands these are meant to keep cattle in—not to keep

Soaring Navajo sandstone cliffs dwarf backpackers in Paria Canyon, Arizona

you out; always remember to leave gates as you find them. In general, you can assume that land is public if you do not see dwellings, No Trespassing signs, or other evidence to the contrary. The Indian reservations of the Southwest are an important exception to this rule; please respect their property rights.

Another alternative when a full campground disappoints you is to obtain a backcountry permit for tent camping elsewhere in a park. In most cases, regulations allow you to camp almost anyplace you want, as long as you are at least a half mile off the trail. The exception to this is in archaeological parks like Chaco, Mesa Verde, and Hovenweep, where backcountry camping is forbidden.

Using This Book

This book is designed to take some of the burden of trip planning out of your hands. It groups many of the most enjoyable trails and awe-inspiring scenic attractions of the high desert into six itineraries, each about two or three weeks in length. Because the loops overlap in spots, those with extra time will find it easy to integrate them into longer trips. For illustrative purposes I have assumed that you will begin and end at a particular town, but naturally you can join an itinerary at any point. If your home is a long distance from the Four Corners region, you can fly to a major urban area such as Denver, Albuquerque, Phoenix, Las Vegas, or Salt Lake City, rent a car, and drive from there to intersect your chosen loop.

With each itinerary, I have minimized driving and maximized time to explore the desert on foot. As you will discover, driving is a pleasure and not a chore in the desert Southwest, since the sweep of country is so expansive and the landforms so exotic. Certain road trips are "classics," worth doing for their own sakes, such as the Burr Trail, AZ-98 across the Navajo Reservation to Lake Powell, and UT-128 north of Moab, along the Colorado River.

I built as much diversity as possible into each loop, to provide a fair sampling of high desert scenery and culture and to strike a balance between day-hiking and backpacking. A few itineraries may have a special appeal to certain audiences. Readers especially intrigued by archaeology should select the Anasazi Loop, while serious backpackers would probably be happiest with the Canyons Loop.

For each hike, I specify its distance (rounded to the nearest quarter mile, except where greater precision seems vital), the time an average hiker needs to complete it (with estimates on the conservative side), and the topographic map(s) that correspond to it. Moreover, each hike has been assigned a difficulty rating on a scale of *very easy* to *very strenuous*. A brief description of each rating follows.

Very easy trails have good walking surfaces, and in some cases may even be paved. They are usually short, more or less level, utterly unproblematic to follow, and suitable for almost everyone. Such trails are generally found in national parks and are highlighted in their brochures.

Easy trails demand minimal physical exertion. Although they may involve some elevation loss or gain, it is of the slow, steady variety. They are usually well marked with signposts or cairns (rockpiles) and well maintained, and although they tend to be longer than their "very easy" counterparts, they still remain good family hikes.

Moderate trails ask somewhat more of the hiker in terms of both skill and endurance. Some of them, by virtue of their length, are practical only for backpackers. They presuppose a certain degree of route-finding ability, in addition to a tolerance for ups and downs. Climbs may be short and steep or may be longer, with a more gentle gradient.

Strenuous hikes put significant demands on the traveler. Often located in remote areas, they generally involve at least some advance planning. Most of them are backcountry trails not suitable for day-hiking. The complications involved may include dramatic elevation gains on steep exposed slopes; deep wading; rock scrambling or boulder hopping; long waterless treks; unmarked or poorly marked routes; and precipitous drops.

Very strenuous routes are recommended only for experienced backpackers in top physical condition. The same hardship factors evident in strenuous hikes also apply here, but to a higher degree of difficulty, or in greater concentration.

Legend

▬▬▬▬	paved road	🚙	drive
▬ ▬ ▬	dirt road	👢	hike
══════	jeep road	📷	overlook
••••••••	trail or route	▲	camping
Ⓢ	start of hike or drive	🏠	ranger station or visitor center
cliff	cliff		rock art
mesa	mesa		ruin
butte, temple or hoodoo	butte, temple or hoodoo		pueblo
peak or dome	peak or dome	目	ladder
natural arch or bridge	natural arch or bridge	] [	bridge
cave	cave	[ ]	tunnel
waterfall	waterfall		park boundary
♂	spring		reservation boundary

Chapter 2

DESERT RIVERS LOOP

Utah

This seventeen-day itinerary promises something for everyone: natural bridges, waterfalls, narrow slot canyons, and prehistoric artifacts. Balancing day trips with backpacking, and involving minimal driving, it explores portions of the Green, Fremont, Escalante, and Paria drainages. The area's oasislike streams carve through some of the driest high desert country around.

The Fremont River in Capitol Reef National Park, Utah, slices through Waterpocket Fold

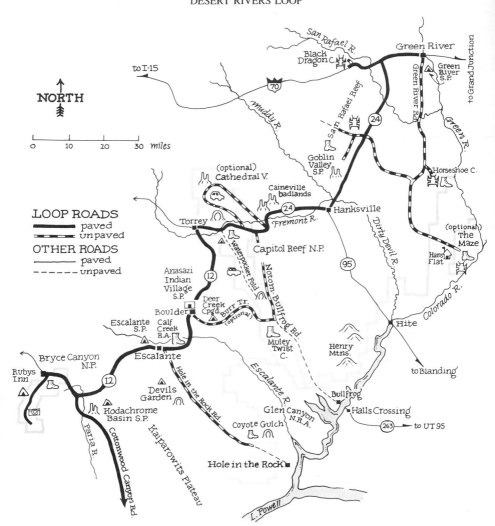

DAY 1: GREEN RIVER TO GOBLIN VALLEY

- **A 45-mile drive along the spectacular San Rafael Reef**
- **Short, conditioning hikes amid bizarre hoodoos**
- **Camping and showers at Goblin Valley State Park**
- **Gas, groceries, and showers available in Green River**

Your trip begins in Green River (population 1050), situated in east-central Utah where the Colorado's main tributary runs underneath I-70 (see map, p. 42). A sleepy town, Green River nevertheless provides the essentials. Fill your gas tank and stock up here, for the next settlement scheduled on the loop—Hanksville, on Day 3—is even tinier than Green River!

Drive west 12 miles on I-70 and take the exit for UT-24. Turn south on this lonely road, which parallels the **San Rafael Reef** virtually all the way to Hanksville. Resembling the backbone of a stegosaurus, the reef is the eastern edge of the San Rafael Swell, a huge anticline born millions of years ago when subterranean forces thrust up and deformed overlying rock strata. It creates a striking contrast to the featureless, arid land on your left, which gives little hint of the Edenic canyons lying just beyond. Through these canyons—the Labyrinth and Stillwater sections of the Green River—one can float 120 miles from the highway bridge at Green River State Park to the Green's confluence with the Colorado, without negotiating a single rapid. (Required permits are available through Canyonlands National Park.)

Reach **Goblin Valley State Park** by turning right (west) onto the good dirt and gravel road to Temple Mountain, 25 miles south of I-70. In

Whimsical hoodoos populate Goblin Valley State Park, Utah

about 5 miles turn left at a junction marked by a sign. Now the San Rafael Reef is on your right, and inspiring views of the lonely Gilson Buttes are on your left. Goblin Valley is 7 miles down this road, just beyond Wild Horse Butte. Despite washboards and occasional encroachment by dunes, this all-weather road rarely presents serious problems.

The goblins of this magical, 3654-acre park are carved out of cocoa brown Entrada sandstone and capped by the greenish white Curtis formation. When the area was discovered in the late 1920s, it was named "Mushroom Valley" in honor of its wildly eroded, toadstool-shaped mudhills. Its treeless campground, complete with showers, flush toilets, and other modern conveniences, serves as an excellent base of operations for trips into the San Rafael Reef and Swell. After setting up your camp, drive another mile down the paved road to its end at the Observation Point, a sheltered overlook with picnic tables and pit toilets. The only access into the main part of the valley is by foot on a short path that descends from here. About 50 yards down, the trail peters out and you're left to follow your own inclinations in this otherworldly setting.

Goblin Valley also has two official trails, both accessible from the Observation Point parking lot. Plan to hike these today, to acclimate yourself to the heat and altitude. The **Carmel Canyon Loop** (1.5 miles) is the shorter and easier of the two. From the northeast corner of the lot, it descends into Carmel Canyon, winds left through some badlands toward a prominent butte called Mollys Castle, and then enters a short narrows section before climbing back to the road a few hundred yards north of the trailhead. More interesting is the **Curtis Bench Trail** (2 miles), which involves many ups and downs. It begins near the campground and ends at the parking lot. A spur trail from the benchland affords marvelous views of the Henry Mountains to the south. This remote and wild chain was the last major range in the continental United States to be discovered by white men.

For further information, write to Goblin Valley State Park, Box 93, Green River, UT 84525-0093.

DAY 2: THE SAN RAFAEL REEF

- ■ **A memorable day hike through narrow sandstone canyons**
- ■ **Camping and showers at Goblin Valley State Park**

For the Day 2 hike, choose among three wonderful, high-walled canyons chiseled into the San Rafael Reef: Little Wild Horse (paired here with Bell to make a loop), Crack, and Chute. All have deep narrows bounded by soaring cliffs and afford ease of passage. You can complete both the Chute and Crack Canyon trips in one day, if you are feeling ambitious. Be sure to fill your water bottles before starting out.

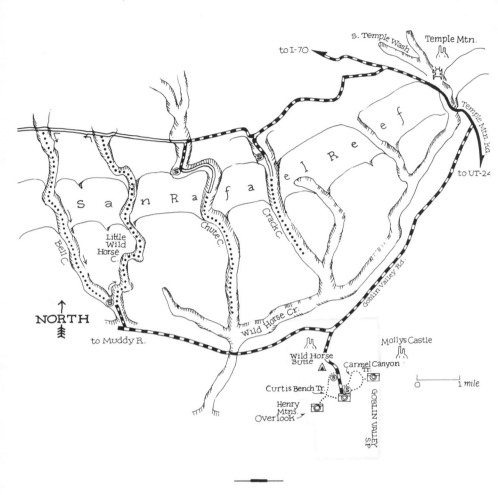

Day Hike 1: Little Wild Horse and Bell Canyons

Distance: 7.5 miles, round-trip
Time: 1 day
Map: USGS quad for Wild Horse
Difficulty: easy

With extensive sections of tight narrows, Little Wild Horse Canyon is a visual and tactile delight (see map, p. 45). Its southern end joins Bell Canyon, making this an exciting but leisurely loop trip. It is also a cool one, for the sun penetrates these deep slots only at midday. Do not enter the canyon if rain threatens, for few exit routes are available to escape a flash flood.

The access road to Little Wild Horse Canyon is 5.75 miles west of the Goblin Valley Entrance Station. Leave the state park and turn left at Wild Horse Butte onto a generally good dirt road. You may have trouble at mile 2.75, where the road crosses Wild Horse Creek; gun it here to avoid getting stuck in the sand. At mile 5.75, a sign on the main road reads "high clearance vehicles only." Turn right just past this sign and follow the jeep track as far as you feel comfortable driving; the road extends for about a mile. Park when you start getting nervous. Past a grove of cottonwoods you climb two dry waterfalls in quick succession. These present little difficulty. After that, you come to a fork with Bell Canyon, your return route, on the left. Go right into **Little Wild Horse.**

Before long you reach the extremely twisty Navajo sandstone narrows that continue, on and off, about two-thirds up the canyon. At times you will have to turn sideways and remove your daypack to proceed; you may also have to jump or wade across a few small pools. Where the canyon opens out at its end, there are several chockstones and pour-offs, but all can be overcome without much difficulty.

After about 3.5 miles, a jeep road crosses the canyon. Turn left here and follow the road for about 1.25 miles over a pass to the head of **Bell Canyon.** Upper Bell is narrower, prettier, and shadier than upper Little Wild Horse, and a rough dirt road extends into it almost as far as its narrow section. Despite some obstructions near the upper end, you can maintain a rapid pace here. In no time, you'll be back at the junction with Little Wild Horse and then to your car.

Day Hike 2: Crack Canyon

> **Distance: up to 7 miles, round-trip**
> **Time: up to 3.5 hours**
> **Map: USGS quad for Temple Mtn.**
> **Difficulty: moderate**

Although you can enter this canyon from either the bottom (via Wild Horse Creek, near the butte) or the top (via a road that parallels the reef), the latter access avoids a sandy slog over 2 miles of featureless desert (see map, p. 45). Drive northeast on the Goblin Valley road for 7 miles to its junction with the road to Temple Mountain. Turn left (north). In about 0.75 mile look for the South Temple Wash Fremont pictograph panel on the right. A half mile farther, the pavement stops, and 1.25 miles past that point, turn left (west) onto a good dirt road (normally suitable for all vehicles as far as Chute Canyon). Magnificent views of **Temple Mountain** (a prime source of the uranium used in the Manhattan Project of the 1940s) and the top of the San Rafael Reef can be enjoyed here, marred only by abandoned shacks, cars, and other debris left by miners in years past.

The entrance to **Crack Canyon** is 4.25 miles down this road. A jeep track extends south into the canyon for about 0.75 mile. As it slices through the reef, the canyon exposes the Navajo and Kayenta formations. In each strata is a colorful set of narrows. Though very short, the Navajo narrows, with rock pockmarked like Swiss cheese, have an overhang that creates an illusion of total enclosure. The Kayenta narrows, much longer and deeper, begin about 2 easy miles down the canyon. A few dryfalls and other obstacles make these narrows somewhat tricky to negotiate, so those without moderate athletic ability may wish to stop here. When you have seen enough, backtrack up the canyon to your car.

Day Hike 3: Chute Canyon

> **Distance: 5 miles, round-trip**
> **Time: 2.5 hours**
> **Map: USGS quad for Wild Horse**
> **Difficulty: very easy**

This canyon is Crack's nearest neighbor to the west; some people combine the two into a long loop hike. But since that involves a dusty trek down Wild Horse Creek, and nearly 2 miles of walking the jeep road north of the reef, investigating each canyon separately is more sensible. With no really tight narrows or obstructions of any kind, Chute is an easy walk (see map, p. 45).

Approach **Chute Canyon** from the road at the top of the San Rafael Reef (see Day Hike 2, Crack Canyon). The entrance into Chute is 6.75 miles down this road, or 1.75 miles past Crack. The road itself actually goes a long way into Chute before climbing out to the west. A good place to turn back is at the end of the narrows section, before the canyon joins Wild Horse Creek.

DAY 3: GOBLIN VALLEY TO CAPITOL REEF

- **A drive through the desolate Caineville Badlands**
- **Short hikes in the Waterpocket Fold country**
- **Camping at Capitol Reef National Park**
- **Gas, groceries, and showers available in Hanksville**

Leave the Goblin Valley area today and head 19.5 miles south on UT-24 to Hanksville, where you should gas up and reprovision, buying two days' worth of food. From here it is 37 miles to Capitol Reef National Park. Continue on UT-24, which follows the Fremont drainage to an eye-blinker of a town, Caineville, in 20 miles. The Henry Mountains rise to the south, and the gray and tan **Caineville Badlands,** most appealing when the sun is low in the sky, are on the north; the most prominent of these is **Factory Butte.** The landscape becomes more lush and inviting as you near **Capitol Reef National Park.**

Called "the land of the sleeping rainbow" by the Navajo, this photogenic and geologically unusual park is somewhat off the beaten track. Water erosion has cut intricate canyons, domes, arches, and spires out of the cross-bedded slickrock, which comprises most of the park. One of the largest domes here, carved from sandstone, resembles the Capitol Building in Washington, D.C. This dome is clearly visible from the highway.

The dominant landform is the 100-mile-long **Waterpocket Fold,** a rocky ridge warped and uplifted sixty million years ago by subterranean pressures. Throughout this region numerous small potholes, or "pockets," in the rock collect rainwater. The Fremont River, named after the famous nineteenth-century explorer John C. Fremont, drains the area.

Between A.D. 800 and 1200, Fremont Indians lived along the river, and their rock carvings (or petroglyphs) are still amply in evidence today; a large grouping can be seen, for example, at an official highway pullout on the north side of the river about 1.25 miles east of the park visitor center. Centuries later, the park's canyons were frequented at different times by Ute and Paiute Indians, law-evading polygamists, and even members of Butch Cassidy's "Wild Bunch." The Fremont River valley itself was colonized by Mormon settlers who planted and irrigated orchards that the Park Service still maintains; in season, visitors are allowed to pick and purchase the apples, cherries, pears, and peaches that these fruit trees produce.

Scenic Drive: Capitol Reef

Distance: 25 miles
Time: 2 hours

You can begin your exploration of Capitol Reef by taking the 25-mile, round-trip scenic drive. It begins at the visitor center, located on UT-24, and ultimately leads to picturesque **Capitol Gorge.** Make the Capitol Reef campground, about a mile down this scenic road, your first stop, to assure yourself of a site. Farther along, are canyons that have cut all the way through the folds, exposing the tilted rock strata that comprise it. As you travel from west to east through the gorges, you move forward in geologic time, beginning with the early Triassic Chinle formation and passing through the majestic "Glen Canyon Group": first Wingate sandstone, then the Kayenta formation, and finally Navajo sandstone. At the end of the road to Capitol Gorge is a shelter where you can eat a picnic lunch. Trails branching off from this point allow you to explore Capitol Gorge's narrows and side-canyons. One popular destination, about a mile's walk from the picnic area, is The Tanks, a series of small, water-filled potholes.

Capitol Reef presents wonderful opportunities for day or overnight hikes. After completing the scenic drive to Capitol Gorge, select two of the following short hikes.

For more information, write to the Superintendent, Capitol Reef National Park, Torrey, UT 84775.

Day Hike 1: Hickman Bridge

> **Distance: 2 miles, round-trip**
> **Time: 2 hours**
> **Map: USGS topo for Capitol Reef National Park**
> **Difficulty: moderate**

The well-marked trailhead to **Hickman Bridge** (see map, p. 50), named after a local man who was instrumental in securing federal protection for the area, is 2 miles east of the visitor center on UT-24. For a short distance, the trail follows the river before climbing rapidly about 400 feet to the top of the gorge. Where the trail splits, 0.25 mile from the trailhead, take the left fork, which will drop into a shallow wash before arriving at the 130-foot-long Kayenta sandstone bridge 0.75 mile past the junction. The plateau offers a striking view of nearby **Capitol Dome** and other petrified sand dunes. On the way back, look for a small granary above the wash and to the right about 0.25 mile shy of the bridge. Hikers willing to extend their excursion by a 4-mile round-trip can pick up the **Rim Overlook Trail** by turning left at the junction. Beautiful views of the area near the visitor center are yours from the trail's end.

Day Hike 2: Fremont River Overlook

> **Distance: 2 miles, round-trip**
> **Time: 1.5 hours**
> **Map: USGS topo for Capitol Reef National Park**
> **Difficulty: initially very easy, then strenuous**

The Fremont River Trail (see map, p. 50) begins at the back end of the Capitol Reef campground, indicated by a stone sign. The first 0.5 mile is a level, leisurely walk along the riverbank, past orchards and horse pastures. Look for yellow-bellied marmots around the bushes here. Passing through a gate, the trail begins a merciless 800-foot ascent over some rock switchbacks to the top of the ridge, marked by a huge cairn. From the crest are

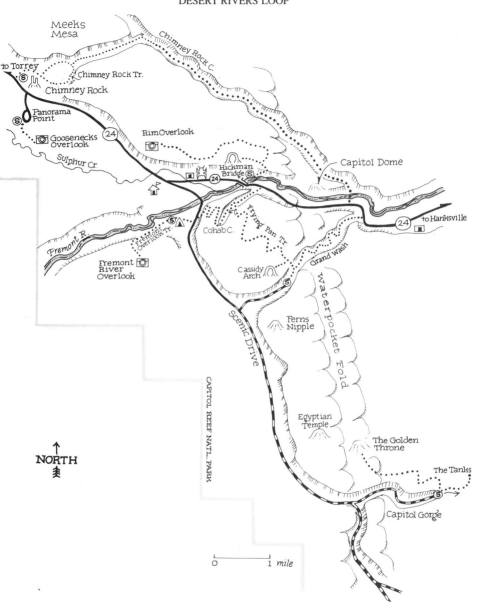

views of the canyon of the upper Fremont River cutting back into Boulder
Mountain, as well as many of the prominent Navajo sandstone domes
along the reef. Currently, the Fremont River canyon can be hiked (a strenuous trip involving many stream crossings), though county officials have
proposed building a dam upstream.

Day Hike 3: Grand Wash ✓

> **Distance: 2.25 miles, one way**
> **Time: 1.5 hours**
> **Map: USGS topo for Capitol Reef National Park**
> **Difficulty: very easy**

Grand Wash has carved through the Waterpocket Fold a sheer-walled canyon with a short but unusually beautiful section of narrows. The elevation gain on this trip is negligible, so you can start at either end. If you have two cars, there is a marked pullout on UT-24, 4.5 miles past the visitor center, to indicate that end of the hike. Otherwise, retrace your steps.

The trailhead for **Grand Wash** is at the end of a spur 3.5 miles south of the visitor center on the scenic park road (see map, p. 50). A trail parallels the streambed on the right for about the first 0.25 mile, but most of the way you will be walking in the wash. Because this 500-foot-deep canyon has few exit routes, do not enter it when rain threatens. Within about a mile, the narrows begin; at some points the canyon is only 20 feet wide. After another mile, the canyon opens up again somewhat, and the hike ends just past the point where power lines cross the wash overhead.

The short side-canyons to the right of Grand Wash are worth exploring. Especially enjoyable are Bear Canyon, which intersects the wash just before the narrows, and a small, unnamed slot canyon that comes in at the heart of the narrows where the wash bends sharply to the left.

DAY 4: MORE IN CAPITOL REEF

- Narrow canyon or ridgetop hike
- Camping at Capitol Reef National Park Cedar Mesa Campground
- Gas, groceries, showers, and laundry available in Torrey

Choose today between two long trails, both with incredible allure. One traverses a high, exposed bench, yielding sweeping views of the top of the Waterpocket Fold; the other explores a narrow canyon memorable for sandstone spires and the play of light and shadow on towering walls. If you opt for the ridgetop trail, you should also have time to visit other places in the park, such as the **Goosenecks Overlook** of Sulphur Creek. Sometime today, decide whether your upcoming backpacking trip (see Days 5 and 6) will be Upper or Lower Muley Twist Canyon. Secure a permit at the visitor center, and buy three days' worth of supplies in oasislike Torrey, 10 miles west of the park on UT-12.

Camp at Capitol Reef Campground or at Cedar Mesa Campground, 20 miles down the Notom–Bullfrog Road (see Days 5 and 6 for directions; map, p. 54). Take along plenty of water (several gallons per person), as the Cedar Mesa Campground and most of the Muley trips are dry.

———

Day Hike 1: Frying Pan Trail

**Distance: 6.25 miles, one way, including side trip to
Cassidy Arch
Time: 5 hours
Map: USGS topo for Capitol Reef National Park
Difficulty: moderate**

Most of the Frying Pan Trail traverses the high slickrock terraces of the Kayenta formation overlooking the park. Because this trail can become ovenlike at midday without a stiff breeze, begin the trip in the early morning. To reach the trailhead (see map, p. 50), drive south from the visitor center on the scenic drive as far as Grand Wash. Turn left here and continue to the road's end, where you begin your hike.

After 0.25 mile, the trail branches off to the left, climbing briskly about 900 feet to the rim of Grand Wash Canyon. In 1 mile a 0.5-mile spur trail to the left leads to **Cassidy Arch,** a graceful span named for the outlaw Butch Cassidy. Return to the main trail and turn left.

The Frying Pan Trail winds through eroded uplands for 3 miles before dropping into **Cohab Canyon,** where you again turn left, proceeding up the canyon to its head. This narrow chasm, with its Swiss cheese walls and even narrower side-canyons, was once a refuge for some Mormon polygamists, or "cohabitationists," trying to evade a federal posse. From the canyon's head, the trail drops steeply in the next mile, switchbacking down a precipitous cliff to the scenic drive. It ends just across the road from the campground, 3.5 miles north of your car.

Day Hike 2: Chimney Rock Canyon

**Distance: 9 miles, one way
Time: 6 hours
Map: USGS topo for Capitol Reef National Park
Difficulty: moderate**

Narrow Chimney Rock (aka Spring) Canyon runs parallel to the axis of the Waterpocket Fold for many miles before cutting through it. The trail into this exquisite canyon starts at the Chimney Rock pullout north of UT-24 on the western end of the park (see map, p. 50), about 3.25 miles from the visitor center. **Chimney Rock** itself, a great spire carved from Moenkopi sandstone and capped by harder Shinarump sandstone (a member of the Chinle formation), can also be visited by those with an extra hour to spare. Otherwise, the hike is slightly downhill and relatively cool most of the way.

From the trailhead, climb onto the tableland behind Chimney Rock to the junction with the **Chimney Rock Trail.** Continue straight ahead under the soaring Wingate cliffs of Meeks Mesa, passing the other portion of the Chimney Rock Trail loop on your right. Following a drainage, you descend gradually until you intersect **Chimney Rock Canyon,** 2.5 miles from the parking lot. There is a drift fence here. Go right and follow the canyon for 6.5 more miles down to its confluence with the Fremont River.

Chimney Rock Canyon, chiseled out of Wingate and Kayenta sandstone, is narrow, twisty, and quite spectacular, its depth averaging about 500 feet. Navajo sandstone domes loom high above. At one point, you'll have to climb a bit onto the eroded left bank to avoid two small pour-offs, but otherwise you remain in the streambed all the way. About halfway down the canyon to your left is a natural arch in the cliff. Just past an enormous alcove, the hike ends where Chimney Rock Canyon empties into the Fremont River, 3.5 miles east of the visitor center on the main highway. From here it is 6.75 miles back to your car, via UT-24. But you must ford the stream to reach the highway.

DAYS 5 AND 6: MULEY TWIST

- **A drive down the Notom–Bullfrog Road along the Waterpocket Fold**
- **An overnight canyon wilderness excursion**
- **Arches, alcoves, and breathtaking scenery**

Both the Upper and Lower Muley Twist hikes match any in the Southwest for diversity and aesthetic appeal. Reserve an extra day for Lower Muley Twist if you plan to investigate side-canyons and walk back to the parking lot. Get an early start, and carry at least 1 gallon of water apiece per day. It's also possible to take day hikes on portions of each canyon instead of backpacking them.

It is a 1.5-hour drive to either of the trailheads, which are close together, from the Capitol Reef visitor center. From the visitor center, proceed east on UT-24 just past the park boundary. Turn right (south) on a dirt road toward Notom, a private ranch and Lake Powell's Bullfrog marina. Cedar Mesa Campground, a primitive campground with five sites, is 20 miles down this road.

About 15 miles past Cedar Mesa, turn right onto the famous **Burr**

Cottonwood leaves shimmer against Muley Twist walls in Capitol Reef National Park, Utah

Trail, which climbs to the top of Waterpocket Fold on some thrilling switchbacks. After 2.5 miles, once the road has topped out, a sign on the left indicates access into Lower Muley Twist Canyon. The turnoff for the Upper Muley trailhead is a mile beyond this point.

Whatever hike you choose, camp near Boulder on the evening of Day 7, perhaps at one of the national forest campgrounds north of town on UT-12. Calf Creek Recreation Area south of town also offers camping, but its few sites fill quickly. For the most direct route to Boulder, continue west through Long Canyon on the spectacular Burr Trail. Deer Creek Campground is conveniently located near the road's end, about 26.5 miles past the turnoff for Upper Muley Twist. Check at the Capitol Reef visitor center in advance to make sure the Burr Trail is not closed for construction. In recent years the status of this road has been a bone of contention between developers, who want it paved, and environmental groups, who oppose paving.

Backpack (or day hike) 1: Lower Muley Twist Canyon

Distance: 17.5 miles (or 6.5 miles), one way
Time: 2 to 3 days (or 1 full day)
Map: USGS topo for Capitol Reef National Park
Difficulty: easy, with strenuous exit on cutoff trail

This historically important, exceptionally scenic canyon got its colorful name from early Mormon pioneers passing through on their way to settle in southeastern Utah; according to local folklore, they declared it sinuous enough to "twist a mule." Running in the Waterpocket Fold, the narrow canyon is chiseled out of the Navajo, Kayenta, and Wingate formations. Although the entire canyon offers outstanding hiking, a cutoff trail allows you to do a 6.5-mile day trip (see map, p. 56). Unless you have two cars, plan on walking back up the Burr Trail to your car, 4.25 miles from The Post, a point on the Notom–Bullfrog Road where the trail ends. Keep in mind that the canyon has no reliable water source. Also, because flash-flooding poses a danger, check with a ranger about weather predictions.

Park at the trailhead near the top of the Burr Trail switchbacks and descend into the canyon, which is shallow at this point. There is no trail, but the wash bottom is generally free of rocks and vegetation. About 2 miles down Muley Twist a large side-canyon comes in from the right; stay in the main canyon by bearing left here. After 4 miles, a sign on the left marks **The Post Cutoff** in the red Kayenta formation. There is an excellent slickrock campsite on the right bank a short distance up the canyon from this sign.

If you have opted for a day trip, leave the canyon here, ascending a cairned trail that follows a tributary of Muley Twist to the system's eastern rim. From the crest of the Waterpocket Fold on, the strenuous trail prefers slickrock for most of its route. Because the way down is not always predictable, be sure to locate each cairn before proceeding. Your route traverses far to the right, sometimes climbing unexpectedly or passing through notches in the low Navajo domes near the top of the reef. Eventually, the trail plunges into the reddish Kayenta formation. At the bottom it crosses a wash to arrive at a spur road, 2 miles from the start of the cutoff.

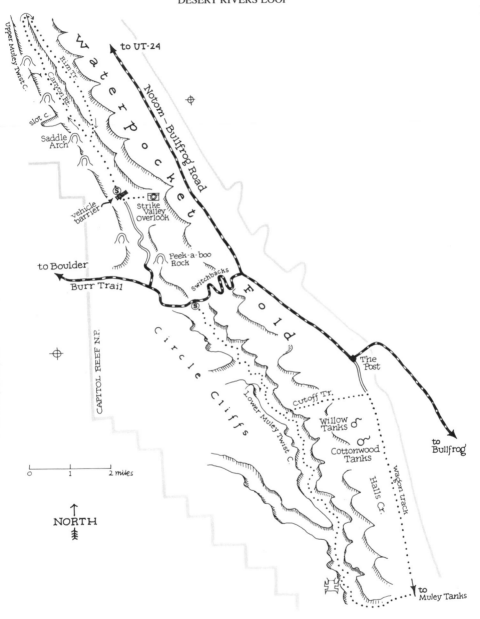

Turn left at the spur road, passing a corral, and within another 0.5 mile you will reach The Post on the Notom–Bullfrog Road.

If you continue your hike down Muley Twist instead of taking the cut-off, you have 8 more miles to the head of the canyon and 5.5 miles back to The Post. Past the cutoff, the serpentine canyon slices deeply into the

Kayenta and Wingate formations, older rock layers than the white Navajo sandstone that sits above them. After encountering some tremendous over-hangs on your left in the next few miles, you arrive at a major drainage entering from the right. This tributary showcases nature's artistry, with its remarkable desert varnish, Swiss cheese cliffs, and hat-wearing gremlins, and it can be easily explored for about 1.5 miles, until a dryfall and some narrows impede upstream progress.

Back in Muley Twist itself, a very long and straight golden cliff presents itself on the left. Where a smaller side-canyon comes in on the right about a mile past the major tributary, a slickrock bench offers excellent camping. There are more alcoves on the right between here and the point where the canyon finally forces its way through the fold. On the rear wall of the largest and southernmost of these amphitheaters, at the head of a big bend, is a sort of register onto which numerous cattlemen from years gone by carved their names. Unfortunately, an overabundance of cow chips makes this an unappealing place to spend the night, but there are nicer spots in the mile remaining between here and the canyon's 90-degree turn into the reef. The canyon walls close in at the end, opening up again near the junction with Halls Creek.

At the junction the route turns left (north), following an old, deterio-rated wagon track toward The Post, 5.5 miles distant. If you are short of water, first detour 0.5 mile to the south and refill your canteens at Muley Tanks, pools of water located near a grove of cottonwoods. The only other water sources in the vicinity are Cottonwood Tanks and Willow Tanks, over a mile south of The Post.

About 0.5 mile below The Post is the east end of the cutoff trail. You can return to your car via this trail, retracing the northern section of Lower Muley (6 miles). Or, you can simply proceed to The Post, returning to your car from there along the Burr Trail (4.25 miles).

Backpack (or day hike) 2: Upper Muley Twist Canyon

> **Distance: 9.5 miles (or 4 miles), round-trip from vehicle
> barrier; 14.5 miles (or 9 miles), round-trip
> from beginning of jeep road
> Time: 1.5 to 2 days (or 1 day)
> Map: USGS topo for Capitol Reef National Park
> Difficulty: initially easy, with strenuous trip to the fold**

Bring along plenty of film for this visual feast of a hike, which will re-gale you with magnificent views both within the canyon itself and along the crest of the Waterpocket Fold.

Your mileage depends on the kind of vehicle you drive, for the 3-mile access route is designated a jeep road after the first 0.5 mile, where others

Saddle Arch casts a dramatic shadow in Upper Muley Twist, Capitol Reef National Park, Utah

can park. However, with high clearance you may be able to go the full distance; the worst stretch of road is at the very beginning, just past the first parking area. Those who must walk the road through this wide portion of the canyon will find the extra 5 miles (round-trip) not only quick and easy but also highly scenic. Peek-a-Boo Rock (a window in the Navajo sandstone) on the right and two unnamed red Kayenta sandstone arches on the left of the road can be more fully savored by those on foot than by those jostling along in a car.

The turnoff for the jeep road is 1 mile above the Lower Muley trailhead at the top of the Burr Trail switchbacks (see map, p. 56). At the end of the jeep road is a large parking area; the easy **Strike Valley Overlook Trail** (0.75 miles, round-trip) is on the right, with the main canyon straight ahead, past a vehicle barrier. The first 2 nearly flat miles of the official hiking route would make an interesting day trip, suitable for all age groups.

Immediately before **Saddle Arch** at mile 2, the second of two significant Kayenta formation arches on the left, a sign on the right indicates the **Rim Trail,** a cairned route to the top of the Waterpocket Fold. Consider establishing a camp either near Saddle Arch on one of the benches (never in the canyon, because of the flash flood danger!), or, preferably, on top of the fold via the cairned route. Campsites become very scarce as the canyon continues to narrow, and much of the route is very difficult, even treacherous, with a backpack. You should establish camp in this vicinity and hike the rest of the canyon with only a daypack containing water and other essentials.

Between Saddle Arch and the upper end of Muley Twist, several more unnamed arches are visible to the left of the wash. About 0.5 mile past Saddle, a slot side-canyon opens on the left; a chockstone here complicates to some degree your exploration of the grotto on the other side. Within another 0.5 mile skirt a very short set of narrows by ascending slightly up the right bank. After about 100 yards, drop back into the streambed and follow it for the next mile.

At a sharp bend to the right, a small jug-handle arch stands directly in front of you. The true narrows start about 0.25 mile past this point, or 4 miles from the vehicle barrier. Leave the canyon floor and climb very steeply up the right bank, following a physically challenging but clearly marked route. The route stays high above the chasm for about 0.75 mile, offering excellent views across Muley Twist. Watch your footing, especially where there are sheer drops.

Once the narrows end, the trail returns briefly to the stream level. Hikers with extra energy can scramble to the head of the canyon, 6.5 miles beyond the vehicle barrier. Others will prefer to proceed to the Rim Trail, which begins immediately after a small chute, 0.25 mile past the narrows, at mile 4.75. Although the trail to the rim seems nearly vertical at times, requiring some hand-over-hand climbing, it is not as dangerous as the narrows section. Cairns mark the rather improbable route.

At the top is a prominent Navajo dome with a tall sign reading "Canyon Route." From here, it's a freestyle trek south along the rim. The route is generally uncairned, so take your bearings by close observation of the side-canyons, arches, and other landmarks you saw from below. On the knife-edged ridges between domes, passage is often hazardous and difficult. But before you to the east stretches a stunning tableau that incorporates Strike Valley, the Henry Mountains, the Little Rockies, Tarantula Mesa, and Halls Creek.

Near Saddle Arch, the cairned Rim Trail route descends to the canyon through an obvious break in the otherwise impenetrable Navajo sandstone cliffs. The descent is not difficult, but spotting the unobtrusive sign marking its beginning may be a problem. Saddle Arch is your best landmark here, and from above it is evident that this arch was aptly named. At the bottom, go left to return to your car.

Calf Creek's falls create a pellucid pool

<u>DAY 7:</u> CALF CREEK

- **A brief visit to an Anasazi ruin**
- **An easy day hike to a desert waterfall**
- **Camping and showers at Escalante State Park**
- **Gas and groceries available in Escalante**

If you camped near Boulder, you won't have far to drive today. Your first stop, **Anasazi Indian Village State Historical Park,** is immediately north of Boulder on UT-12. This excavated, multiroom structure was abandoned by its neolithic residents around A.D. 1300. Nearby are a museum and a full-scale replica of an intact Anasazi dwelling.

South of Boulder, UT-12 switchbacks down a narrow ridge between two canyons in the Escalante system. At the bottom, **Calf Creek Recreation Area** is on the right, 11.5 miles past Boulder. The entrance sign, positioned at a sharp angle to the highway, may be hard to see. Park at the picnic area and fill your canteens in preparation for today's hike to Lower Calf Creek Falls.

At the conclusion of your hike, you will drive southwest on UT-12 to the small town of Escalante (population 800), located 28 miles past Boulder. The drive is engaging, especially after you cross the river and ascend to a canyon viewpoint west of town. Resupply in town, then go west about a mile on UT-12 to the turnoff for **Escalante State Park,** on the right, where you will camp. Here you can take the short Wide Hollow Trail and the adjoining Sleeping Rainbow Loop (which total 1.75 miles, round-trip); originating at the campground, these trails wind through beautiful petrified wood deposits. Other attractions here include fossilized dinosaur bones and prehistoric Fremont artifacts.

For additional information, contact the Bureau of Land Management, Escalante Resource Area, P.O. Box 225, Escalante, UT 84726; and Escalante State Park, P.O. Box 350, Escalante, UT 84726.

Day Hike: Lower Calf Creek Falls

Distance: 5.5 miles, round-trip
Time: 3 hours
Map: USGS quad for Calf Creek
Difficulty: easy

The main attraction of this pleasant, interpretive trail is a 125-foot waterfall, but it also has various archaeological treasures to offer. Proximity to a verdant streamside campground makes this an immensely popular destination for family outings.

From the picnic area, walk a short distance up the road through the campground; look for the trailhead on the left. The trail, mostly over sand and shaded for much of the day, runs along the left bank of the perennial Calf Creek. In addition to a few pictograph panels, there are two ruins high in the Navajo sandstone cliffs: one in the main canyon and another in a side-canyon on the left. Below the waterfall, located in a sort of grotto, is a

Pastel spires descend a slope, Bryce Canyon National Park, Utah

large pool ideal for wading and swimming. Sheer cliffs around the falls prevent the trail from going farther; to return to your car you must double back.

DAY 8: BRYCE CANYON NATIONAL PARK

- **Scenic drive along the canyon rim**
- **Day hikes amid the hoodoos**
- **Camping at Bryce Canyon National Park**
- **Gas, groceries, laundry, and showers available in Rubys Inn and Bryce Canyon**

This should be a relaxing day, involving only a one-hour drive to the Bryce entrance station and a subsequent trip down the scenic park road, punctuated by overlook-stopping and short hikes into the canyon. From Escalante, follow UT-12 west for about 45 miles, then turn south on UT-63 at **Rubys Inn.** Entering the park, select a campsite at Sunset or (better) North Campground, where you can garner a choice site fairly close to the rim if you arrive early enough. Then continue south on the park road to Yovimpa and Rainbow points, stopping at overlooks on the way back to savor the panorama spread before you.

Bryce Canyon is one of those special places that stir the imagination and encourage metaphor. The Paiute Indians called it "red rocks standing like men in a bowl-shaped canyon"; to Ebenezer Bryce, the immigrant rancher after whom the canyon was named, it was simply "a hell of a place to lose a cow." Technically, it is not a single canyon, but a huge amphitheater carved out of the Paunsaugunt Plateau, which on this side is drained by the Paria River (a Colorado tributary). Like neighboring Cedar Breaks, Bryce's high altitude—up to 9100 feet—makes it a much cooler and more comfortable place to visit in the summer months than most other desert spots.

About 60 miles of trails wind through the park's needles and spires, carved out of the Claron formation by physical and chemical weathering. Most trails are under 5 miles in length, but, with the exception of the Rim Trail, all are at least moderately difficult, requiring tough climbs of several hundred feet back up from the canyon floor. You will have the opportunity to sample several of them during your two days in the park.

For further information, contact the Superintendent, Bryce Canyon National Park, Bryce Canyon, UT 84717.

Day Hike 1: Navajo Loop

> **Distance: 1.5 miles, round-trip**
> **Time: 1 hour**
> **Map: USGS topo for Bryce Canyon National Park**
> **Difficulty: Moderate**

The Navajo Loop and the Queens Garden Trail (see Day Hike 2, below) can be hiked independently or together. They are Bryce Canyon's most popular routes, for they allow visitors direct access to the hoodoos in the heart of the park.

The **Navajo Loop** begins at Sunset Point (see map, p. 64). Just below the rim, the trail forks. Take the left fork and descend 525 feet to the canyon floor, enjoying a close-up view of the Two Bridges, The Pope, and Thors Hammer, a slender orange pinnacle capped by a mallet-shaped

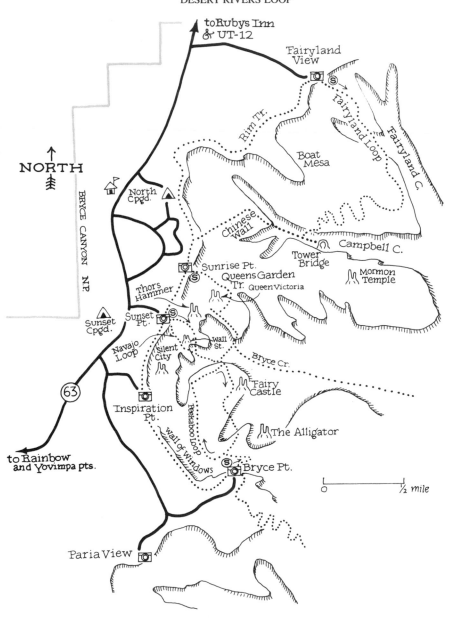

stone. Within 0.75 mile, the connector to the Queens Garden Trail comes in on the left. Bear right to continue on the Navajo Loop. Rounding a bend, you soon reach Wall Street, which consists of two parallel rows of closely-spaced pinnacles. The trail threads through this passageway as it begins its steep climb back to the rim. Near the top, a spur to the left passes through a window in the rock to an overlook of the Silent City.

Day Hike 2: Queens Garden Trail

Distance: 1.5 miles, round-trip
Time: 1 hour
Map: USGS topo for Bryce Canyon National Park
Difficulty: Moderate

Beginning at Sunrise Point (see map, p. 64), the **Queens Garden Trail** is the easiest of the trails that descend to the floor of the Bryce amphitheater. It switchbacks steeply down 325 feet, past Gullivers Castle and Queens Castle, before ending at a viewpoint of the Queen Victoria profile formation. From here you can retrace your steps back to the rim, or take the connecting trail to the Navajo Loop. If you do ascend on the Navajo Loop, a very easy 0.5-mile walk to the right along the Rim Trail will return you to Sunrise Point.

Day Hike 3: Rim Trail

Distance: variable, up to 11 miles, round-trip
Time: up to 4 hours
Map: USGS topo of Bryce Canyon National Park
Difficulty: easy

The incomparable Rim Trail follows the lip of Bryce Canyon from Fairyland View to Bryce Point (7800 and 8300 feet, respectively). Since it connects with Sunrise, Sunset, and Inspiration points, all accessible by car, there are many different places to begin and end the hike (see map, p. 64). Arguably the most beautiful section extends from Sunrise to Inspiration, where the walking is especially easy. The Rim Trail presents the hiker with continual tableaus of the canyon's pastel cliffs and hoodoos, as well as of more distant features, such as the Navajo Mountain and the Kaiparowits Plateau.

DAY 9: MORE EXPLORATION OF BRYCE CANYON

- **Glorious day-hiking amid spires and needles**
- **Camping at Bryce Canyon**
- **Gas, groceries, showers, and laundry available in Rubys Inn and Bryce Canyon**

Each of the following day hikes gives you an opportunity to see the strange and wonderful formations of Bryce Canyon close up.

Day Hike 1: Fairyland Trail

> **Distance: 8 miles, round-trip**
> **Time: 4 or 5 hours**
> **Map: USGS topo of Bryce Canyon National Park**
> **Difficulty: moderate**

One of the longest trails in the park, the delightful Fairyland Loop can be hiked in either direction. It can also be shortened by 2.5 miles with a car shuttle from Sunrise Point to Fairyland View.

From the trailhead at Fairyland View overlook near the park entrance, the route descends 850 feet along a scenic ridgeline to cross the upper reaches of colorful Fairyland Canyon (see map, p. 64). After circling to the east and south of Boat Mesa in a series of moderate ups and downs, and passing exotic formations such as the Palace of the Fairy Queen and the Ruins of Athens, you reach Campbell Canyon. The trail then intersects a short spur on the left leading to **Tower Bridge,** one of the two significant natural bridges in the park. Past the Tower Bridge turnoff, the trail starts its steep ascent, offering views of the Chinese Wall to the left. At the top the trail forks; the path on the left leads immediately to Sunrise Point, while the Rim Trail on the right climbs to North Campground, hugging the lip of the bowl back to Fairyland View.

Day Hike 2: Peekaboo Loop

> **Distance: 5.5 to 7 miles, round-trip, depending on trail-**
> **head**
> **Time: 3 or 4 hours**
> **Map: USGS topo of Bryce Canyon National Park**
> **Difficulty: moderate**

With its seemingly constant ups and downs, the Peekaboo Loop deters the more casual visitor. Another deterrent is the sights and smells left in the wake of horse concession operations that use this trail. Any unpleasantries are quickly forgiven, however, when you catch sight of the Alligator, the Fairy Castle, the Silent City, the Wall of Windows, and other interesting formations along the route.

The Peekaboo Loop is connected to the rim by trails leading down from Sunset, Bryce, and Sunrise points; the round-trip mileages are 5.5, 6.5, and 7, respectively (including in each case 3.5 miles on the loop itself). The ascent to Bryce Point is about 300 feet greater than it is to the other trailheads—a factor to consider when selecting a point of departure (see map, p. 64).

From Bryce Point, the trail takes off to the northeast, then doubles back and descends very steeply on several switchbacks to meet the Peekaboo Loop. Turn left to proceed clockwise around the loop arriving at a picnic area with pit toilets. The trail continues past the Wall of Windows and Inspiration Point on the left, then reaches the junction with the trails from Sunrise and Sunset points. Turn right here, climb a few hundred feet, and then descend to meet a wash. Catch your breath before rejoining the trail back to Bryce Point.

DAY 10: KODACHROME BASIN AND DEVILS GARDEN

- Encountering the "sand pipes"
- Camping and exploring at Devils Garden
- Gas and groceries available in Escalante
- Showers available in Kodachrome Basin State Park

Today you should make preparations for a three-night backpack trip in the Escalante River drainage. However, purchasing supplies and obtaining a backcountry camping permit at the Bureau of Land Management (BLM) office won't be the only things you do. A stopover at Kodachrome Basin before you drive into Escalante, and a primitive, waterless campsite tonight at the Devils Garden, will make this day memorable.

The turnoff to **Kodachrome Basin State Park** is 12 miles west of Bryce Canyon on UT-12. Go south for 7.75 miles on the Cottonwood Canyon Road, which follows Cottonwood Wash. The state park, a left turn off the road, protects a geologically singular area. From its valley floor rise almost seventy tall, tan needles called "sand pipes"—columns of rock produced by subterranean pressures and then exposed as the surrounding Entrada sandstone eroded away. Hiking opportunities in the park include walks on the Shakespear Arch Trail (0.75 mile, round-trip); the Panorama Trail (3 miles round-trip; inspects the sand pipes); the Angels Palace Trail (0.5 mile, round-trip); and the rather treacherous Eagles View Trail (1.25 miles round-trip, involving a steep 450-foot climb).

For further information, contact Kodachrome Basin State Park, P.O. Box 238, Cannonville, UT 84718.

Conclude your business in Escalante (remember to fill your canteens!), then drive to your campsite at Devils Garden. Devils Garden can be reached by driving southeast on the **Hole in the Rock Road,** which begins 4.5 miles east of Escalante off UT-12. This road, which extends all the way to Lake Powell, was named for an event in Mormon history, when a party of settlers, stymied by the high walls of the Colorado River's Glen Canyon, blasted a notch through sheer cliffs, lowered their wagons and stock, and forded the river. Travel 12.5 miles down this graded road, then look for a sign toward the **Devils Garden** BLM area on your right. A quar-

Storm clouds build behind Metate Arch, Devils Garden, Utah

ter mile down a spur road is the picnic ground and parking area.

Kids of all ages will love this fascinating area of goblins, arches, and strange erosional forms. There are no trails here, but one can wander around at will. Two arches—one named Mano, the other Metate (words referring to stone implements used to pulverize seeds and grain)—are a few hundred yards south of the picnic area, and a short, shallow red canyon with sheer walls is less than 0.5 mile down the wash. Despite the lack of water, this is a wonderful spot for camping.

DAYS 11 THROUGH 14: ESCALANTE RIVER

- **Discovering four major natural spans**
- **Splashing through a watery canyon**
- **Narrows, alcoves, and gardens galore**

Rise early for your 20.5-mile drive down the Hole in the Rock Road to the trailhead of an exceptional hike through Hurricane Wash and Coyote Gulch to the Escalante River. The Hole in the Rock Road runs parallel to the Kaiparowits Plateau for its 55-mile length. Although it has washboards, it should be drivable as far as the parking area for Hurricane Wash, 33 miles from the UT-24 turnoff. The parking area is adjacent to a big cottonwood on the right just before the road dips into a gully.

The placid, shallow Escalante River, named after a Spanish missionary who pioneered the exploration of the Southwest, is a tributary of the Colorado. It was the last major river to be discovered in the continental United States; John Wesley Powell's second expedition is credited with this achievement. Much of the river's lower end is now an arm of Lake Powell, created after the controversial Glen Canyon Dam was built in 1963 over the Colorado River.

The serpentine, cottonwood-lined canyons of the Escalante, with their fantastic arches, amphitheaters, and hanging gardens, contain flowing water (which you will need to treat). Because you'll be wading for some of the way, wear old boots or sneakers and bring along extra socks. Patches of quicksand often develop during the rainy season; if it is present near the beginning of your hike, it is likely to pose a significant problem as you proceed down the canyon. Carry about 1 gallon of water apiece as insurance until you start seeing pools and springs.

The featured hike takes you as far as the river, requiring you to double back over the same route to your car. More adventurous backpackers might want to begin at **Harris Wash,** 10.5 miles up the Hole in the Rock Road toward Escalante, and then return via Coyote Gulch. That trip, which totals 63 miles, necessitates a car shuttle. Its feasibility depends on the lake level, which may force you to exit prematurely at 25 Mile Wash.

Where you decide to camp at the conclusion of your trip will depend on how early you get out and how keen you are for hamburgers and showers. One suggestion is to reprovision in Escalante and spend the night in one of the national forest campgrounds off UT-12 on Boulder Mountain, between Boulder and Torrey.

For more information, write to the Bureau of Land Management, Escalante Resource Area, P O. Box 225, Escalante, UT 84726; or the National Park Service, Glen Canyon National Recreation Area, Escalante Ranger District, Escalante, UT 84726.

Backpack: Escalante River via Coyote Gulch

> **Distance: 26.5 miles, round-trip**
> **Time: 4 days**
> **Maps: USGS quads for Big Hollow Wash, King Mesa,**
>   **and the Rincon**
> **Difficulty: moderate**

This hike starts at the Hurricane Wash parking lot at mile 35 along the Hole in the Rock Road (see map, p. 70), where you pick up a jeep road heading east. The road leads to **Hurricane Wash.** After a level, dry, and sandy stretch, gradually the Navajo sandstone cliffs begin to rise. At about

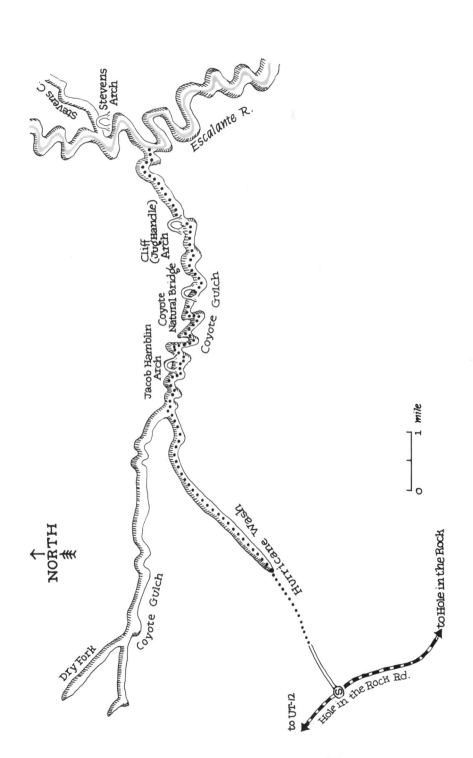

NORTH

Dry Fork

Coyote Gulch

Stevens C.

Stevens Arch

Escalante R.

Cliff (Jughandle) Arch

Coyote Natural Bridge

Coyote Gulch

Jacob Hamblin Arch

Hurricane Wash

1 mile

0

to UT-12

Hole in the Rock Rd.

to Hole in the Rock

5.5 miles from the trailhead, the wash empties into Coyote Gulch. Camping is good in this vicinity. Turn right here, continuing downstream past two dramatic erosional formations: **Jacob Hamblin Arch** (at mile 7) and **Coyote Natural Bridge** (at mile 8.5).

About 1 mile past Coyote Bridge, the trail climbs onto the left bank of the canyon above a rockfall, then arrives at a series of pour-offs. Skirt the one near Cliff (aka Jug Handle) Arch on the right at mile 10.5. The canyon deepens and narrows near its mouth, and you have to climb the cliff to the right, assisted by ladders. Cairns mark the spot where you go up.

Approaching the **Escalante River,** at mile 13.25, you come within sight of exceptional **Stevens Arch** far above the stream. Unless the lake level is too high, you should be able to turn left at the river and splash upstream about 0.5 mile or so to a sandy bank on the left where you can camp if there is no flash flood danger. When you have seen enough, double back to your car.

Splashing through Harris Wash, a tributary of the Escalante River, Utah

DAY 15: CATHEDRAL VALLEY

- **A loop drive through phenomenal badlands and/or more day hikes in Capitol Reef**
- **Camping at Capitol Reef National Park**
- **Gas, groceries, showers, and laundry available in Torrey**

This morning, drive over Boulder Mountain on UT-12 toward the town of Torrey (35 miles from Boulder). Be sure to stop at the designated overlooks along this route to enjoy views of the Henry Mountains and Waterpocket Fold country. After resupplying in Torrey select a campsite in Capitol Reef.

If your car is a "low rider," you should not attempt the Cathedral Valley loop described below. Instead, hike one of the Capitol Reef trails you missed before (see Days 3 and 4). If your car has reasonably good clearance, however, the road to Cathedral Valley should present no problems, as long as you take it slow. The half-day drive leads to the wild and remote northern sector of the park, frequented more by cowboys than by tourists. Check at the visitor center that the roads are in decent condition, and avoid them in the event of rain, since their clay beds make them impassable when wet.

Scenic Drive: Cathedral Valley

Distance: 59 miles
Time: half day

To begin the scenic loop, continue east on UT-24 for 11.5 miles past the visitor center. Turn left at a sign for the Fremont River ford (see map, p. 73), testing the rocky-bottomed stream for depth before crossing it. For the first several miles, you pass through the rainbow-hued Bentonite Hills. This area, with its barren, clay-like mounds, is geologically younger than other sections of the park, a part of the Morrison formation. The Henrys loom on the southern horizon. At miles 14 and 27 (from the UT-24 turn-off), spur roads lead to overlooks of the **South Desert** basin, bounded on the west by the Waterpocket Fold. (An overlook of Upper Cathedral Valley is located 0.5 mile up another spur just short of mile 27.5.)

Immediately past this spur, turn right at Hartnet Junction and descend on switchbacks into **Upper Cathedral Valley.** The road veers close to the flank of Thousand Lake Mountain here, going over some rough high spots. The Park Service maintains a small, primitive campground (Cathedral Campground) in this vicinity. At the bottom of the switchbacks are fluted

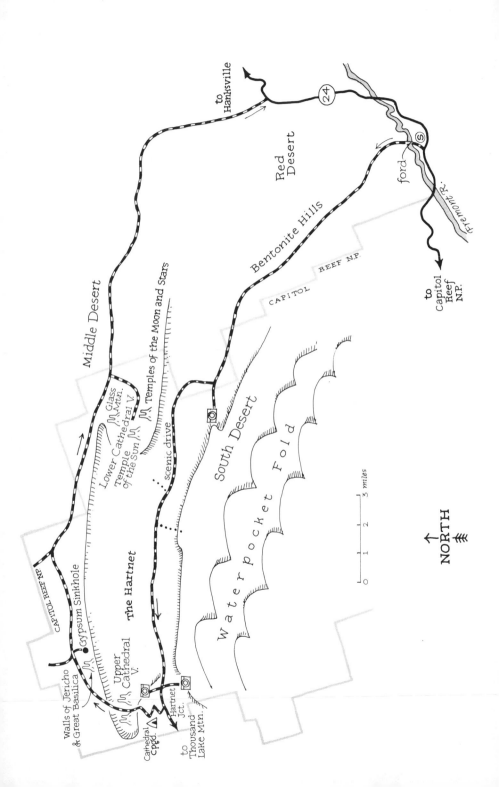

to Hanksville

24

Red Desert

ford

Fremont R.

to Capitol Reef N.P.

Bentonite Hills

CAPITOL REEF N.P.

Middle Desert

Glass Mtn.
Lower Cathedral V.
Temple of the Sun
Temples of the Moon and Stars

scenic drive

South Desert

W a t e r p o c k e t   F o l d

CAPITOL REEF NP

Gypsum Sinkhole

The Hartnet

Upper Cathedral V.

Walls of Jericho & Great Basilica

Cathedral Cpgd.

Hartnet Jct.

to Thousand Lake Mtn.

0   1   2   3 miles

NORTH

rock pyramids composed of Entrada sandstone. Here begins the most scenically compelling part of the drive, which continues as you descend slowly toward **Lower Cathedral Valley.** You pass the Walls of Jericho and the Great Basilica on your right at mile 31, continuing straight ahead at a junction 2 miles down the road. Be sure to notice the Layercake Wall, with its tortelike horizontal bands of sandstone, on the right about a mile after crossing the irregular boundary line of the park. Past here a spur road on the right goes to the Temples of the Sun, Moon, and Stars, and sparkling Glass Mountain (a gypsum formation). Look for a small arch about 4 miles beyond the spur. Rejoining UT-24, turn right to the Capitol Reef Campground, 20 miles away.

DAY 16: HORSESHOE CANYON

- **The Great Gallery pictographs**
- **Camping at Horseshoe Canyon**
- **Gas, groceries, and showers available in Hanksville**

Drive west out of the Capitol Reef Park on UT-24 to Hanksville, and resupply for an overnight backpack trip in Horseshoe Canyon, a detached unit of the Maze District of Canyonlands National Park. At Hanksville, continue north on UT-24 (a left turn) for about 19 miles to a sign for the

Admiring the Great Gallery's Ghost King, Canyonlands National Park, Utah

Maze on the right, just south of the turnoff to Goblin Valley. Turn east on this dirt road, continuing for 24 miles. When you come to a fork, turn left onto the Green River Road and continue on for 5 more miles. Then turn right onto another dirt road. Proceed for about 2 miles (the last mile or so may be rough) to the lip of the canyon. Brochures describing Horseshoe Canyon are available in a box at the trailhead, as are overnight camping permits. Because campsites in Horseshoe Canyon are limited in number, it is advisable during the busy spring season and on Labor Day weekend to camp at the trailhead on BLM land, planning to hike to the Great Gallery and back the following day.

An alternative backpacking trip in the Maze District, much longer and more challenging, is presented below.

For more information, contact the Superintendent, Canyonlands National Park, 125 West 200 South, Moab, UT 84532.

Backpack (or day hike): Horseshoe Canyon

Distance: 6.5 miles, round-trip
Time: 1 day (or overnight)
Map: USGS topo for Canyonlands National Park
Difficulty: easy, with a moderate ascent

Horseshoe Canyon (see map, p. 76) (aka Barrier Creek), a tributary of the Green River, contains some exquisite pictograph panels, including the famous 200-foot-long Great Gallery, the Louvre of the Southwest. The cottonwood-lined canyon, cut from Navajo sandstone, is lovely in its own right, though it looks somewhat uninviting from the top. Since springs are not reliable (they tend to dry up in the summer months), bring along plenty of water (at least 1 gallon per person per day).

An abandoned jeep road takes you from the parking area to the floor of the canyon. Near the top you pass a vehicle barrier and then an old trough and water tank. Cairns mark the way over the 800-foot, 1.5-mile descent. The first half of the hike is over slickrock, though the roadbed turns to sand near the bottom. At the bottom, turn right and select one of the designated sites between here and the mouth of Water Canyon, the first side-canyon to the left. Be sure to visit the pictograph panels in this area, one on either side of the canyon. You can go on to the Great Gallery today or wait until the morning.

From a second vehicle barrier just past Water Canyon, it takes about an hour of leisurely strolling to arrive at the solemn **Great Gallery,** 1.75 miles upstream on the right, where the canyon opens up slightly. Archaeologists previously regarded the life-sized pictographs in this splendid panel as Fremont creations; but most now attribute them to Archaic age nomads,

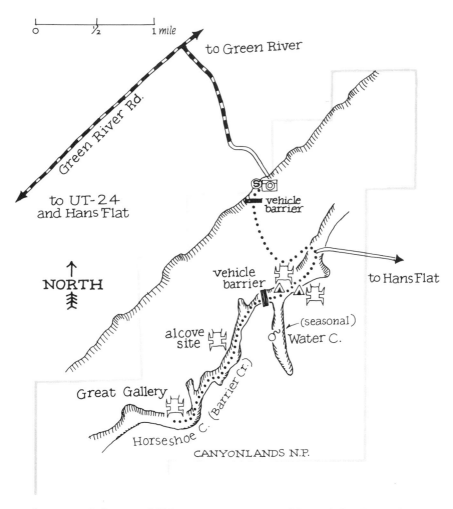

who roamed the area 2000 or more years ago. Most of the figures have small heads and elongated, jug-shaped or trapezoidal bodies. The most memorable painting depicts a white, ghostlike being. It is thought that the figures had religious significance. On your return, stop at a large alcove on the left, about halfway back to the campsites, to see a fourth panel. This one, unfortunately, has been vandalized.

It is sometimes possible to find water in Barrier Creek near the Great Gallery. In addition, there may be a flowing spring about 0.25 mile up Water Canyon, located among some cattails to the right of the streambed. You can walk up this charming tributary of Barrier Creek for over a mile until it ends in a box canyon.

Alternative Backpack: Horse Canyon

Distance: 33 miles or more, round-trip
Time: 4 or 5 days
Map: USGS topo for Canyonlands National Park
Difficulty: strenuous

This trip (see map, p. 78) involves a long trek to the floor of the Maze, with its intricate canyons and ancient rock art. It should not be attempted in very hot weather, because it involves a 14-mile waterless slog over open desert. You can reach the Maze Overlook either by jeep or on foot, but only hikers can actually penetrate its branching canyons.

Before you set forth, stop at the Hans Flat Ranger Station, located 46 bumpy miles past the UT-24 turnoff to the Maze District. Follow the road signs to get there. Be sure to bring in plenty of water, up to 2 gallons per person, for the hike to the overlook. There should be water in the Maze canyons themselves; the rangers will have information on current conditions.

After obtaining your camping permit, drive a few miles farther to the North Point Road. On foot, take the North Point Road to your left for about a mile through a wooded area. Then pick up the **North Trail Canyon Trail** to your right. For the first 0.5 mile, the trail descends gradually onto a slickrock terrace, and then drops precipitously into North Trail Canyon about 1500 feet below. This part of the route is rugged, with rocks and tree roots conspiring to slow you down. Canyon wrens seem ubiquitous here.

In the next 3.5 miles, the canyon will narrow and become hotter, but also more level. You may even find pockets of water in its lower reaches. As you approach the intersection with the jeep roads that marks your halfway point, the sand in the wash gets deeper. Bear right at the first junction and left at the second, heading east toward **Maze Overlook.** From here on you can expect no water and little shade, though the road permits you to make good time. It takes you through Elaterite Basin (Horse Canyon and its tributaries will be to the left) and around **Elaterite Butte,** a many-armed monster. Within a mile, the unparalleled spectacle of the Maze unfolds before you.

The Maze consists of a rather confusing canyon system made of white and red sandstone in alternating bands. The Cedar Mesa and Cutler formation cliffs are graceful and curving, with trees and bushes lining the washes. Four very prominent reddish brown slabs of Organ Rock shale called the **Chocolate Drops** stand in a neat row on top of one of the canyon walls, surveying the scene; these can help to orient you in this labyrinth when you reach the bottom.

Exploring to the left of the official overlook, you'll find a cairned route that starts near the Nuts and Bolts, tower-like formations with white

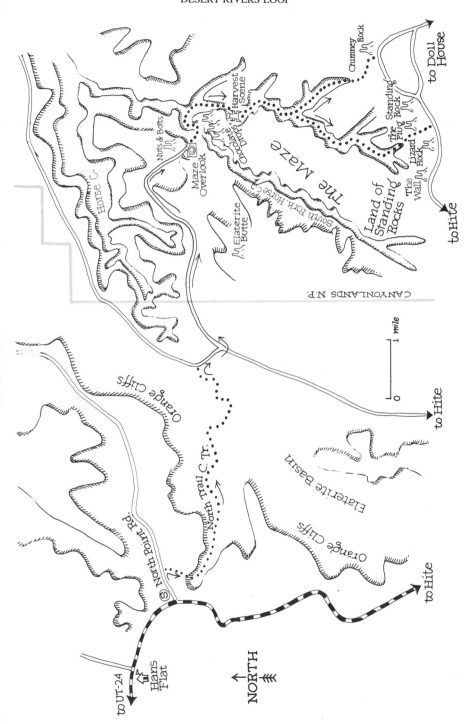

caps, and leads 650 feet down to the bottom of the canyon in the next mile. There are many steep spots, and in a few places you might want to remove and lower your packs. Lowering packs will be easier if you bring along a 20- to 30-foot long rope for this purpose. A slickrock "slide," exposed ridges, and a narrow cleft nearby make you feel as though you've stumbled across a wilderness amusement park. The route to the bottom deposits you into the South Fork of Horse Canyon. You will find shade and probably some water here.

Possibilities for exploration in the Maze are limitless. Don't miss the side trip to the famous pictograph **Harvest Scene,** located 2.5 miles from the overlook, on the back side of the Chocolate Drops. In it are many large figures in a long row, one holding a sheaf of rice grass. From the base of the overlook trail, walk north down the South Fork of Horse Canyon. At the first fork, bear right, proceeding upstream to a second fork, where you again turn right, following cairns. Walk up this canyon, which is significant in size. Not far ahead stands a tall minaret, isolated in the center of a large open area. It is clear why prehistoric peoples regarded this as a place of powerful magic. Proceed slowly, examining the smooth cliffs to your right to find the pictograph. From here you can continue up the canyon, which forks after about 1.5 miles, the right fork leading to **the Plug** and the left (past some minor obstructions) to **Chimney Rock.**

DAY 17: BLACK DRAGON CANYON

- Studying some sublime pictographs
- Camping and showers at Green River State Park
- Gas, groceries, and laundry available in Green River

Your last day in the desert begins with a climb out of Horseshoe Canyon. From the parking lot, drive back to the first junction, turning right here toward the town of Green River (42 miles to the north) on the Green River Road. This good, unpaved road provides multiple access points to canyons and overlooks on the western side of the river.

In Green River, resupply, and pitch a tent at Green River State Park. Then head west on I-70 for 15 miles in order to inspect the rock art of Black Dragon Canyon. About 0.75 mile beyond the I-70 bridge across the San Rafael River, near milepost 145, is a good dirt and gravel road to the north. Pass through a gate designed to keep stock off the highway and drive over a mile up the dirt road until you come to a wash, which is **Black Dragon Canyon.** Park here just off the road or drive up the wash a short distance until you reach a large overhang on the left. Although the pictograph panels are quite close to the mouth, you may want to walk farther up the canyon if time permits. When you are finished here, return to the campground in preparation for tomorrow's trip home.

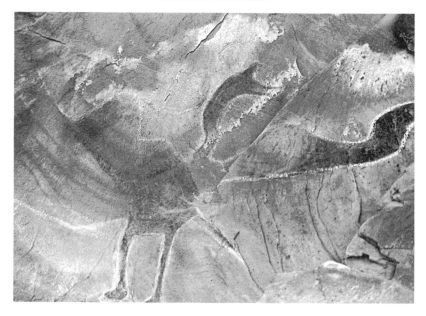

This Fremont, Utah, "dragon" pictograph suggests a prehistoric pterodactyl

Day Hike: Black Dragon Canyon

Distance: up to 5 miles, round-trip
Time: up to 3 hours
Map: USGS quad for San Rafael Desert
Difficulty: very easy

Noted for its Fremont pictographs, this deep, lovely canyon of Navajo, Kayenta, and Wingate sandstone slices through the San Rafael Reef to join the San Rafael River to the east.

About 400 yards up-canyon on the right, around a big bend to the left, is a pictograph panel high on the wall of the canyon. The most unusual of the drawings resembles a (red, not black) dragon; it has been outlined in white to make it more visible. Some of the other drawings have an "expressionist" quality, being composed entirely of short lines that lend them a certain dynamism.

Black Dragon Canyon can be hiked through the reef and beyond. Past the pictographs the canyon widens. A jeep road makes the walking here fast and relatively easy. Rock layers include the Entrada, Carmel, Navajo, Kayenta, and Wingate formations. You'll have to double back to your car when you are ready to leave.

Chapter 3

REDROCK LOOP

Colorado, Utah

Originating in Grand Junction, this circuit minimizes driving time by confining itself to the eastern side of the Green and Colorado rivers, a fractured landscape replete with exquisite arches, towering mountains, and sweeping panoramas. It is ideal for people interested in devoting their vacation time to relatively short and easy day hikes and backpacking trips. White-water rafting options add to the excitement of this memorable loop.

DAY 1: COLORADO NATIONAL MONUMENT

- **Wonderful views of Grand Valley**
- **Day hikes amid soaring pinnacles**
- **Camping at Colorado National Monument**
- **Gas, groceries, showers, and laundry available in Grand Junction and Fruita**

Grand Junction, a pleasant city of 28,150 near the Utah border, is different from the other towns in this region, both in its size and in the diversity of its services. Poised on the western flank of the Rockies, within easy reach of the high desert, it's a natural gateway community. Buy food, ice, and other supplies here. Your first destination is very close: **Colorado National Monument** (see map, p. 82). Take CO-340 across the river to the east entrance station and begin the 23-mile Rim Rock Drive, which traverses the park and returns to CO-340 near Fruita. The visitor center and campground are at the western end of the drive.

The national monument occupies a high mesa on the Uncompahgre Plateau, which erosion has cut into a series of deep canyons and isolated sandstone towers. Up to 1500 feet higher than the surrounding desert, it offers exciting views into the valley below and north to the Book Cliffs. The Colorado River was once known as the "Grand," so the valley in which the towns of Grand Junction and Fruita sit is also called by that name. Irrigated patchwork fields add a pastoral, amber and green contrast to the mesa's wilderness of monoliths.

Book Cliffs

Grand Junction

Fruita

to Denver

Colorado N.M.

Green River

Sego C.

Cisco

Colorado R.

to I-15

Crescent Junction

Thompson

70

128

Arches N.P.

Fisher Towers

Green R.

313

Moab

La Sal Mtns.

Dolores R.

Island in the Sky

Dead Horse Pt. S.P.

(optional)

191

Glen Canyon N.R.A.

Canyon Rims

LaSal Jct.

46

The Maze

(optional)

The Needles

211

Newspaper Rock S.P.

Canyonlands N.P.

Monticello

Colorado R.

Abajo Mtns.

to Blanding

UTAH | COLORADO

LOOP ROADS
paved
unpaved

OTHER ROADS
paved
unpaved

↑
NORTH

0   10   20   30 *miles*

Several interesting trails of varying lengths either hug the rim of the mesa or descend into the canyons from breathtaking overlooks along Rim Rock Drive. Especially memorable are two easy trails near the east end of the drive: the **Serpents Trail** (2.5 miles, one way), which follows the incredibly crooked bed of the old road into the national monument, and the adjacent **Devils Kitchen Trail** (1.5 miles, round-trip), which crosses No Thoroughfare Canyon before ascending to a sandstone rock garden. Short paths lead to the Coke Ovens, Grand View Point, and the Pipe Organ. You may wish to stop at some or all of these on your way to the visitor center and campground, where nature trails originate. Establish your campsite, then drive back to the Coke Ovens area and take the Monument Canyon Trail.

For further information, contact the Superintendent, Colorado National Monument, Fruita, CO 81521.

A collared lizard sports vivid green and yellow markings

Day Hike: Monument Canyon Trail

Distance: 5.5 miles, one way
Time: 3 or 4 hours
Map: USGS topo for Colorado National Monument
Difficulty: moderate

This fascinating trail (see map, p. 82), like many others in the area, was built early in the century by John Otto, a wilderness enthusiast who sought national park status for these cliffs and buttes. Unless you have two cars, you may wish to ask at the visitor center about hiring someone to drive you to the trailhead, leaving your own vehicle at the trail's end.

Originating at the Coke Ovens Overlook, the shadeless path quickly switchbacks to the floor of **Monument Canyon,** 600 feet below. (The total descent is 1400 feet.) At the bottom it turns left and parallels the rim, descending gradually much of the way. Along the route, which cuts through the Wingate and Chinle formations to Precambrian rock, views of many of the monument's most prominent and interesting formations appear, including the Kissing Couple and Independence Monument.

Near Independence Monument, the trail veers to the right, passing a boulder garden formed as the sandstone cliffs weathered. At the bottom of the canyon, bear left, walking alongside the fence until the trail intersects CO-340 near the monument's west entrance.

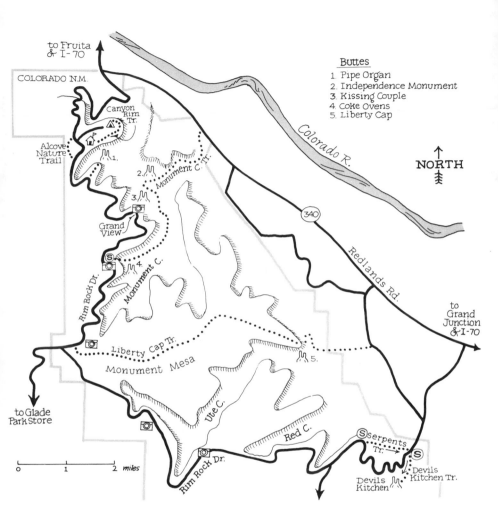

Buttes
1. Pipe Organ
2. Independence Monument
3. Kissing Couple
4. Coke Ovens
5. Liberty Cap

DAY 2: SEGO CANYON AND FISHER TOWERS

- **Exceptional prehistoric pictographs**
- **A scenic drive along the Colorado River**
- **A hike through tall red spires**
- **Camping in the Moab area**
- **Gas, groceries, showers, and laundry available in Moab**

Leave Colorado National Monument and head west for 69 miles on I-70 from Fruita. Your first destination is the prehistoric pictographs of

Sego Canyon, near the whistle-stop town of Thompson, Utah. The country becomes drier and bleaker with each passing mile; you would hardly guess that the Colorado River is gouging out Horsethief, Ruby, and Westwater canyons, with their outstanding rafting opportunities, immediately to the south. Equally hard to imagine is that the desolate-looking, 250-mile-long **Book Cliffs** region to the north is cut by fairly well-watered canyons, through which Neolithic hunters and gatherers once roamed.

The rock drawings of these ancient peoples are located north of Thompson, at the junction of **Sego** and **Thompson canyons.** Take exit 185 off I-70 and enter Thompson on UT-94, driving across the railroad tracks. The pavement ends here, but the dirt road is graded. Continue for 3.5 miles past the tracks until the canyon opens up. Park in the small lot on the left just after the road crosses a wash. Three major panels are on the left side of the road, and two additional ones are about 100 yards up-canyon on the right. These remarkable pictographs are probably from the Fremont culture. Some contain vase-shaped figures like those in Horseshoe Canyon's Grand Gallery (see Chapter 2, Desert Rivers Loop, Day 16). Unfortunately, because the Sego Canyon panels are so easily accessible, they have been badly vandalized.

From Thompson, backtrack eastward on I-70, taking exit 212 toward

The noxious jimson weed in bloom

Hikers explore redrock wilderness below Fisher Towers, Utah

the hamlet of Cisco. Within a few miles you pick up UT-128, a classic among desert roads. After traversing a depressingly barren plateau, the road suddenly dips to cross the **Colorado River,** which it then parallels all the way to Moab, 47 miles from the interstate. Next to the new bridge across the river is its more charming predecessor, Dewey Bridge, a rickety, white one-laner that lent its name to a rock stratum found in various parts of the Southwest. Below Dewey Bridge, the cloud-covered La Sal Mountains, a high chain of laccoliths, soon come into view. River rafting from here to Moab is wonderful—long placid stretches alternating with exciting rapids and riffles. Whether by car or boat, the trip through the canyon is a textbook lesson in Four Corners geology. Most of the way, dramatic Wingate cliffs predominate, dipping beneath the earth's surface near Moab to be succeeded by Navajo sandstone bluffs.

In the shadow of the La Sals, about 20 miles northeast of Moab, loom the **Fisher Towers**—brick-colored monoliths hewn from the Moenkopi and Cutler formations. As you approach them, look for a short dirt and gravel road on your left, which leads to a parking lot, picnic area (with pit toilets and covered tables), and trailhead, all maintained by the BLM. This is where you begin your day hike to Fisher Towers, described below.

At the conclusion of your hike, continue driving southwest on UT-128. At a T-intersection, leave the Colorado River and turn left (southeast) on US-191 toward Moab, a friendly, diverse community of 4000. Numerous wilderness-oriented businesses have been established in this poor man's Sedona, most notably river rafting companies, which offer trips of varying lengths on the Colorado.

Moab will serve as your base of operations for the next few days. You can stay at one of the local RV parks (where showers are available), or, after filling your tank with gas and your cooler with two days' worth of food and ice, backtrack north on US-191 toward Arches National Park, a few miles past the highway bridge over the river. Inquire at the entrance station about campsites. If all have been taken, make other arrangements for the night and plan to claim a site early the next morning. One option is to request a permit for backcountry camping at the visitor center. This commits you to walking out of sight and at least 0.5 mile off one of the trails or secondary roads in the park before establishing your camp. If vacancies do exist in the campground, drive to the end of the spectacular scenic road to select your spot.

Day Hike: Fisher Towers

> **Distance: 4.5 miles, round-trip**
> **Time: 2.5 hours**
> **Map: USGS quad for Castle Valley**
> **Difficulty: moderate**

The clearly designated trailhead is located adjacent to the BLM picnic area. After crossing a shallow canyon, the trail gradually ascends, winding along the right-hand side of a cliff broken into a series of striated pinnacles. Views are splendid along the entire route. To the west is the Colorado River's Professor Valley; to the south is labyrinthine Onion Creek, with its maroon cliffs and short section of narrows. The **Titan,** biggest of the towers at 900 feet high, is visible a mile up the trail. The top of the climb rewards you with an outstanding panorama of the La Sal Mountains and the buttes of nearby Castle Valley.

DAY 3: ARCHES NATIONAL PARK

- **Four fabulous day hikes**
- **Camping in Arches National Park**

Arches National Park is a slickrock wonderland situated on a plateau high above the canyon of the Colorado River. The park is celebrated for its fins and towers, balanced rocks, petrified sand dunes, and, of course, for its over 1500 natural arches and windows, formed by the action of ice, water, and wind on Entrada sandstone. An 18-mile paved road stretches from one end of the park to the other, providing access to these outstanding natural treasures.

At the visitor center, reserve a spot in a ranger-led hike into the Fiery Furnace. Also, obtain a permit for overnight camping near Dark Angel on Day 4. Although water is available at the campground, the visitor center is a convenient place to fill canteens.

Leave the visitor center and take the park road up a well-engineered set of switchbacks, which climb a golden cliff face. This ascent treats you to exceptional views of Spanish Valley (in which Moab is located), the Colorado River and its so-called "Portal" (where the canyon closes in again after the river has crossed the valley), and the impressive La Sal Mountains in the distance. Along the road, take advantage of the many scenic viewpoints and short trails the park has to offer.

For further information, write to the Superintendent, Arches National Park, P.O. Box 907, Moab, UT 84532.

Day Hike 1: Park Avenue

> **Distance: 1 mile, one way**
> **Time: 0.5 hour**
> **Map: USGS topo for Arches National Park**
> **Difficulty: easy**

A must for visitors to Arches is a leisurely stroll down Park Avenue, 2 miles from the entrance station, in the **Courthouse Towers** section. The easy, well-marked trail (see map, p. 89) gently descends 325 feet toward Courthouse Wash, with its huge sandstone buttes. You walk between cliffs topped by flat, waferlike Entrada sandstone projections, which somehow seem vaguely Egyptian. At the end, either retrace your steps or follow the road back to the parking lot.

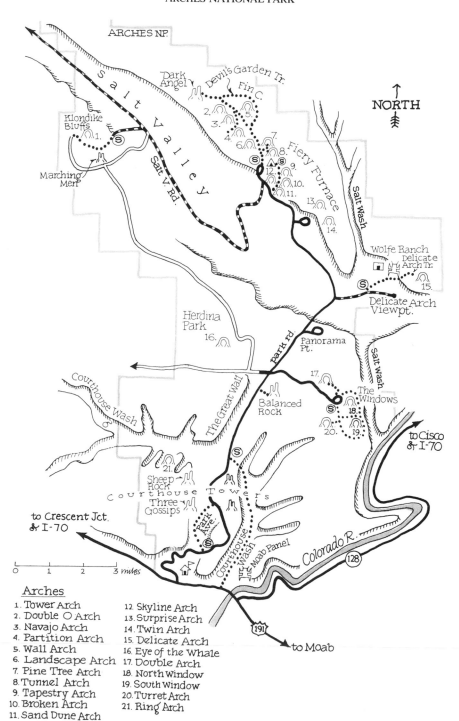

Arches

1. Tower Arch
2. Double O Arch
3. Navajo Arch
4. Partition Arch
5. Wall Arch
6. Landscape Arch
7. Pine Tree Arch
8. Tunnel Arch
9. Tapestry Arch
10. Broken Arch
11. Sand Dune Arch
12. Skyline Arch
13. Surprise Arch
14. Twin Arch
15. Delicate Arch
16. Eye of the Whale
17. Double Arch
18. North Window
19. South Window
20. Turret Arch
21. Ring Arch

Day Hike 2: The Windows

Distance: 1 mile, if all trails are hiked
Time: 1 hour
Map: USGS topo for Arches National Park
Difficulty: very easy

The popular Windows section is reached by turning right off the park drive onto a 2.5-mile paved spur road near **Balanced Rock** (see map, p. 89), 9 miles past the visitor center. Very short, well-kept trails lead to several major arches here, including the famous **Double Arch, Turret Arch,** and **North** and **South Windows.** Climb the rocks on the left behind North Window to get a wonderful "framed" view of Turret Arch. From the South Window a primitive trail drops behind the arches to return to the parking area.

Day Hike 3: The Fiery Furnace

Distance: 2 miles, round-trip
Time: 2 hours
Map: USGS topo for Arches National Park
Difficulty: moderate

The mazelike **Fiery Furnace** (see map, p. 89), a natural amusement park of sorts, is not a place for the claustrophobic hiker. It's strongly advisable to take the ranger-guided tour your first time through, because even an experienced person could easily get lost in this confusing, nearly trackless area, or miss some of its special attractions, such as Surprise and Twin arches. The parking lot is off a short spur to the right of the park road, at about mile 14.5. Reservations, which are required, must be made in person at the visitor center.

Day Hike 4: Sand Dune, Broken, and Tapestry Arches

Distance: 2.25 miles, round-trip
Time: 2 hours
Map: USGS topo for Arches National Park
Difficulty: easy

Winding through the upper Fiery Furnace is a cairned trail to Broken Arch (see map, p. 89), with a very short spur to its unique neighbor, Sand Dune. This is a fine hike to schedule for after dinner, for it starts at the rear of the campground, ending at a designated pullout on the park road about

Fins seen through an upper opening, Double O Arch, Arches National Park, Utah

16 miles from the visitor center. Your first landmark, Tapestry Arch, is a few hundred yards in on the left. Its backdrop and namesake is a wall coated with long, black streaks of "desert varnish" (composed of iron and manganese oxide). Then the trail passes through Broken Arch, a fairly sizable specimen, whose "break" is revealed upon closer inspection to be illusory. After crossing an open area, take the left-hand spur, which passes through fins to tiny Sand Dune Arch, named after the drifts around and below it. The highway pullout is only a hundred yards past the trail junction. You can walk back to the campground along the park road (a 1.75-mile distance). To shorten the hike considerably, start at the pullout, visit Sand Dune and Broken arches, and then return to the road.

DAY 4: ARCH-HUNTING IN ARCHES

- **The Parthenon of arches**
- **And seven or eight others**
- **Backcountry camping in the Devils Garden area**
- **Gas, groceries, showers, and laundry available in Moab**

Today is an arch-finding extravaganza. In the morning, hike to Delicate Arch (bring water). After purchasing food for two nights in Moab, put on your pack and walk through the arch-studded Devils Garden to your chosen backcountry camp site.

Day Hike: Delicate Arch

Distance: 3 miles, round-trip
Time: 3 hours
Map: USGS topo for Arches National Park
Difficulty: moderate

This perfect freestanding natural arch is a favorite among photographers. Originally it was known as Landscape Arch, because it frames the La Sals in the distance. But a cartographer's error resulted in the old Delicate Arch being officially named Landscape Arch, and vice versa. To reach the trailhead drive 11.5 miles past the visitor center on the park road (see map, p. 89). Turn right and go about 1.5 miles down this road to the parking lot on the left at Wolfe Ranch, an old pioneer cabin.

The trail to Delicate Arch is spectacular. First you cross a suspension bridge over Salt Wash (it may be buggy here), then pass through a Morrison formation badlands area and begin a brisk 500-foot ascent. Cairns mark the route up the slickrock. At the top, look carefully for trail markers. The trail goes up a small wash, then hugs the right wall of a canyon, where it has been blasted out of sandstone. A large "potty" arch is straight ahead. A "window" in the rock above the trail gives you your first glimpse of Delicate Arch. The trail continues around a bend to a sandstone bowl with steep sides. At its far end is **Delicate Arch.** With caution, you can safely make your way over to it. Like the park's other arches and fins, it is made of Entrada sandstone.

Return to your vehicle by retracing your steps. You can stop at a petroglyph panel near the right bank of Salt Wash by turning right on a path at the end of your descent, before reaching the bridge. Walk along the cliff for about 100 yards; the petroglyphs are in the rocks to the right. For a different perspective on Delicate Arch, drive past the Wolfe Ranch parking area to the end of the spur road and walk 0.25 mile on an easy trail to a viewpoint.

Backpack (or day hike): Devils Garden

> **Distance: 5 miles, round-trip**
> **Time: 4 hours (or overnight)**
> **Map: USGS topo for Arches National Park**
> **Difficulty: very easy to Landscape Arch, moderate thereafter**

The Devils Garden trail system (see map, p. 89) is much traveled, and with good reason, for along its paths are seven natural arches. Although the circuit described below can be completed in half a day, this fascinating area warrants a longer visit. Pack in 1.5 gallons of water apiece for an overnight. The trailhead and parking area are at the end of the park road, 18 miles from the visitor center.

For most of the way, the trail threads through sparse pinyon and juniper vegetation. Less than 0.25 mile from the parking lot is a branch trail to your right, which soon divides, with one fork leading to Tunnel Arch and the other to Pine Tree Arch. Retrace your steps to the main trail and continue on toward **Landscape Arch.** Just before reaching the arch, you pass a trail on the right that winds through Fin Canyon on its way to Double O Arch. Landscape Arch, the length of a football field, is among the largest in the world. A steep spur takes you up under the span before looping back to the main trail.

The trail gets rougher here and begins to climb, following cairns. After passing Wall Arch on the right, take the short spur trail on the left to Navajo and Partition arches, 0.25 mile away. Past this junction, the main trail favors slickrock and much of the time winds along the tops of various fins. From Fin Canyon Overlook try to pick out Black Arch. **Double O Arch** consists of a large, round opening on top of a smaller one in a significant sandstone fin. Ease your way through the arch to the other side and continue 0.5 mile to rocket-shaped **Dark Angel.** The trail here, although cairned, is hard to follow in spots; it bends to the left, arriving at a vantage point with stunning views of Salt Valley and the La Sal Mountains. The wild, trailless country beyond Dark Angel is rarely explored.

From Dark Angel, backtrack a short distance past Double O Arch. You can retrace your steps back to the parking lot, or return via scenic Fin Canyon, a slightly longer (3.5 miles) and more rugged route. It begins near Double O Arch and rejoins the main trail near Landscape Arch.

DAY 5: HIKER'S CHOICE

- ■ **Afoot in more remote parts of Arches National Park**
- ■ **Camping at the campground**

This afternoon, after registering for a site in the campground, you can stroll down lower Courthouse Wash or visit Klondike Bluffs. In either case, carry at least 2 quarts of water per person.

Day Hike 1: Lower Courthouse Wash

Distance: 6 miles, one way
Time: 4 hours
Map: USGS topo for Arches National Park
Difficulty: easy

This pleasant day hike begins where the park's main road crosses **Courthouse Wash,** 4.25 miles past the entrance station (see map, p. 89). Head downstream (a right turn from the bridge). Very soon the Navajo sandstone cliffs deepen and the canyon narrows. Because intermittent water may be in the wash, wear appropriate footgear: old boots or sneakers. You may find a few small pools for cooling off.

Courthouse Wash is quite pretty and interesting, and requires little stamina or physical skill. You may, however, meet up with deerflies in reedy places, and there is sometimes quicksand in the last 0.5 mile of the canyon (which you can avoid by picking up a trail on the bank). The hike ends at US-191, about 2 miles southeast of the Arches entrance station. Before returning to your car, climb to the Moab Panel of pictographs, on the cliff face to the left, paralleling the highway.

Day Hike 2: Klondike Bluffs

Distance: 3 miles, round-trip
Time: 2.5 hours
Map: USGS topo for Arches National Park
Difficulty: moderate

Reach this unspoiled part of Arches National Park by turning west from the main park road onto a dirt road near Skyline Arch, 17 miles from the visitor center (see map, p. 89). The road runs the length of Salt Valley, which is rich in both flowers and wildlife. **Klondike Bluffs** is about 8 miles up the road. (Don't use this road before or after a rain, because it crosses a wash.) Turn left onto a tertiary road to the Klondike Bluffs parking area.

Delicate Arch in Arches National Park, Utah, commands the far end of a slickrock bowl

The trail begins to the left of here. It rapidly ascends a cliff, rewarding hikers with splendid views of the Fiery Furnace and Devils Garden areas of the park, as well as of the lower end of the Island in the Sky. Then it veers to the right between two widely spaced rock walls, descending slowly toward a small drainage. Look for an unnamed arch on the left near the trail's low point. Crossing the wash, the trail goes up a sandy hill, then turns right and continues over sand for about 0.25 mile. From this spot, **Tower Arch** is visible in a fin to the right. An enormous pinnacle next to the arch lends this gorgeous span its name. On the arch's right abutment is an inscription carved by Alexander Ringhoffer and his family. Generally regarded as a founding father of Arches Park, Ringhoffer operated a mine in Salt Valley in the 1920s. Just 100 yards to the south, in another fin, is an unnamed double arch very close to the trail. On your way out, explore the wash you crossed earlier in the downstream direction for a closer inspection of a row of isolated monoliths called the Marching Men.

An easy—but longer (4 miles) and less shady—alternative route back, begins near the small sign for Tower Arch. This cairned route climbs in a westerly direction, soon joining a jeep track, which can be followed back to the Salt Valley Road. Where the jeep road swings hard to the left is an attractive slickrock mass. At the halfway mark, an intersecting jeep road takes off toward Balanced Rock, 9 miles distant; the road you want goes straight ahead, toward the top of a big hill. Cresting the hill, it drops down and eventually meets the Salt Valley Road, where you turn left. After a few hundred yards, another left onto the Klondike Bluffs spur road takes you back to your car.

DAY 6: THREE HIKES NEAR THE RIVER

- ■ **A canyon-bottom or canyon-rim day trip**
- ■ **Camping at Dead Horse Point State Park**
- ■ **Gas, groceries, showers, and laundry available in Moab**

This morning, drive into Moab and stock up on three days' worth of groceries and supplies. If you want to take a raft trip down the Colorado later in the week (see Days 9 and 10), make reservations with one of the local companies. Then select one of the day hikes described below.

Tonight, after your hike, you'll be camping at Dead Horse Point State Park. To reach the park from Moab, drive northwest 9 miles on US-191 to UT-313 and turn left. The road crosses some railroad tracks and climbs to the mesa top, offering views of nearby **Monitor** and **Merrimac buttes** as well as of a good portion of Arches National Park.

About 29 miles from Moab the road will fork. Tomorrow you'll take the right fork, leading to the Island in the Sky. Tonight, however, turn left and proceed to **Dead Horse Point,** 4 miles away. The campground offers covered shelters, running water, and electric lights, all for a reasonable fee. Dead Horse Point itself—best viewed at sunset—juts out over the erosional basin of the Colorado River and is connected to the main body of the mesa by an isthmus only 30 yards wide. According to local legend, the point got its name when wild mustangs were rounded up and then accidentally left to die out on the mesa. The vista from the point is one of the most incredible in the entire Southwest. The Colorado makes a bowknot bend directly below, and buttes, needles, and benchlands extend as far as the eye can see. The rock strata visible here, from top to bottom, include the Entrada, Navajo, Kayenta, and Wingate sandstone layers as well as the Chinle, Moenkopi, Cutler, and Honaker Trail formations.

For more information on the trails featured below, contact the Bureau of Land Management, Grand Resource Area, Sand Flats Road, P.O. Box M, Moab, UT 84532.

Day Hike 1: Negro Bill Canyon

> **Distance: 4 miles, round-trip**
> **Time: 3 hours**
> **Map: USGS quad for Moab**
> **Difficulty: easy**

A tributary of the Colorado River, lovely, steep-walled **Negro Bill Canyon** got its name from William Granstaff, a nineteenth-century mulatto prospector, farmer, and rancher who grazed his cattle here. In the late 1970s, the canyon was the scene of a skirmish in the so-called Sagebrush Rebellion of the pro-development Westerners resisting federal proposals to designate more wilderness areas. But the Negro Bill system is also famous for Morning Glory Bridge, an enormous Navajo sandstone span that commands the end of a short side-canyon.

Drive 3 miles northeast on UT-128 from the Colorado River bridge at Moab; Negro Bill Canyon (see map, p. 98) is the second side-canyon on your right. Park here in the designated lot.

The canyon floor is green, thanks to a perennial stream that supports cottonwoods and Gambel's oaks. Beginning on the left side of the canyon, a primitive hiking trail, maintained by the BLM, crosses and recrosses the stream. About 1.5 miles from the highway, turn up into the second side-canyon on the right. Follow the trail on the left bank of this box canyon 0.5 mile to the impressive, 250-foot-long **Morning Glory Bridge,** one of the Southwest's largest. Underneath this vaulting span is a sizable pool, created by a seep spring. But beware of poison ivy, which thrives here. You can explore farther up Negro Bill—it extends for some 10 miles toward its origin in the La Sal foothills—before backtracking to your car.

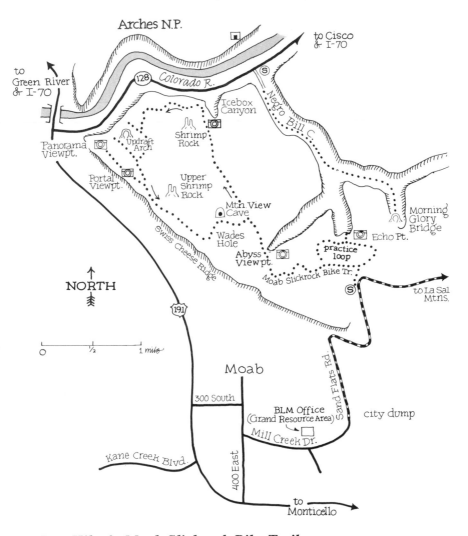

Day Hike 2: Moab Slickrock Bike Trail

> **Distance: 2.25 miles for practice loop, or 10.25 for main loop, round-trip**
> **Time: from 1.5 hours, or full day**
> **Map: USGS quad for Moab**
> **Difficulty: moderate**

Although designed originally for motorcyclists and used now almost exclusively by mountain bikers (advanced biking skills required), this trail makes for interesting hiking on petrified dunes of Navajo sandstone. Avoid the area on weekends, however, when it receives heavy mountain bike traffic.

From Moab, turn east off US-191 onto 300 South (3 blocks south of the center of town) (see map, p. 98). Follow this street to a T-intersection with 400 East and bear right. Two blocks down begins Mill Creek Drive, which soon runs into the Sand Flats Road; look for signs. Proceed up the Sand Flats Road for over 2.25 miles, passing the city dump along the way. The trailhead and large parking lot are on the left.

The Colorado River in Utah is placid below the Slickrock Bike Trail

The route is indicated by white dashes, painted directly on the slick-rock. Alternate routes, usually more challenging, are marked by a series of white dots, with yellow paint reserved for major junctions and hazardous drops. To stay out of the way of bicyclists, who generally have a tough time of it, keep to one side of the line.

The practice loop takes off to the right after 0.25 mile. Its highlight is the appropriately named Echo Point, which overlooks a large side-canyon of the Negro Bill system. A nice 3.75-mile day trip involves taking the practice loop, continuing on to Abyss Viewpoint, then taking the main trail back to your car.

Past Abyss Viewpoint, the main trail forks. Take the right-hand trail to Shrimp Rock, an oddly shaped butte on the edge of short Icebox Canyon, whose intermittent waters feed into the Colorado River. The rock takes its name from a pool at its base that contains fairy shrimp and other tiny creatures that thrive in this sort of micro-environment. Do not disturb any of the potholes encountered along the way. Three short spurs lead to other spectacular overlooks. From the first and second of these, potty-type Updraft Arch can be admired; the third goes to Portal and Panorama viewpoints. The main trail then swings south and closes the loop near Wades Hole.

Day Hike 3: Corona, Bowtie, and Pinto Arches

> **Distance: 3 miles, round-trip**
> **Time: 2.5 hours**
> **Map: USGS quad for Moab**
> **Difficulty: moderate**

Corona Arch, formed from the weathering of a fin, is also known as "Little Rainbow Bridge" because of its resemblance to famous Rainbow Bridge on the Utah-Arizona border. Two other arches, Pinto (aka Goldbar) and Bowtie (a pothole-type formation), are close by. All three are composed of Navajo sandstone.

To reach the trailhead, drive north from Moab on US-191 for 1.5 miles past the Colorado River Bridge. Turn left at UT-279 (Potash Road) and proceed about 9 miles. Following the west bank of the Colorado, this road passes through the Portal at mile 2.75, where the river unexpectedly abandons Spanish Valley to slice back through Navajo sandstone domes, becoming imprisoned once again in a deep gorge. You will notice a ruin, some rock art panels, and a turnout for dinosaur tracks as you progress down the road. A sign indicates where to park your car for the hike.

The cairned trail, maintained by the BLM, ascends a steep embankment to cross railroad tracks, whose bed was blasted out of the cliffs decades ago. Pinto Arch is barely visible in the distance to your left. Past the tracks, the trail goes to the right of a shallow gorge, climbing gradually while bearing left toward golden-hued cliffs. As it nears the cliffs, it contours to the right and rounds a bend. At a small scallop in the cliff, two cables, carved-out footholds, and a ladder will help you negotiate rough spots.

From the top of the ladder, you can see both Bowtie and Corona arches in the next bay over. The cairned route leads across the slickrock to each of these giants. **Bowtie** is the arch at the midpoint of the amphitheater, while its even more impressive companion, **Corona,** commands the bowl's far end. Poetry in stone, this arch measures almost 150 feet across, and from it you gain fine views into the railroad canyon. Double back over the same route to your car.

<u>DAY 7:</u> TOURING THE ISLAND

- **Day hikes to craters, arches, and overlooks**
- **Watching the sunset from Grand View Point**
- **Camping at Canyonlands National Park**

On today's agenda is a leisurely exploration of the Island in the Sky, part of **Canyonlands National Park.** Fill your canteens at Dead Horse Point before you go as no water is available at the island. Rugged and magnificent, Canyonlands is really several parks rolled into one. This 260,000-acre preserve, divided into three distinct sections by the Y-shaped confluence of the Green and Colorado rivers, covers some of the wildest land in the entire country. The Island in the Sky is the northernmost sector, a high mesa located between the two rivers; to the west is the mysterious Maze District, with the Needles District to the east. The park has everything a visitor to the Southwest could want, including thrilling white water in Cataract Canyon, ancient pictograph panels in the Maze, canyons filled with ruins and arches, hair-raising jeep roads extending deep into the desert, and 360-degree overlooks of spires, buttes, and goosenecks.

Return to the fork you took to Dead Horse Point (see Day 6) and turn left on a paved road to the **Island in the Sky,** 4.5 miles distant. Like Dead Horse Point, the Island—6000 feet above sea level—is a peninsula separated from the rest of the plateau by a skinny neck. This high, rolling mesa, dotted with pinyons and junipers, drops precipitously on three sides to the **White Rim,** a broad, flat terrace almost 1000 feet above the Green and Colorado rivers. From The Neck, a mile south of the ranger station, you are treated to outstanding views into both Taylor Canyon (a tributary of the Green) and Shafer Canyon (a tributary of the Colorado). To the left is the beginning of the Shafer Trail, a jeep road that descends precariously to the White Rim and eventually hooks up to UT-279. The waterless, no-fee Willow Flat Campground is off the Green River Overlook spur near the end of

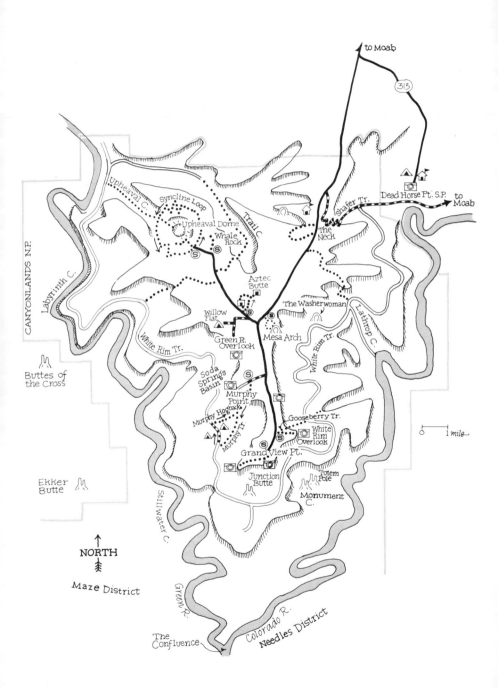

the park road. On your way there, stop at scenic turnouts and hike a couple of the following short but intriguing trails.

For more information, contact the Superintendent, Canyonlands National Park, 446 South Main Street, Moab, UT 84532.

——————

Day Hike 1: Mesa Arch Trail

> **Distance: 0.5 mile, round-trip**
> **Time: 0.5 hour**
> **Map: USGS topo for Canyonlands National Park**
> **Difficulty: very easy**

This nearly level loop trail leaves the park road 5.75 miles past the ranger station (see map, p. 102). It heads east toward the Navajo sandstone **Mesa Arch,** on the edge of a 500-foot drop-off to the floor of Buck Canyon, which cuts down another 700 feet to the White Rim. Framed through Mesa Arch is another formation known as the **Washerwoman,** a distinctive butte containing a small window.

Day Hike 2: Aztec Butte Trail

> **Distance: 1.25 mile, round-trip**
> **Time: 1 hour**
> **Map: USGS topo for Canyonlands National Park**
> **Difficulty: very easy, with a moderate climb to the butte**

The turnout for this hike is located roughly opposite the start of the Green River Overlook spur road (see map, p. 102). Of the two rock mounds visible from the trailhead, Aztec Butte is the higher one farther from the parking lot. Early on, the trail splits, and you go right, looping around to the back of the first butte. Look here for a spur trail branching off to the right. This trail ascends 200 feet up the steep face of Aztec Butte, rewarding you at the summit with a small roofless ruin as well as some marvelous views of the countryside. The one-room ruin explains the name of the formation—early settlers believed that area cliff dwellings were built by tribes from Mesoamerica. Return to the main trail and look for yet another spur, very faint, almost directly opposite the first (you should be able to spot it from Aztec Butte). Follow this spur to the top of the low mound, then bear right along the rim until you notice a break. Just below the break is a pair of granaries in excellent condition. These are also visible from the main trail, which loops back around the base of the mesa to the parking area.

Day Hike 3: Crater View Trail

Distance: 1.25 miles, round-trip
Time: 1 hour
Map: USGS topo for Canyonlands National Park
Difficulty: easy to first viewpoint, moderate to second

Beginning at the end of the scenic drive on the western side of the Island (see map, p. 102), this trail climbs 200 feet in less than 0.5 mile to an overlook of **Upheaval Dome,** a cavernous depression whose origins are shrouded in mystery. Some geologists believe it to be an eroded salt dome (hence its name); others theorize that it is an eroded meteorite impact dome. Tomorrow's itinerary will offer you a chance to circumambulate the dome and even enter it from the bottom, if time allows. For now, content yourself with walking along the rim of the 1000-foot-deep, mile-wide depression, marveling at the colorful, tilted, wildly eroded badlands at its center. A rather steep and rough trail extending 0.5 mile from the initial vantage point affords an even better view. It veers to the left and quickly drops down a sandstone defile, with the aid of hacked-in steps, before ending at a second overlook.

Day Hike 4: Whale Rock

Distance: 0.5 mile, round-trip
Time: 0.5 hour
Map: USGS topo for Canyonlands National Park
Difficulty: easy

While in the vicinity of Upheaval Dome, don't miss the view from adjacent **Whale Rock** (see map, p. 102). With the aid of handrails, climb 100 feet to the summit of this slickrock mass on a cairned route. From this lofty perch you peer into Trail Canyon, a tributary of Taylor, and beyond to the whole northwestern sector of the park. You can also see the entire perimeter of Upheaval Dome.

Day Hike 5: White Rim Overlook Trail

Distance: 1.5 miles, round-trip
Time: 1 hour
Map: USGS topo for Canyonlands National Park
Difficulty: very easy

Near the south end of the mesa, a short, level hike on a finger of slickrock takes you to **White Rim Overlook** (see map, p. 102), an incredibly scenic place that affords vistas into sheer-walled **Monument Canyon.** This canyon sports rows of chocolate-colored, Cutler formation pinnacles capped with erosion-resistant White Rim sandstone "hats." The most impressive of these pinnacles is known as the Totem Pole. It is possible to hike to the White Rim from this vicinity on the strenuous Gooseberry Trail (6 miles, round-trip), but the only nontechnical way to enter Monument Canyon is from the Colorado River.

Day Hike 6: Grand View Trail

> **Distance: 2 miles, round-trip**
> **Time: 1.25 hours**
> **Map: USGS topo for Canyonlands National Park**
> **Difficulty: easy**

At the southernmost tip of the Island is **Grand View Point** (see map, p. 102), whose name contains no exaggeration. The views are similar to those from Dead Horse Point, though vaster in scope; the surrounding landforms seem remote and almost surreal. The rivers are 2000 feet below, and on a clear day you can see landforms up to 100 miles distant, including the Maze and Needles districts of the park, the confluence of the Green and

The towers of Monument Canyon, Canyonlands National Park, Utah, lure photographers at Grand View Point

Colorado, and the blue cones of each of Utah's major laccolithic ranges: the Henrys, Abajos, and La Sals. To the right off from Grand View Point is a cairned, mostly level trail that continues along the island's rim to the tip of the peninsula. From the overlook, Junction Butte is immediately to the south, and the intricate canyons, fins, and standing rocks of the Maze District across the Green River are almost palpable.

DAY 8: ISLAND DAY HIKE

- Into the backcountry
- Camping at Willow Flat Campground

Assuming that the Island isn't too hot or too buggy, you can choose one of the long day hikes described below. Either could be done as a backpack trip.

———

Day Hike (or backpack) 1: Murphy Trail

Distance: 9 miles, round-trip
Time: 1 full day (or overnight)
Map: USGS topo for Canyonlands National Park
Difficulty: strenuous

This shadeless loop begins at a pullout about 1 mile down the dirt road to Murphy Point, an overlook (see map, p. 102). The road is easily negotiable as far as the trailhead in almost any kind of vehicle; beyond that, 4-wheel drive is required. The trail heads toward the rim of the canyon, then cuts across Kayenta ledges, dropping about 100 feet to a break in the Wingate sandstone. The next mile of trail, though carefully constructed, traverses steep and rocky terrain. Low walls minimize the risk of injury and a rickety footbridge helps you cross a chasm. Plunging through the Wingate layer in a knee-busting 750-foot descent, the trail deposits you at the base of the cliff. At the fork, go left; you'll return via the other route.

The trail follows the canyon bottom for a few miles, slowly descending, until it intersects the **White Rim Trail,** a jeep road that contours around the base of the Island in the Sky. Turn right here, walking along the road to the top of **Murphy Hogback.** You can expect outstanding views, particularly as you peer into Soda Springs Basin to the north.

Past the Hogback's primitive campgrounds on the right, leave the White Rim road to rejoin the Murphy Trail and complete the loop. All the way from here to the cliff base, the trail is level and the scenery sublime. Rest a while at the bottom in preparation for the grueling climb to the top.

Day Hike (or backpack) 2: Syncline Loop

> **Distance: 8 miles (or longer), round-trip**
> **Time: 1 full day (or overnight)**
> **Map: USGS topo for Canyonlands National Park**
> **Difficulty: strenuous**

This glorious trail (see map, p. 102) provides access into Upheaval Dome through its outlet, Upheaval Wash, and also permits easy exploration all the way to the Green River's Labyrinth Canyon. Those options add, respectively, 3 miles and 6 miles round-trip to the hike, and therefore are best reserved for backpackers who can spend a night or more in the area.

The two ends of the Syncline Loop begin a short distance up the Crater View Trail to the overlook of Upheaval Dome. Turn right onto the loop. After a long, fairly level stretch, the trail drops steeply through the Breach, a wide gap between Navajo sandstone cliffs. Reaching crescent-shaped **Syncline Valley,** you continue to descend, first gently and then very rapidly, even treacherously, at an enormous pour-off. The views beginning here are outstanding, but watch your step on the loose, slippery scree. You may find springs at both the top and the bottom of this difficult drop. The trail then proceeds more easily to the junction with the signed, unmaintained route into Upheaval Dome, on the left. Backpackers might consider camping in this vicinity and trekking into the dome (or down to the river) without all their gear.

From the junction, the loop trail dips to the floor of Upheaval Canyon. It proceeds down the canyon for several hundred yards to intersect a big side-canyon, which you enter in preparation for the tough 1300-foot climb back out. Your efforts are compensated with views into the canyon of the Green River that improve with every step. The trail levels off in the last mile.

DAYS 9 AND 10: LANDLUBBER'S DELIGHT

> ▪ **White-water rafting on the Colorado**
> ▪ **Day-hiking options**
> ▪ **Or an overnight stay "Behind the Rocks"**
> ▪ **Camping on Day 9 at Newspaper Rock State Park**
> ▪ **Gas, groceries, showers, and laundry available in Moab or Monticello**

Visitors in the mood for a different kind of adventure can participate in one of the many river-running expeditions that depart regularly from Moab. Common destinations include Westwater and Cataract canyons,

Many cultures contributed petroglyphs to Newspaper Rock, Utah

with their ferocious rapids, and especially the much tamer stretch of river from Fisher Towers to Moab (called "the Daily" in the local jargon). Make arrangements in advance to join such trips. Also, you may need to camp closer to Moab than at the Island in the Sky, the night before your trip. If your raft trip lasts only one day, use the following section for ideas about how to spend Day 10.

From Island in the Sky return to Moab and buy food for two days. Your destination is **Behind the Rocks,** a slickrock wonderland with awe-inspiring domes, fins, and arches. There are few trails on this high, broken plateau, but jeep roads provide good access to the most picturesque spots, and cross-country hiking opportunities for those who can read topographic maps are superb. The only problem is an absence of water, which mandates full canteens (1 gallon per person per day for summer backpacking). For those who would prefer to car camp and take day hikes, some options are presented below. Good car camping opportunities exist both along Kane Creek Boulevard and along the dirt roads to the south of Behind the Rocks.

When you emerge from Behind the Rocks, you'll have plenty of time to shower, wash clothes if necessary, and buy food for the next four nights before heading toward your campsite at Newspaper Rock State Park. From Moab, drive south on US-191, stopping at **Wilson Arch,** visible from the road just south of La Sal Junction. About 42.5 miles past Moab, you'll see Church Rock on the left. Turn right (west) at the sign for the Needles District of Canyonlands National Park (UT-211). The road descends from a plateau and follows the Indian Creek drainage to the Needles, 34 miles from the turnoff. Where you pick up Indian Creek, and the road bends to the right, look for enchanting **Newspaper Rock,** called Tse Hani (or "rock that tells a story") by the Navajo. This flat slab of Wingate sandstone is decorated with 2000 years of petroglyphs from many cultures: Desert Archaic, Anasazi, Fremont, Navajo, and Ute. Just across the highway, adjacent to the creek, is a small primitive campground. No drinking water is provided.

For more information about Behind the Rocks, contact the Bureau of Land Management, Moab District, 82 Dogwood Avenue, Moab, UT 84532; and Newspaper Rock, contact Utah Parks and Recreation, Southeast Regional Office, 115 West 200 South, Moab, UT 84532.

Backpack (or day hike) 1: Pritchett Canyon

> **Distance: 10 miles, round-trip**
> **Time: 1 day (or 1.5 days)**
> **Map: USGS quad for Moab**
> **Difficulty: easy, with moderate climbs to the arches**

Pritchett Canyon's exceptional beauty is complemented by three large, named arches and several unnamed ones, all surrounded by breadloaf-shaped domes of Navajo sandstone. Although it's possible to day hike part or all of the canyon, backpacking will permit more leisurely exploration.

To enter this redrock fantasyland, head south on US-191 from the center of Moab and turn right onto Kane Creek Boulevard, which parallels the Colorado River on its eastern bank (see map, p. 110). Follow this road for about 4.5 miles, stopping to appreciate the rock art (vandalized, unfortunately) in Moon Flower Canyon at mile 3.25. Park your car just downstream past **Pritchett Canyon's** mouth, beyond the end of the pavement on Kane Creek Boulevard.

Begin by walking a jeep road toward the canyon's head, passing several interesting side-canyons on the left. At about mile 2, the road forks, and a spur enters one of the side-canyons; detour to see a small natural bridge that spans the side-canyon's wash within 0.25 mile of the confluence. The main trail bears right at the fork. Around mile 3, it climbs to cross a weathered fin separating two upper branches of Pritchett Canyon. **Window Arch,** with its large triangular opening, is in this fin. Once you drop back down, you can spot Pritchett Arch looming on the far rim.

Here the road forks again. To walk to Halls Bridge (0.5 mile distant), go right here past the Ostrich, a distinctively shaped butte, and then take another right, passing the roads that lead into Pritchett's upper reaches.

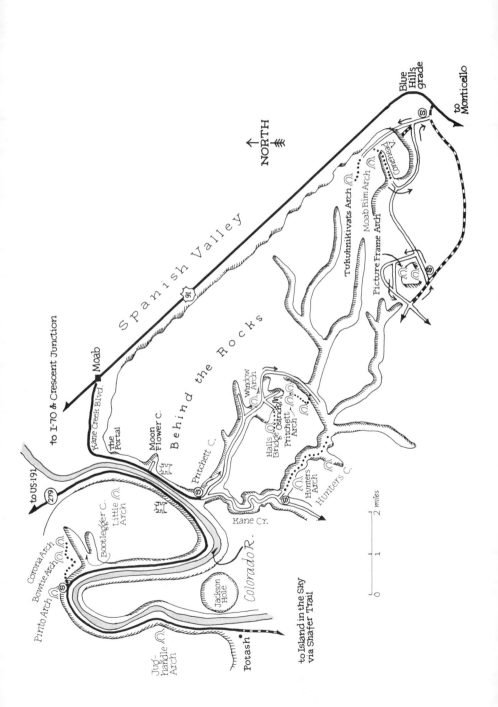

to I-70 & Crescent Junction

Spanish Valley

Moab

NORTH

Kane Creek Blvd.

The Portal

Moon Flower C.

Behind the Rocks

to US-191

279

Corona Arch
Pinto Arch
Bowtie Arch

Bootlegger C.
Little Arch

Pritchett C.

Window Arch

Halls Bridge
Ostrich
Pritchett Arch

Jug-handle Arch

Kane Cr.

Jackson Hole

Colorado R.

Hunters Arch
Hunters C.

Tukuhnikivats Arch

Moab Rim Arch

Picture Frame Arch

Coneheads

Blue Hills grade

to Monticello

Potash

to Island in the Sky via Shafer Trail

0   1   2 miles

The road you want heads back down the canyon a short distance, following the rim closely. When it ends, pick up a faint footpath marked by a cairn, which enters the left fork of the first side-canyon you meet. It is a bit steep, especially where it climbs up a slickrock slot to avoid a dryfall. Continue on for a few hundred yards until muscular Halls Bridge (really an arch) appears in the fin to your right. You can climb up the cleft at the head of the side-canyon and cautiously work your way underneath the arch from its back side.

Hikers who are very skilled at reading a topo map can proceed cross-country from here over the high slickrock terraces to Pritchett Arch. But the more common route requires a backtrack to the jeep road between the Ostrich and Window Arch. Follow this road up the canyon to a pass, then descend into upper Hunters Canyon, which parallels a massive sandstone escarpment. In the valley, after passing an isolated rock obelisk and a small arch on the right, the road crosses a wash twice, forking at the second crossing. Go right here and follow the spur to its end under the cliffs. Pritchett Arch will be visible on the ridge to the right.

Look for a cairn indicating where an obscure footpath ascends to the mesa top through a notch behind a split column of sandstone. Once on top, bear right, contouring around the base of the cliff into a hanging side-canyon. Within the next 0.25 mile you will notice a cave and an unnamed potty arch on the left. The trail peters out except for an occasional marker, but it's impossible to lose your way here if you just continue straight ahead. Near the far end of this hanging side-canyon, **Pritchett Arch** peeks out from behind a slickrock mass on the left. You can climb the slope to get underneath the arch, a classical and graceful span. Follow the side-canyon just a bit farther to an overlook of the Pritchett Canyon fork you hiked in earlier. Window Arch is clearly visible from the rim, as is another big potty arch in the side-canyon itself. But it's far too risky to attempt to return to Pritchett Canyon this way. Your best bet is to retrace your steps.

Day Hike 2: Hunters Canyon

> **Distance: 6 miles, round-trip**
> **Time: 4 hours**
> **Map: USGS quad for Moab**
> **Difficulty: easy**

Lower Hunters offers delightful day hiking up to the point where it ends in a box canyon. Its sandy mouth, distinguishable by a parking area and jeep track (which continues for a short distance) is about 8 miles from Moab on Kane Creek Boulevard. Be sure not to confuse Hunters with a short canyon located near a dripping spring at the bottom of the Kane Creek Boulevard switchbacks.

The narrow, watery gorge contains several natural spans, including unusual **Hunters Arch** at mile 0.5 and an unnamed beauty a few hundred feet up a significant side-canyon on the right at about mile 2. Past this side-canyon, progress is hampered by heavy brush. Hikers who persist will reach a pour-off grotto 3 miles above the canyon mouth, graced by a deep pool and a small natural bridge. To continue past the pour-off into upper Hunters Canyon and the Pritchett Arch area requires free-climbing skills.

Day Hike 3: Conehead Valley

> **Distance: 4 miles, round-trip**
> **Time: 3 hours**
> **Maps: USGS quads for La Sal Junction and Hatch Point**
> **Difficulty: easy, with moderate climb to Tukuhnikivats**
> **Arch**

The fascinating dome-bounded area that some locals call Conehead Valley (see map, p. 110) marks the southern end of Behind the Rocks. Excellent day-hiking possibilities abound on the rough jeep tracks that honeycomb this otherwise very wild and unspoiled area. To get there, drive 13 miles south of Moab on US-191 to the top of a grade, and look for a marked BLM dirt road taking off to the right. Although this dirt road soon deteriorates, its initial section does not require high clearance. After 0.5

Bare sandstone domes encircle Conehead Valley, Utah

mile turn right at a fork and then park along the shoulder wherever it seems convenient.

Hike this road all the way to Conehead Valley, clearly visible about 1 mile distant. Continue straight ahead past intersecting jeep tracks and dirt roads until you reach a triple fork. You will return on the left fork, but now take a hard right along the rim, skirting the slickrock domes, enjoying incomparable views of the La Sals and Spanish Valley, and passing upper Conehead Valley and the sizable Moab Rim Arch on the left. At another fork, go right and continue to the end of the road. A small but uncommonly shaped arch will come into view on the left horizon. To get there, climb the moderately steep side-canyon in front of you, skirting small pour-offs on the left. At the top, look to your left about 25 yards to see the arch, named Tukuhnikivats ("the land where the suns shines longest") after the mountain peak that it frames.

Backtrack down the side-canyon to the road and proceed to the upper end of Conehead Valley. Although there is no trail to guide you, it is easy to drop down into the valley and intersect an old jeep road there. As it leaves the valley at the lower end, this road climbs rapidly up a steep sand hill, angling back around to the left for a good view of the "cones." From the top you can see all three of southern Utah's mountain ranges. The road takes you back to three forks mentioned earlier. Turn right here to return to your car.

Day Hike 4: Picture Frame Arch

> **Distance: 0.75 mile, round-trip**
> **Time: 1 hour or less**
> **Map: USGS quad for Hatch Point**
> **Difficulty: easy**

If your car has high clearance, you can also visit lovely **Picture Frame Arch** (see map, p. 110) nearby, 5.75 miles from US-191. From the highway take the same dirt road as for the Conehead Valley hike, but turn left rather than right at the fork at mile 0.5. Follow the signs for Pritchett Arch until you reach the short Picture Frame spur, which loops around a prominent redrock mass just past a dune area on the right. Park here and tackle the 0.75-mile spur road on foot. Walking counterclockwise around the base of steep cliffs, you pass a large, inaccessible arch within the first 100 yards, then come to Picture Frame Arch, located around the back of the mesa. Picture Frame can be reached from a sloping terrace, provided you can boost yourself up over a low cliff. The old ladder here may be unsafe. Just behind the arch's square opening is a small chamber that makes a great place to relax out of the sun. Continue on the road around the mesa to return to your car.

DAYS 11 THROUGH 13: NEEDLES DISTRICT

- Wandering through cities of stone
- Making a pilgrimage to Druid Arch
- Camping at Chesler Park and Devils Kitchen
- Gas, groceries, and showers available seasonally at Needles Outpost

Today you'll begin your stay in the **Needles District** of Canyonlands Park, an area defined by standing rocks in all colors, shapes, and sizes. On your left as you approach the park are the distinctive Six Shooter Peaks (with tops of Wingate sandstone) and two lovely canyons full of arches and ruin sites: **Davis** and **Lavender,** both accessible only by 4-wheel drive vehicle. Wooden Shoe Arch stands guard over Squaw Flat Campground inside the park.

Stop at the ranger station for a two-night permit to camp in the Chesler Park region. Inquire about the water situation (you'll probably have to carry 1 gallon each). On Day 13, plan to camp at Squaw Flat after you're showered and resupplied at Needles Outpost, just outside the park.

For further information contact the Superintendent, Canyonlands National Park, 125 West 200 South, Moab, UT 84532.

—■—

Backpack: Chesler Park

> **Distance: 22 miles, round-trip**
> **Time: 3 days**
> **Map: USGS topo for Canyonlands National Park**
> **Difficulty: moderate**

Chesler Park (see map, p. 115), a meadow surrounded by sandstone towers, is one of the great beauty spots of the desert. In late spring and early summer the area is carpeted with paintbrush, sego lilies, and other flowers characteristic of the Colorado Plateau.

At Squaw Flat's Campground A, take either the Squaw Canyon or the Big Spring Canyon trail, roughly equal in length, which intersect (to make a nice 7.5-mile loop) in about 3.75 miles. The Big Spring route is a bit harder because it crosses a slickrock pass, but also more scenic. Both trails are cairned and have signs at junctions. Soon after the trails converge, the path seems to disappear on a slickrock bench, but actually goes through a narrow fracture to the right between two fins. Logs jammed into this "joint" protect hikers from injury. Shortly thereafter, you cross a sandstone pass into a tributary of the Elephant Canyon system, with the help of ladders.

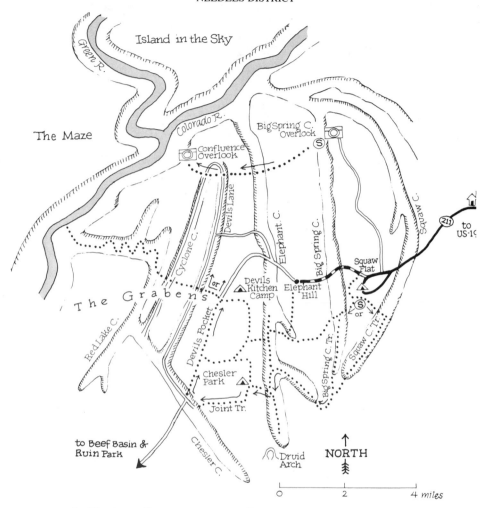

At Elephant Canyon proper (mile 6), bear left, heading toward its source. Springs and pools appear in this canyon when the water table gets close to the surface. You'll be grateful for these miniature oases in the summer months, as Elephant Canyon can be very hot around midday. Treat any water you find here.

Plan to spend your first night in magical **Chesler Park.** The trail to Chesler Park (which begins 6.25 miles from Squaw Flat) climbs rapidly through remarkable country dominated by rows upon rows of tall, spindly monoliths or "needles" composed of Cedar Mesa sandstone. A loop trail defines Chesler Park's perimeter. Camping here is restricted to certain areas; check with the ranger for details.

In the morning, leave your packs behind (taking along your valuables plus any canteens that need refilling) and return to Elephant Canyon for a

The Needles of Chesler Park, Canyonlands National Park, Utah, ring lush meadows

memorable side trip. Up the canyon about 2 miles is the magnificent, 200-foot-tall **Druid Arch,** with its twin vertical openings. This idyllic area is closed to camping, but you can get water from shallow pools nearby.

From Druid Arch, backtrack to Chesler Park, retrieve your pack, and locate the start of the **Joint Trail.** This trail, under a mile in length, follows a slender passageway between towering walls of sandstone. The fracture sometimes opens into cool, charming grottoes. Where the joint ends, the trail drops to a jeep road below. Turn right here, picking up a trail to Devils Kitchen's primitive campground. You can camp in this vicinity.

At Devils Kitchen take either of two jeep roads to **Elephant Hill.** The road to the left is somewhat longer but perhaps more interesting, as it incorporates the Silver Stairs, a challenging 4-wheel drive roadbed formed entirely of slickrock. Descend Elephant Hill on the jeep road, passing a parking lot to the right (as far as regular passenger cars can go). From this point you have about 3 easy miles of road-stomping back to Squaw Flat.

DAY 14: A TRIP TO THE CONFLUENCE

- **Watching the Green merge with the Colorado**
- **Camping at Squaw Flat**
- **Gas, groceries, and showers available at Needles Outpost**

This interesting journey takes you to a viewpoint about 1000 feet above the junction of the Green and Colorado rivers. Although it can be completed in one long day, you may prefer to camp out; check with rangers about camping restrictions.

Day Hike (or backpack): Confluence Overlook

Distance: 11 miles, round-trip
Time: 1 day (or 2 days)
Map: USGS topo for Canyonlands National Park
Difficulty: moderate

The trail to Confluence Overlook takes off from the road to Big Spring Canyon Overlook, 3.5 miles north of Squaw Flat Campground (see map, p. 115). The only tiring part of the hike occurs at its very beginning (and end, since you'll be doubling back) when you cross Big Spring Canyon. Expect little shade and no water along the route.

The trail may lack some of the drama that characterizes its rivals in the area. But it does acquaint you with the lower reaches of Elephant Canyon, and from a high ridge more than halfway to the confluence you can feast your eyes on the needles around Chesler Park. From the ridge you descend and cross Cyclone Canyon, one of many "grabens" that continue the rest of the way to the Colorado River.

In Cyclone Canyon you join a jeep road, which you follow to its end. **Confluence Overlook** is only 0.5 mile farther on, near the top of a rise. The Green River, coming in from the northwest, does in fact look noticeably greener than the muddy Colorado. Inside the V made by the rivers at their junction lies the Island in the Sky; the Maze section of the park is directly across the river from where you stand.

Canyon-bottom habitat encourages a profusion of wildflowers

<u>DAY 15:</u> A SCENIC FAREWELL

- **Car touring the Canyon Rims**
- **And/or the lofty La Sals**
- **Returning to Grand Junction**

On your way back to Grand Junction, you can opt for scenic drives in Canyon Rims Recreation Area and the La Sal Mountains. Of the two, the Canyon Rims trip is longer. The La Sal Mountains Loop replaces most of the drive between Moab and the Fisher Towers region on UT-128.

For more information on these areas, write to the Bureau of Land Management, Grand Resource Area, Moab District, P.O. Box M, Moab, UT 84532; and the Moab District Ranger Station, Manti-La Sal National Forest, 125 West 200 South, Moab, UT 84532.

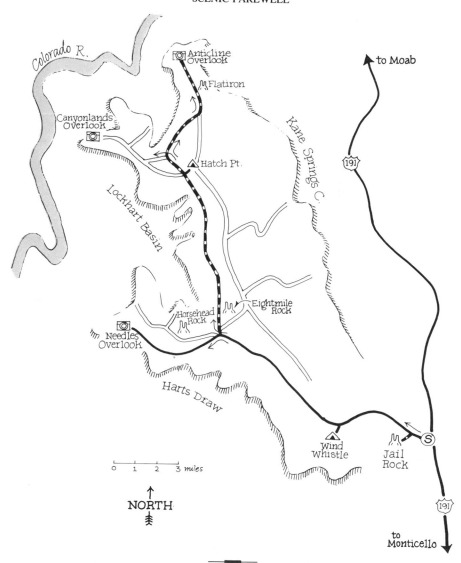

Colorado R.

Anticline Overlook

Flatiron

Kane Springs C.

to Moab

191

Canyonlands Overlook

Hatch Pt.

Lockhart Basin

Eightmile Rock

Horsehead Rock

Needles Overlook

Harts Draw

0 1 2 3 miles

↑
NORTH

Wind Whistle

Jail Rock

S

to Monticello

191

Scenic Drive 1: Canyon Rims

Distance: up to 74 miles, round-trip
Time: 3 hours

Canyon Rims Recreation Area, administered by the BLM, is perched between the La Sal Mountains and the gorge of the Colorado River, 1400 feet below. From the Needles District, turn north on US-191 and drive 7 miles to a signed road on the left, where you turn off. Three outstanding vantage points, Needles, Anticline, and Canyonlands overlooks, provide excellent views of the canyon system carved out by the Colorado and its tributaries. A round-trip to Needles and Anticline overlooks from the main highway covers about 74 miles (see map, p. 119).

The paved road into the recreation area passes Jail Rock and Wind Whistle Campground before arriving at a junction at mile 15. The left fork, still paved, goes to **Needles Overlook,** the closest of the three at 22 miles from the main highway, where you can enjoy sweeping views of the BLM-administered lands in lower Indian Creek and the Needles District of Canyonlands Park.

The right fork at mile 15, a gravel road, eventually leads past Hatch Point Campground (23 miles from the main road) near where you turn off to **Canyonlands Overlook.** (The Canyonlands Overlook road requires 4-wheel drive.) Seven miles beyond Hatch Point, the road terminates at dizzying **Anticline Overlook,** with vistas of the canyons of both the Colorado River and its tributary, Kane Creek.

Scenic Drive 2: La Sal Mountains Loop

Distance: 36.5 miles, one way
Time: 1.5 hours

This interesting and varied route ascends into the cool alpine uplands and meadows of the **La Sal Mountains** (see map, p. 119). A 61-mile loop beginning and ending in Moab requires about three hours, but the route described below is substantially shorter. The roads are almost completely paved and therefore suitable for passenger cars, although people with jeeps can anticipate extra hours of enjoyment on the numerous mining tracks that climb to the mountaintops or circle around to the back side of the range.

Begin at milepost 118 south of Moab on US-191 by turning right and intersecting the La Sal Loop Road (a right turn) in 1 mile. The winding road steadily climbs out of Spanish Valley, heading Mill Creek on its way to its crest in the mountains. Often snowcapped even into summer, La Sals are a geologically young range. Like the Abajos to the south, they are laccoliths, or igneous intrusions into sedimentary rock that were exposed when the surrounding layers eroded away. **Mount Peale,** at 12,700 feet, is the highest peak in the range.

Around the top of the loop are short spur roads to Oowah and Warner lakes. Under normal conditions, most cars can negotiate these roads easily, though high clearance would be welcome. Both lakes have campsites, tables, and outhouses, and are beautifully situated in basins just below the high peaks. Farther on, you pass an old road to Miners Basin, a cirque where prospectors in the 1890s established a little town. Nearby is the site

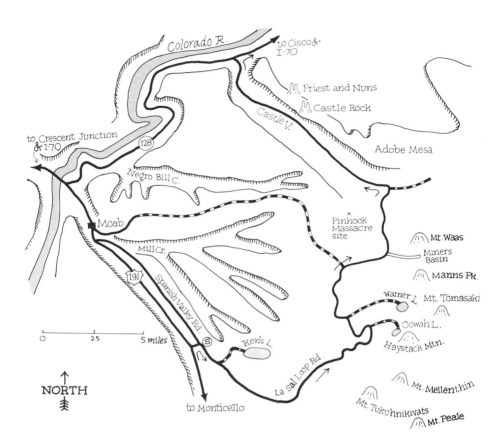

of the Pinhook Massacre, where members of a white posse were killed in 1881 by a band of Indians trying to evade capture for murder and horse theft.

Up in the aspen belt you enjoy extravagant, unblocked views of both the La Sals and the redrock wilderness far below. You soon drop down breathtaking **Castle Valley,** bounded on the left by two unusual formations, called the Priest and Nuns, and Castle Rock. Eventually you wind your way back to UT-128 south of Fisher Towers, where you turn right and continue toward I-70.

Chapter 4

CEDAR MESA LOOP

Utah

Most of this short loop explores the Cedar Mesa country between the Abajo Mountains and the San Juan River (see map, p. 123). Prehistoric ruins, natural bridges, and high-walled canyons add to the circuit's allure. Since the towns in this part of Utah are small and rustic, offering few amenities, the tour demands that you be willing to "rough it." It is, moreover, a very active tour, with substantial day hikes or short backpacking trips scheduled for almost every day. Opportunities to raft the San Juan River and see Lake Powell by boat are other options.

<u>DAY 1:</u> BLANDING TO NATURAL BRIDGES

- **Meeting the Anasazi**
- **Driving through a spectacular monocline**
- **Camping at Natural Bridges National Monument**
- **Gas, groceries, showers, and laundry available in Blanding**

Unlike other "host" cities in this book, Blanding (population 3100) is not located on an interstate highway. But this southeastern Utah community can be reached in a few hours from either I-70 or I-40 via US-191. The town's ultra-wide streets and prohibition on the sale of alcoholic beverages are legacies of its Mormon heritage. A more subtle influence is provided by local Utes, whose reservation south of here was established in the early 1920s in the wake of a skirmish that killed two of their people. Blanding is nestled under the Abajo (aka Blue) Mountains, a laccolithic range whose peaks soar to over 11,300 feet. Buy gas, ice, and groceries for three days before striking off into the desert.

On the outskirts of Blanding is your first stop, **Edge of the Cedars State Park,** an Anasazi ruin complex. It consists of a cluster of six buildings (five of them unexcavated) on the mesa above shallow Westwater Canyon. A short trail winds around the ruins, passing an unusual "great kiva," the northernmost of its kind in Utah. Unlike smaller kivas, asso-

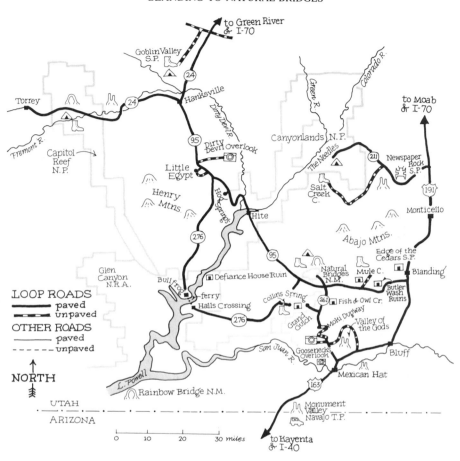

ciated with each household, great kivas were employed by the community as a whole for religious and social functions. The masonry style here shows mainly Mesa Verdean influence, as would be expected, but also some degree of borrowing from far away Chaco Canyon in New Mexico. The park museum ranks among the best of its kind, providing exhibits and information about prehistoric sites on Cedar Mesa, as well as an outstanding collection of Anasazi pottery.

For further information, contact the Superintendent, Edge of the Cedars State Park, Box 788, Blanding, UT 84511-0788.

From Blanding, drive a few miles south on US-191 and turn right on scenic UT-95 toward Natural Bridges National Monument, 31 miles away. Take the turnoff on the right at mile 10.5 for **Butler Wash Ruins.** A short, easy loop trail of under 1 mile round-trip leads to an overlook of a cliff dwelling, perched in an alcove on the opposite side of the canyon. The ruin contains four kivas—one done in the square Kayenta style and three in the round Mesa Verdean variety. Walk about 50 yards to the left of the

Tiny insects are attracted to a saffron cactus flower

overlook to see an arch just to the right of the main ruin. The petroglyph panels, for which Butler Wash is also known, are at its confluence with the San Juan River, between Bluff and Mexican Hat, and are best approached by boat.

About 2.5 miles farther on, the highway cuts through the tremendous Comb Ridge monocline, which extends for some 80 miles from the Abajo foothills through Arizona's Monument Valley. Nine miles to the west is a spur road to **Mule Canyon Ruins,** a 700-year-old complex with twelve small rooms, a restored kiva, and the remains of a tower. On Day 3, you will hike in Mule Canyon proper.

Continue west for 11 more miles to Natural Bridges National Monument, where you'll spend the next three nights. About 42 miles from Blanding is the turnoff. Be warned that the park's small, no-fee campground can fill up quickly. If no vacancies exist, ask at the entrance station or visitor center for the information sheet showing where "overflow camping" is available and acceptable.

DAY 2: NATURAL BRIDGES

- ■ **Encountering three wondrous spans**
- ■ **Searching for ruins and pictographs**
- ■ **Camping at Natural Bridges**

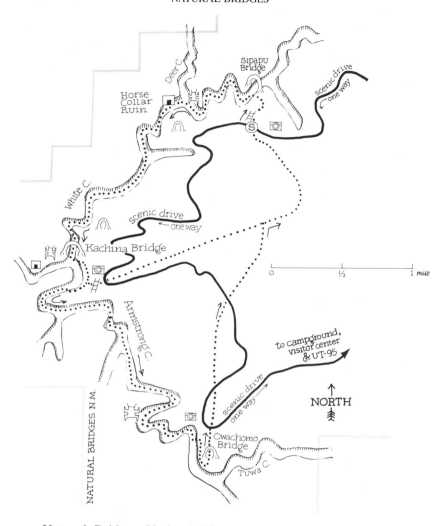

Natural Bridges National Monument contains three spectacular bridges: Kachina (named after spirits in the Hopi religion), Sipapu (a word used to designate a legendary opening to the underworld, from which traditional Hopi believe their ancestors emerged), and Owachomo (meaning "rock mound" in Hopi). Given that natural bridges are fairly rare phenomena, the proximity of three such beauties is just short of miraculous. No matter how their size is calculated, all rank among the largest in the world. Made of Cedar Mesa sandstone, the bridges were "discovered" by a prospector, Cass Hite, in the 1880s, though the area was long known to local Indians such as the Paiute (whose word for a natural bridge means "under the horse's belly"). Even earlier, Anasazi inhabited these canyons, and the

Each canyon bend beckons anew in Natural Bridges National Monument, Utah

national monument contains numerous ruins from their prehistoric culture.

An 8.75-mile loop trail through White and Armstrong canyons connects the bridges and returns over the mesa top, but you can also see and visit them from designated overlooks along the scenic drive. Each bridge is accessible from the road by a short trail; of these, the one to Owachomo is easiest.

The loop trail through the canyons comes highly recommended. You can easily day-hike it, or break it up into two segments, or even make it an overnight trip. (In that case you must walk an extra 1.5 miles past Kachina Bridge down White Canyon to cross over into BLM land, since backcountry camping is not permitted in the national monument. During the late summer rainy season, camping in White Canyon is not recommended due to the flash flood danger. Overnight parking along the scenic drive is always prohibited.) Those who are inclined to do only part of the canyon trail might find the section from Sipapu to Kachina Bridge more picturesque.

For further information, write to the Superintendent, Natural Bridges National Monument, Box 1, Lake Powell, UT 84533.

Day Hike: Natural Bridges Loop

Distance: 8.75 miles, round-trip
Time: 1 day
Maps: USGS quads for Natural Bridges and Bears Ears
Difficulty: easy

Your route starts at the parking lot near Sipapu Bridge, 2.75 miles past the visitor center (see map, p. 125). In the course of a steep 0.5-mile, 500-foot descent of the cliff, aided by ladders and stairs, you pass a small ruin on the left just before a spur to an overlook, then drop down to the floor of White Canyon. Turn left here and pass under **Sipapu Bridge,** the biggest of the three, with a span of 270 feet. Past Sipapu, look for handprint pictographs on the alcove wall at the junction with Deer Canyon, and a hundred yards farther on, a multiroomed cliff dwelling named Horse Collar Ruin, opposite a small arch.

About 2.25 miles past Sipapu, **Kachina Bridge,** the youngest of the trio, spans an idyllic spot where White Canyon meets Armstrong Canyon. Look for pictographs on both abutments; more rock art and small ruins are a short distance past the bridge. To proceed, turn left up Armstrong Canyon. The trail ascends the left bank of the streambed temporarily, then intersects with the trail up to the Kachina parking lot. Continue straight ahead here, dropping back into Armstrong Canyon after passing a section of narrows. In about 1.5 miles, the wash takes a big rightward turn below a prominent undercut formation shaped like an anvil. Look for a pictograph panel around the bend to the right.

The trail soon goes up onto the left bank, about 50 feet above the canyon floor. About 2.75 miles past Kachina, **Owachomo Bridge**—the oldest, smallest, and most eroded in the monument—comes into view. Owachomo is adjacent to Armstrong Canyon, since it was cut by a different stream. The trail goes under the bridge and climbs to the overlook in the next 0.25 mile. Cross the park road, joining the easy, pleasant mesa trail, which winds through a pinyon and juniper forest for about 3 miles, back to the Sipapu parking lot.

DAY 3: MULE CANYON

- **Discovering cliff dwellings**
- **Camping at Natural Bridges**
- **Gas, groceries, showers, and laundry available in Blanding**

Retain your campsite in Natural Bridges while you complete the following day hike. The trip provides a good introduction to wilderness travel: Although trailless, it is short and not terribly challenging. To reach the mouth of **Mule Canyon,** backtrack about 15 miles on UT-95 in the direction of Blanding. Go 0.5 mile past the sign for the roadside ruin and turn left onto the good dirt road to Texas Flat. Pull off to park where this road crosses the south fork of Mule Canyon, in another 0.5 mile.

When your hike is over, drive to Blanding to purchase supplies for three more days, two of which will be spent backpacking. Then return to Natural Bridges for the night.

Desert varnish decorates an overhang above a ruin in Mule Canyon, Utah

Day Hike: South Fork, Mule Canyon

Distance: 6 miles or more, round-trip
Time: 1 day
Maps: USGS quads for Bears Ears and Brushy Basin
Wash
Difficulty: moderate

Mule is a shallow, unremarkable canyon cut into Cedar Mesa sandstone. Though it gets prettier toward its upper end, few people would find it worth exploring except for the magnificent, unusually well-preserved Anasazi ruins that grace both of its forks. (As you visit these ancient ruins, remember that disturbing them or their contents in any way is against the

Mule Canyon, Utah, harbors well-preserved cliff dwellings

law. Please leave everything as you found it for others to enjoy.)

You can hike up the 7-mile-long South Fork as far as you wish. Since no trail penetrates it, you will be walking in or frequently crossing the creekbed, so old sneakers are the recommended footwear. For the first 0.5 mile, and occasionally thereafter, you must fight your way through brush. During the rainy season, pools and quicksand can impede your progress. The cliff dwellings, about six in all, occupy the south-facing (right hand) wall of the canyon, beginning about a mile in (see map, page 129). A particularly extensive ruin is nestled into the cliff 3 miles from the trailhead.

DAYS 4 AND 5:   FISH AND OWL CREEKS

- **Strolling through remote canyons**
- **Spying ruins along the cliffs**
- **Camping near the confluence and in Valley of the Gods**
- **Gas, groceries, showers, and laundry available in Mexican Hat**

The next two days include an overnight backpack to deep sandstone canyons boasting numerous ruins, unusual rock formations, and a large arch, and a visit to the Valley of the Gods.

To start the hike in Fish and Owl creeks, register and check on water availability at the Kane Gulch Ranger Station, 4.5 miles down UT-261 from its junction with UT-95, just east of Natural Bridges. Normally, these canyons contain pools and running springs, but remember to treat all drinking water.

For more information, contact the Bureau of Land Management, 284 South First West, P.O. Box 7, Monticello, UT 84535.

―――

Backpack: Fish and Owl Creeks

Distance: 15.5 miles, round-trip
Time: 2 days
Maps: USGS quads for Cedar Mesa and Bluff
Difficulty: moderate, with strenuous ascent at end

To reach the trailhead, go south on UT-261 about 1 mile past Kane Gulch. Turn left onto a graded dirt road and follow it for 5 miles through a pinyon and juniper forest to its end at a parking lot.

The recommended direction for this hike is to descend into Owl and ascend the west arm of Fish. From the parking area, follow the roadbed on your right for about 50 yards to a wash, which leads to the **Owl Creek** rim and the start of a cairned trail (see map, page 129). A short distance below the rim is the first ruin, off to the right, near a dryfall. The trail winds around past another ruin and another pour-off before dropping into the bed of Owl Creek, by way of a small side-canyon at mile 1.5. At the bottom, look for a spring at ground level. You may also find pools of water over the next few miles.

Follow the wash, passing large Nevills Arch high in a Cedar Mesa sandstone fin on the left at mile 4.25, until Owl and Fish meet at mile 6.75. The confluence makes a good place to camp; there may be more pools in the vicinity. McCloyd Canyon, about a mile below the confluence on the right, also contains some fine ruins.

Turn left at the confluence and walk up **Fish Creek,** which is even prettier than Owl. It also boasts more archaeological sites, though you will have to look sharp to find them. A particularly intriguing area 2 or 3 miles above the confluence is open and grassy, ringed by strangely shaped monoliths.

Six miles above the confluence, Fish Creek forks. Go left here and continue about 0.5 mile to a pour-off and a spring gushing out of the canyon wall to the left. The canyon narrows considerably past the fork, and heavy brush and boulders make walking more difficult. If you have another night to spare, consider camping on the right bank opposite the spring on a slickrock terrace.

Immediately past the spring on the left bank begins the very steep 0.25-mile route out of Fish Creek, marked by a large cairn. Although no

The San Juan River in Utah has carved a serpentine canyon

developed trail exists here, occasional cairns mark the 600-foot ascent to the rim. The top rewards you with a great view of both the canyon system and the Bears Ears buttes. Pick up the 2-mile trail here that takes you through the pygmy forest to your car.

———

After the hike, drive south 27.5 miles on UT-261 through rolling country. The road makes a series of hairpin bends down Cedar Mesa's 1100-foot cliff face. Pull off the highway at designated turnouts to enjoy the views. This dizzying stretch of road is called the **Moki Dugway,** after the early Mormon name for the Anasazi; "dugway" means a route carved from solid rock. Near the bottom, look for a sign on the right to **Goosenecks Overlook.** An 8-mile round-trip drive leads to a spot 1000 feet above the twisty meanders of the San Juan River.

Where UT-261 intersects US-163, bear right toward Mexican Hat, 4 miles away, to resupply. Just north of Mexican Hat take a very short dirt road to the east, leading to the unusual butte on the river that gave the town its name; it resembles a person wearing a sombrero. To the east of the road towers Raplee Ridge, a steeply tilted monocline through which the San Juan has cut its canyon. This gray-, rust-, and purple-banded formation is known locally as the "Navajo Rug."

Mexican Hat is home to companies that offer white-water rafting adventures on the San Juan. Outstanding one- and two-day trips begin at

Sand Island BLM Recreation Area south of Bluff (see Chapter 5, Anasazi Loop, Day 3), with longer trips continuing on to Clay Hills Crossing on the periphery of Lake Powell. Check into these trips locally if the prospect appeals to you. Another option for readers with extra time is a tour of nearby Monument Valley (Anasazi Loop, Day 3).

When your business concludes in Mexican Hat, go northeast on US-163 for about 8 miles. Turn left on a well-marked 16.5-mile-long dirt and gravel road that loops through **Valley of the Gods.** Take a right where the dirt road forks just past the highway, then ford a shallow wash. The broad, open valley, which defines the lower end of Lime Creek, contains a series of reddish brown monoliths, many of them pyramidal formations capped by round knobs. Among the most prominent are the Setting Hen, the Seven Sailors, and Scotchman Butte. It's a great place for photography and primitive camping—pull off onto a spur road and flop down your sleeping bag—but there are no trails.

DAY 6: VALLEY OF THE GODS TO GOBLIN VALLEY

- **Visiting another vertiginous overlook**
- **Swimming in Lake Powell**
- **Camping and showers at Goblin Valley State Park**
- **Gas and groceries available in Hanksville**

This morning, complete the scenic drive through Valley of the Gods. At UT-261, turn right and proceed up the Moki Dugway. At the crest, take a good dirt road on the left that parallels Johns Canyon and leads in a few miles to **Muley Point,** another San Juan River aerie more than 1000 feet higher than Goosenecks Overlook.

Continue north on UT-261 to its end and head left (northwest) on UT-95 to Hanksville (about 90 miles). This road gives access to a number of wild places not discussed between these covers, such as Dark Canyon Primitive Area. West of Natural Bridges, UT-95 hugs the edge of White Canyon, bestowing heart-stopping views. Unmistakable buttes called the Cheese Box and Jacobs Chair soon appear on the right; between them on the other side of the road is Fry Canyon Store, which sells gasoline and basic grocery items.

After the highway crosses the Colorado and Dirty Devil rivers near **Hite Marina,** it stays on the shore of Lake Powell's narrow northernmost arm for a few miles before climbing quickly to the badlands to the west. Hite derives its name from a prospector who ran a store in this vicinity during the late nineteenth-century uranium rush; a ferry was established to transport people and livestock across the Colorado. You'll find many uncrowded swimming spots along the lake.

Past Hite, UT-95 follows North Wash for a long way as it proceeds toward Hanksville. Attractions along the route include **Hog Springs** (where the BLM has established a picnic area and short trail; a small Fremont pictograph panel is across North Wash in an alcove 50 yards down the road), **Little Egypt** (a miniature Goblin Valley), and **Dirty Devil Overlook** (11 miles of dirt road off the highway). The **Henry Mountains** in the background provide a refreshing contrast to the hot, dry country you're traversing.

In Hanksville, resupply, and travel north on UT-24 for 19.5 miles to the turnoff for **Goblin Valley State Park,** your camping spot. Consult Day 1 of Chapter 2, Desert Rivers Loop, for trail information.

DAY 7: GOBLIN VALLEY TO CAPITOL REEF

- **Jaunts to Fremont Overlook and Hickman Bridge**
- **Camping at Capitol Reef National Park**
- **Gas, groceries, and showers available in Hanksville**

After additional exploration of Goblin Valley in the morning, return to Hanksville and buy provisions for two nights. Continue west on UT-24 for 37 miles to **Capitol Reef National Park,** making camp here. In the af-

Petrified dunes near Hite on Lake Powell, Utah

ternoon, hike to Hickman Bridge and examine the Fremont petroglyphs along the riverbank. Later on, try the Fremont Overlook Trail, which commences at the campground.

DAY 8: DAY HIKES ALONG THE SCENIC DRIVE

- **Hiking to Cassidy Arch and Cohab Canyon**
- **Strolling through Grand Wash**
- **Camping at Capitol Reef**
- **Gas, groceries, showers, and laundry available in Torrey**

This morning, organize a daypack and canteen and head south from the campground along the park's scenic drive, 25 miles round-trip. Get an early start on the Frying Pan Trail, which visits Cassidy Arch and Cohab Canyon. After a picnic lunch in Capitol Gorge at the far end of the road, walk the length of Grand Wash in the late afternoon. All of these places are discussed under Days 3 and 4 in Chapter 2, Desert Rivers Loop.

DAY 9: CAPITOL REEF AND BULLFROG MARINA

- **Morning blood-warmer to Chimney Rock Overlook**
- **Optional boat tour (or rental) on Lake Powell**
- **Camping at Natural Bridges or at Grand Gulch trailhead**
- **Gas, groceries, and showers available in Hanksville; laundry available in Bullfrog and Halls Crossing**

How you organize this day depends on whether you prefer to take a morning hike in Capitol Reef or a boat trip on Lake Powell. Whichever you choose, allow time for shopping, laundry, and showers, for tomorrow you begin a multiday backpacking expedition in Grand Gulch. The drive to Grand Gulch includes a half-hour ferry crossing of Lake Powell. Call ahead, either to the Bullfrog (801-684-2233) or Halls Crossing (801-684-2261) marina, to learn the ferry schedule.

The hike option is a moderately difficult 3.5-mile round-trip on the **Chimney Rock Trail** at the western border of Capitol Reef (see Chapter 2, Desert Rivers Loop, Day 4). Allow 2.5 hours for the loop hike, which involves a 500-foot ascent to an overlook, then take UT-12 east to Hanksville and prepare for the upcoming backpacking trip. If you prefer to take the boat ride, drive straight to Hanksville this morning.

From Hanksville, go southeast 27 miles on UT-95, turn right on UT-276, and travel 38 miles to **Bullfrog.** There you can join a guided boat tour of Defiance House Ruin in Forgotten Canyon, 12 miles up Lake Powell. Those with extra time could take a full-day boat trip tomorrow to Rainbow Bridge National Monument. Motor- and houseboats can be rented from both marinas; reservations are recommended.

Take the ferry from Bullfrog to **Halls Crossing;** before leaving the marinas, fill all available canteens. Continue east on UT-276. Tonight's final destination will depend on which Grand Gulch hiking option you select: Collins Spring to Kane Gulch (5 days) or Bullet Canyon (4 days), or Bullet Canyon to Kane Gulch (3 days). For each, a car shuttle or some equivalent is required; the rangers at Kane Gulch may be able to advise you on this matter when you obtain your hiking permit (required even for dayhikers). Plan to camp at your chosen trailhead or at Natural Bridges, saving the shuttle for tomorrow morning.

The Collins Spring turnoff, marked by a sign, is about 40 miles up UT-276 past Halls Crossing. Travel east on a dirt road for about 6.5 miles to the trailhead. Without a high clearance vehicle, you may have to walk the last 2 or 3 miles.

To reach Bullet Canyon, take UT-276 to the junction of UT-95. Turn right here, and then right again onto UT-261. From this junction it is 4 miles to Kane Gulch Ranger Station and 7 more to the signed turnoff to Bullet Canyon. The parking area is 1.0 mile down a dirt road to the right of the highway.

DAYS 10 THROUGH 12: GRAND GULCH

- **Surveying ancient cliff dwellings**
- **Walking between towering canyon walls**
- **Camping in Grand Gulch**

Few canyons house as many unspoiled Anasazi ruins as this picturesque tributary of the San Juan River. For centuries, Indians farmed the canyon floors, and today hikers will find numerous archaeological sites, as well as pictographs, alcoves, and (except in dry years) pools.

From the upper reaches of lovely Grand Gulch to its confluence with the San Juan is 51.75 miles. Most hikers select a shorter alternative; two good ones are given below. When you register, check with the rangers about water availability and be sure to treat or boil whatever water you find.

Whichever hike you choose, you may be too tired upon emerging from the canyon to do much more than retrieve your car. In that case you can make camp at Natural Bridges (or at least obtain fresh water there).

Pulling into a private campground near Blanding is another possibility.

For more information, contact the Bureau of Land Management, Kane Gulch Ranger Station, Box 1, NABR, Lake Powell, UT 84533.

Backpack 1: Bullet Canyon to Kane Gulch

> **Distance: 23 miles, one way**
> **Time: 3 days**
> **Maps: USGS quads for Cedar Mesa, Grand Gulch, and Bears Ears**
> **Difficulty: moderate**

The Bullet Canyon trail starts to the right of the parking area. (See map, p. 138, and Day 9 for driving directions.) Follow the rim a short distance, then, at a large cairn, descend to the canyon floor on a steep trail, turning right at the bottom. Within 0.25 mile, look up to the right as you round a bend to see a square masonry tower. You can reach this ruin easily from the large cairn on the rim.

Less than a mile from the trailhead, pass a large, shallow cave on your left; another mile brings you to a long slickrock ramp, below which hiking becomes tougher as the canyon narrows. Where the trail begins to flatten out, and a side-canyon enters from the left, there may be a spring; look for ruins and pictographs in this vicinity. The trail remains brushy for the next mile, but walking improves when the canyon widens.

Jailhouse and **Perfect Kiva** ruins are on the right side of the canyon about 4.75 miles from the trailhead. Jailhouse Ruin is much easier to see, with its striking, white, circular pictographs (perhaps representing ghost faces, or phases of the moon) and the small, barred window that occasioned its name. Perfect Kiva Ruin contains a kiva with a specially reconstructed roof and a ladder leading down into its interior. This is the only ruin site on Cedar Mesa in which visitors are allowed to walk on a roof and enter a kiva. When the controversial explorer Richard Wetherill visited the canyon in the 1890s, his party excavated this and many other ruins, selling the artifacts to museums.

Across the wash from Jailhouse is a good camping place amid some cottonwoods, and just past the trees flows Jailhouse Spring at mile 5. About 2.5 miles of effortless walking brings you to the confluence with **Grand Gulch,** where there is a heavily used campsite. Turn right here and proceed upstream. Be alert for Anasazi sites in alcoves throughout this area, especially on the south-facing side of the canyon.

Shieks Canyon at mile 8.5, the first side-canyon to the right, is especially rich in rock art and may contain a spring about 0.25 mile up from its junction with Grand Gulch. **Split Level Ruin,** one of Grand Gulch's major

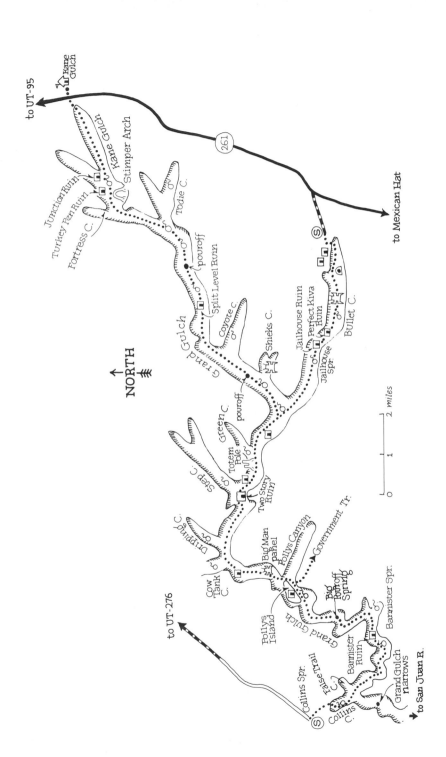

to UT-95

Kane Gulch

261

to Mexican Hat

Junction Ruin
Turkey Pen Ruin
Fortress C.
Kane Gulch
Stimper Arch
Todie C.
pouroff
Split Level Ruin
Coyote C.
Sheiks C.
Jailhouse Ruin
Perfect Kiva Ruin
Jailhouse Spr.
Bullet C.

Grand Gulch

NORTH

Green C.
pouroff
Totem Pole
Two Story Ruin

Step C.

Dripping C.

Big Man Panel
Pollys Canyon
Government Tr.

Cow Tank C.

Pollys Island

Big Pouroff Spring

Grand Gulch

Bannister Spr.

Collins Spr.
False Trail
Bannister Ruin
Collins C.
Grand Gulch narrows

to UT-276

to San Juan R.

0   1   2 miles

houses, is on the left at mile 12.75. Todie Canyon, 3 miles farther, boasts many archaeological treasures. Past Stimper Arch are two very significant ruins—**Turkey Pen** (at mile 18.25) and **Junction** (at mile 19), both on the left side of the canyon. The very large Junction Ruin, situated in a football field-sized alcove, bears John Wetherill's inscription. It marks the confluence of Grand Gulch with **Kane Gulch** (originally known as Wetherill Canyon), the 4-mile-long tributary that is your way out of the primitive area. After a 500-foot ascent, the trail ends at the Kane Gulch Ranger Station parking lot.

Backpack 2: Collins Spring to Bullet Canyon

> **Distance: 30 miles (or 38 to Kane Gulch), one way**
> **Time: 4 days (5 to Kane Gulch)**
> **Maps: USGS quads for Bears Ears, Cedar Mesa, and**
> **Grand Gulch**
> **Difficulty: moderate**

Especially if you opt for the longer trip to Kane Gulch, this ambitious hike introduces you to the best of what the primitive area has to offer. Not only do you cover more ground and view more ruins, but you also experience more solitude on this route than on the Bullet-to-Kane trip. Register at Kane Gulch Ranger Station before setting out.

The trailhead is marked by a large sign. (See map, p. 138, and Day 9 for driving directions.) Follow the trail 2 miles down Collins Canyon to its intersection with Grand Gulch. Careful map reading will prevent your being confused by False Trail Canyon, which joins Collins Canyon in the vicinity of Grand Gulch. If you want to detour to see the Grand Gulch narrows, you can drop your pack at the intersection and turn right, walking 0.25 mile downstream; otherwise, go straight ahead and amble up the canyon past a large slickrock platform. There may be pools here.

In about 2.5 more miles, you will reach Bannister Spring, just 0.25 mile below **Bannister Ruin** on the left. This two-tiered ruin contains an exposed horizontal beam; its intact but fragile kiva should not be disturbed. Big Pour-off Spring is at mile 8.75. About 0.25 mile before you reach it is a slickrock terrace that offers ideal camping.

The trail skirts Big Pour-off on the left. Your next landmark is the junction with the Government Trail at mile 11.75. A campsite, sometimes complete with springwater, is located between this trail junction and Pollys Island, formed by a "rincon" or abandoned meander of Grand Gulch; a ruin is visible here high up in the cliff on the left.

Look for the **Big Man** pictograph panel 1.5 miles past Pollys Island, about 200 feet above the canyon floor on the right. Shortly before you reach the viewpoint for this panel, a shady undercut ledge on the left also

Pictographs of Grand Gulch, Utah, recall modern pointillist techniques

contains some interesting rock art. Water may be available up Cow Tank Canyon, at mile 15.25, and Dripping Canyon, 0.5 mile farther.

Just past Dripping Canyon on the left is another slickrock terrace that could provide a pleasant campsite. Few other spots for camping exist between here and the Totem Pole. In fact, these next 4.25 miles are unquestionably the most tedious and difficult of the trip, since they involve a great deal of bushwhacking. Step Canyon, at mile 18.5, has a small clearing that you can use as your base to explore for ruins. The entire tributary deserves study if time permits. Anasazi sites abound here, and you should persist long enough to find magnificent **Two Story Ruin,** concealed by thick brush on the right bank of the main canyon. Like Green Canyon farther on, Step may contain water.

The Totem Pole, an unmistakable pillar on the left at mile 20, signals the end of the hard stretch. You can relax among the cottonwoods on the high ground past the Totem Pole before pushing on to the Bullet Canyon junction, 2.5 miles beyond. Although this section of trail is characterized by constant ups and downs, you will probably be relieved to be done with the willows. Keep your eyes peeled for small Anasazi sites on both sides of the trail.

DAY 13: GRAND GULCH TO CANYONLANDS

- **Deciphering the messages on Newspaper Rock**
- **Optional jeep trip or plane flight**
- **Camping in Canyonlands National Park**
- **Gas, groceries, showers, and laundry available in Blanding or Monticello**

Today, take UT-95 east to Blanding, then drive north 21 miles on US-191 to Monticello in the Abajo foothills, stopping in either town to buy supplies for four days. Then continue north on US-191 for 15 miles, turning left on UT-211 to the Needles District of Canyonlands National Park. This stretch of road, and scenic attractions along it, is described under Day 10 of Chapter 3, Redrock Loop; remember to stop at **Newspaper Rock State Park** to inspect its fascinating multicultural inscriptions. Either in Monticello or at Needles Outpost on the park boundary, you can arrange a scenic plane flight over the area or a jeep tour of lovely Davis, Lavender, or Horse canyons, all laden with arches and ruins.

Camp at Squaw Flat (see Chesler Park backpack described under Day 11 of Chapter 3, Redrock Loop) and take scenic drives and short nature walks around Canyonlands. At the visitor center, secure a permit and discuss transportation arrangements for a four-day backpacking trip in Salt Creek Canyon. Also inquire about the water situation.

DAYS 14 THROUGH 17: SALT CREEK CANYON

- **Ruins, arches, and pictographs**
- **Camping beneath golden cliffs**
- **The road home**

Salt Creek Canyon begins in the foothills of the Abajos and extends deep into the Needles District. The lower half of the canyon, which is narrow and twisty, is very pretty and worth a trip for that reason alone, but the main attractions for visitors are the canyon's many ruins, arches, and pictographs. The hike terminates at Cave Spring (or, alternatively, Squaw Flat; see below).

At the conclusion of your backpack trip, camp at Squaw Flat before beginning your drive home. If you are headed north, and have extra time for the high desert, Arches National Park won't disappoint you. Those traveling east should consider a stop at Mesa Verde. South of here, major points of interest include Monument Valley, Canyon de Chelly, and the Petrified Forest.

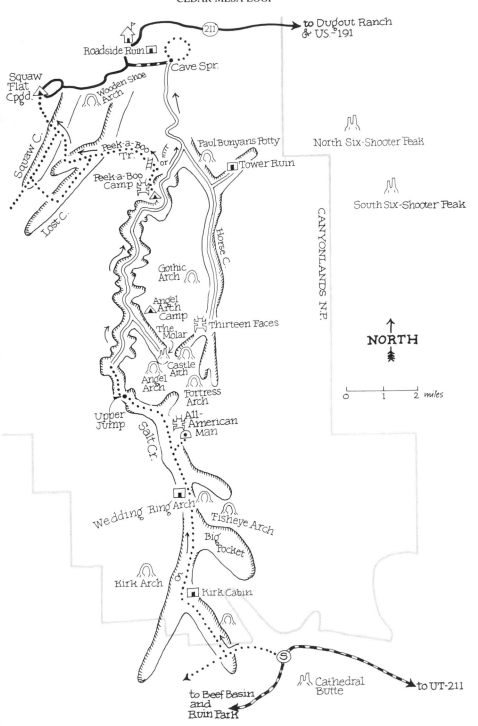

Backpack: Salt Creek Canyon

> Distance: 28.5 miles, one way, including side trip to Angel
> Arch
> Time: 4 days
> Map: USGS topo for Canyonlands National Park
> Difficulty: moderate

To get to the trailhead, drive out of the Needles District on UT-211. Turn south onto a dirt road at Dugout Ranch. In 3.5 miles the road will fork; take the right fork and continue for about 12.5 miles in the direction of Ruin Park and Beef Basin. The Salt Creek system is 0.25 mile past Cathedral Butte, on the right. A bit of scouting should enable you to find the point where the trail drops down into the shallow pink and white drainage.

Salt Creek in its upper stretches is rather brushy, requiring some bushwhacking. You'll be following the streambed the entire distance, and there should be water both in the wash and in springs along the way. The canyon contains numerous Anasazi ruins; enjoy them from a distance, but do not climb in or around them, since this practice hastens the deterioration of the sites.

Your first landmark is Kirk Cabin, 3.5 miles from the starting point, built by a Mormon pioneer in the nineteenth century. Near the cabin look for two natural arches. The first major side-canyon to the right, **Big Pocket,** contains Anasazi ruins, and a cliff dwelling is in the distance to the left of Salt Creek. Be sure to stop at Wedding Ring Arch on your right. In this vicinity, small ruins and granaries line both sides of the canyon. A mile or so past Wedding Ring Arch is an interesting joint cave on the left, formed by the meeting of several large slabs of rock. Just across the canyon from this opening is a cliff dwelling.

Approximately 4 miles past Kirk Cabin look for a little spur trail to the right that heads for a small, inconspicuous cave in the cliff. This cave conceals an amazing pictograph called the **All-American Man,** so named because it's colored red, white, and blue and even sports flaglike stripes. The man looks like a comic book Martian, with a round shield for a body and a lone antler growing from his head.

The streambed narrows within the next mile and a fair amount of water may be in the wash. There are at least two Anasazi sites to the left just before Upper Jump, a pour-off. Here the canyon walls close in, the creek follows a serpentine course, and the scenery becomes much more interesting. About 5 miles past the All-American Man, you'll start to see jeep tracks in the wash, and a mile farther is the junction with the Angel Arch trail to your right.

Don't miss illustrious **Angel Arch,** a Cedar Mesa sandstone span that dominates the end of an attractive side-canyon, only 1.5 flat and easy miles

Joints in Salt Creek Canyon, Canyonlands National Park, Utah, shelter hikers from the summer sun

from where the trails converge. Because a jeep road extends most of the way up this side-canyon, you are likely to meet other people here. Very close to the arch, the right pillar of which resembles an angel in profile, stands a lone rock formation called the Molar.

On your way back to the main trail, notice some ruins about halfway down the side-canyon on your right. From the junction it's a twisty 8.5-mile trek to Peek-a-Boo Spring, now buried under tons of sandstone, the casualty of a slide. The canyon here remains narrow and colorful, with a good deal of vegetation. At Peek-a-Boo primitive campground, under a partially collapsed cliff on the left, look for a trail ascending about 50 feet to a pictograph panel featuring men with shieldlike bodies.

Back in Salt Creek, about a mile past the spring, fabulous **Horse Canyon** (6.5 miles long) comes in from the right. Popular among jeepers, this tributary features several major arches and archaeological sites. If time permits, visit Paul Bunyans Potty, a large arch about 0.5 mile up-canyon, and Tower Ruin, another mile past that, on a spur road that takes off to the left.

Below the Horse Canyon confluence, the main Salt Creek trail is dusty all the way to its end at **Cave Spring,** where an easy 0.5-mile loop trail leads to an old cowboy camp. Deep sand makes hiking these last 2.5 miles a tiring experience, particularly in the heat of early summer, when deerflies inhabit the lower part of the canyon.

An alternative route out of Salt Creek, one that leads to Squaw Flat Campground 5 miles distant, begins a few feet below the Peek-a-Boo Spring petroglyphs. Initially you are on the Peek-a-Boo Trail, whose destination is Lost Canyon. After following Salt Creek's big bend to the right on a sandy bench, the trail ascends through a very narrow cleft to the slickrock above by means of a high ladder. It remains on sandstone rimlands all the way to Lost Canyon, under 2.5 miles from Peek-a-Boo Camp. Indisputably one of the most scenic and imaginatively designed trails in the park, it contours around various small side-canyons, passing through a window in a fin near a 20-foot-high natural arch (hard to see because it is pressed against the cliff). In Lost Canyon, where the Peek-a-Boo Trail ends, go right and pick up the trail toward Squaw Flat, about 2.5 miles away. This trail follows the washbed upstream for a short time, then climbs a slickrock pass before dropping into the Squaw Canyon drainage. Here you intersect the Squaw Canyon Trail, which leads to Squaw Flat.

Chapter 5

ANASAZI LOOP

New Mexico, Colorado, Utah, Arizona

Short in days but long in miles, this loop will appeal especially to people interested in the ancient ruins and modern cultures of Native Americans. Day hikes are showcased, and backpacking minimized. The circuit, while concentrating on New Mexico, is the only one to cross into all the Four Corners states. Though not available at every destination, creature comforts beckon in the Rio Grande Valley from Los Alamos and Taos to Albuquerque.

<u>DAY 1:</u> ALBUQUERQUE TO EL MORRO

- **Getting acquainted with Albuquerque**
- **Puzzling over petroglyphs**
- **Visiting the Sky City**
- **Camping at El Morro National Monument**
- **Gas, groceries, showers, and laundry in Albuquerque**

With almost 332,000 residents, Albuquerque is by far the largest city in the high desert region (see map, p. 147). This metropolis on the Rio Grande offers so much to keep visitors busy that it's tempting to spend half one's vacation here. Local attractions include the restored Old Town section, with its shady plaza bordered by gift shops and New Mexican eateries; the Mountain Road museum district, where the outstanding Museum of Natural History and the Albuquerque Museum of Art are situated; the nearby Rio Grande Nature Center State Park and Indian Pueblo Cultural Center; and the sky-scraping Sandia Mountains (meaning "watermelon" in Spanish) just outside the city limits, whose crest is reachable either by car or by aerial tram.

High on the list of interesting places to visit is **Indian Petroglyph State Park** (proposed for national monument status) in the northwestern part of the city, which features four very short walks along the base of a 17-mile-long talus cliff. The estimated 15,000 Anasazi petroglyphs laboriously pecked into the huge igneous boulders here many centuries ago de-

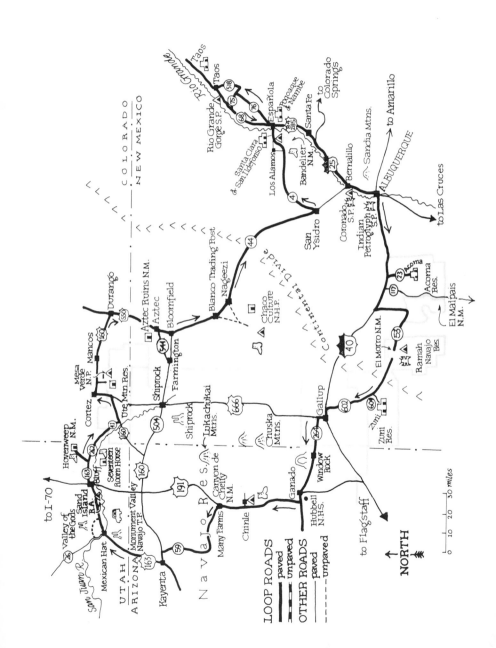

pict birds, reptiles, mammals, people, and kachinas. To see them, turn north at the Coors Road exit off I-40, bearing left at a major Y-intersection onto Atrisco Drive. In a few miles, turn left onto Unser Boulevard and follow it to the park entrance station. The Mesa Trail ascends about 50 feet to the top of a low mesa, winding its way through a rock garden rich with specimens of primitive art. The Short and Cliff trails, beginning near the picnic area, are very easy, involving virtually no elevation change. In the Upper Park (a few hundred yards up Unser Boulevard) is the start of the steep, poorly marked Canyon Trail. One of the petroglyphs along this route is of Kokopelli, regarded by some as the Anasazi version of Pan. This flute-playing figure, with hunched back and prominent phallus, symbolizes fertility.

Buy food and ice for tonight in Albuquerque before heading west on I-40 to the first of several Native American pueblos on this loop: dramatic **Acoma,** the Sky City. This is one of nineteen politically independent communities in New Mexico inhabited by descendants of the Anasazi. Taken together, these communities, concentrated in the Rio Grande Valley, are home to over 40,000 people. They welcome tourists, charging modest entrance fees in most cases (with photography and painting permits costing extra). Several times a year they sponsor sacred traditional dances and hold feasts on saints' days; visitors are allowed to attend these functions, provided they behave in a respectful manner. (Spanish colonial effort to Christianize the New Mexican Indians succeeded only superficially, with the Indians fusing Catholic beliefs with their own traditional ones. Persecution led the residents of many Rio Grande villages to rise up against their conquerors in the Pueblo Revolt of 1680.)

To get to Acoma, drive 52 miles west of Albuquerque on I-40 until you reach exit 108 for NM-23. Turn south here and proceed 12 miles to the town visitor center. Acoma, celebrated for its pottery, seems in many ways representative of contemporary pueblo life. Poor by U.S. standards but picturesque, it is positioned 400 feet above the surrounding country on a forlorn, sheer-sided mesa. Only a small number of people actually inhabit the mesa year-round; most members of the tribe reside in the valley, where there is electricity and running water. A guided tour will include a visit to the San Esteban del Rey church, constructed in the early seventeenth century through the labor of mission Indians. According to legend, some of the forebears of the modern-day dwellers of Acoma starved to death on adjacent Enchanted Mesa when a rockslide prevented them from descending the cliffs.

From Acoma, return to I-40; drive west 26 miles to the Grants exit, and turn south on NM-53. On its way to El Morro, where you will camp tonight, the road swings through **El Malpais National Monument,** a volcanic badlands area complete with ice caves, lava tubes, 1000-foot-deep Bandera Crater, and La Ventana Arch (on NM-117). Nature trails provide access to these attractions, some of which continue to be private, commer-

The Sandia Mountains in New Mexico loom high above the Rio Grande

cial operations. Most ambitious is the 15-mile round-trip Zuni-Acoma Trail, which follows an old Anasazi route, crossing four major lava flows. To extend your visit to El Malpais, drive 10 miles down Route 42 (a high clearance road) to the Big Lava Tubes area. A cairned trail leads to Big Skylight and Four Window caves. One of the nearby lava tubes measures 17 miles in length. Guides or very detailed directions, available at El Malpais Information Center in Grants, are necessary for visiting this area.

Both El Malpais and neighboring **El Morro National Monument** contain prehistoric ruins. From the visitor center at El Morro, the easy Mesa Top Trail ascends to Atsinna, a partially excavated Anasazi pueblo with 850 rooms; allow about 1.5 hours for the 1.5-mile round-trip. El Morro is better known, however, for its remarkable Inscription Rock, a sandstone cliff face into which generations of prehistoric Indians, Spaniards, and Anglo-Americans engraved their messages. The very easy 0.5-mile Inscription Trail leading to messages also passes the freshwater pool that made the area a mecca for so many cultural groups.

For further information contact the Superintendent, El Morro National Monument, Route 2, Box 43, Ramah, NM 87321; and El Malpais Information Center, 620 East Santa Fe Street, Grants, NM 87020.

Spider Rock, a setting for Navaho tales

DAY 2: EL MORRO TO CANYON DE CHELLY

- **Ancient ruins and modern craft shops in Zuni**
- **A trading post and a rock window on the Navajo Reservation**
- **Touring and camping at Canyon de Chelly National Monument**
- **Gas and groceries available in Gallup**

Just east of El Morro on NM-53 is **Zuni,** a large reservation dotted with lakes. Historians believe the ancient Zuni town of Hawikuh, now in ruins, to have been the first pueblo encountered by the Spanish in the sixteenth century. Another archaeological site here is the Village of the Great Kivas, a Chacoan outlier with impressive pictographs. Inquire locally about hiring a Zuni guide if you want to tour these ruins. Zuni's silversmiths craft high-quality jewelry inlaid with turquoise, coral, and other semiprecious stones.

Leaving Zuni, go north on NM-604 and NM-602 to Gallup, on the periphery of the Navajo Reservation. This border town is a good place to refuel and buy supplies for tonight. Your next stop, reached by driving north on US-666 for 7.5 miles and west onto Route 264 for 16.5 miles, is Window Rock, where the Navajo tribe is headquartered. The town gets its name from a large natural arch or "window," which can be reached by a short trail.

Past Window Rock, stop at **Hubbell National Historic Site** in Ganado. The Park Service runs guided tours of the beautifully appointed home of John L. Hubbell, who established a trading post here a century ago that still operates today. Top-quality Navajo rugs and other craft items are sold here.

For further information, contact the Superintendent, Hubbell National Historic Site, Box 150, Ganado, AZ 86505.

Head east 6 miles on AZ-264 to pick up US-191 then drive north on US-191 to the turnoff for **Canyon de Chelly National Monument** (see map, p. 153); set up camp here upon arrival. The national monument, containing over 100 ruins, is in a remote rural area on the windward side of the Lukachukai and Chuska mountains (sometimes called the "Navajo Alps"). It is drained by Chinle Wash, which empties into the San Juan River.

Canyon de Chelly (pronounced de-SHAY; a Spanish/Anglo corruption of "tsegi," the Navajo word for rock canyon) is a gem, but unless you arrange to join a commercial or ranger-guided tour, your access to it is restricted to what you can see from overlooks along the rim, or on the trail to White House Ruin. Free-lance travel here is strictly prohibited, in part because the deep sandstone canyon provides a summer home to about 30 Navajo families.

All of the observation points along the scenic drives are worth visiting. On South Rim Drive, be sure not to miss the 800-foot needle, **Spider Rock,** legendary home of Spider Woman, who supposedly taught the Navajo the art of weaving. On North Rim Drive, stop at the overlooks for Massacre and Mummy caves. In 1805, Spanish soldiers—trying to punish and deter raids on their settlements—slaughtered 115 Navajo who were hiding in what is now called **Massacre Cave.** At nearby **Mummy Cave,** prehistoric burial remains were found in a fifty-room ruin. The 1849 expedition that first explored Mummy Cave named the tributary in which it is located Canyon del Muerto, "the canyon of the dead."

For more information, write to the Superintendent, Canyon de Chelly National Monument, Box 588, Chinle, AZ 86503.

Day Hike: White House Ruin

> **Distance: 2.5 miles, round-trip**
> **Time: 2 hours**
> **Map: USGS quad for Canyon del Muerto**
> **Difficulty: moderate**

This trail, which starts from 6 miles past monument headquarters along the South Rim Drive, immediately switchbacks 600 feet to the canyon floor (see map, p. 153). At the creek, turn left and proceed to the ruin, splashing through shallow water and occasionally encountering patches of quicksand as you walk down the lushly foliaged wash. **White House Ruin,** so named because of the color of some of its adobe, is straight ahead on the right-hand wall of the canyon. Once home to almost 100 people, it has two tiers. The canyon's walls (composed of de Chelly sandstone) are streaked with "desert varnish," dark mineral traces that rains have leached from the rock and washed in long stripes down from the rim. A nice picnic area is here, amid the cottonwoods.

<u>DAY 3:</u> CANYON DE CHELLY TO SAND ISLAND

- **Driving through incomparable Monument Valley Tribal Park**
- **And nearby Valley of the Gods**
- **Visiting San Juan River overlooks**
- **Optional river trip**
- **Camping near pictographs at Sand Island or in Valley of the Gods**
- **Gas and groceries available in Kayenta; showers and laundry available in Mexican Hat**

Today you leave the Navajo Reservation and cross into Utah, driving through strikingly scenic country drained by the San Juan River and its tributaries. From Canyon de Chelly, go north 14 miles on US-191 to Many Farms and take a left at the fork onto Route 59. Follow this road 44.5 miles over remote mesas to its end, turning left onto US-160. Drive 8 miles to Kayenta. In Kayenta, head north 23.5 miles on US-163 to Monument Valley, a Navajo tribal park.

Scenic Drive: Monument Valley

> **Distance: 14 miles**
> **Time: 2 hours**

Monument Valley Tribal Park is not only a mecca for tourists, but also the setting for countless car commercials and a favorite backdrop for Westerns and Bible films. For a small fee, you can take the 14-mile round-trip scenic drive—a serpentine road that descends a few hundred feet to the valley floor and then circles mammoth Cutler formation spires and monoliths. Coming in all shapes and sizes, and looking surprisingly fresh from

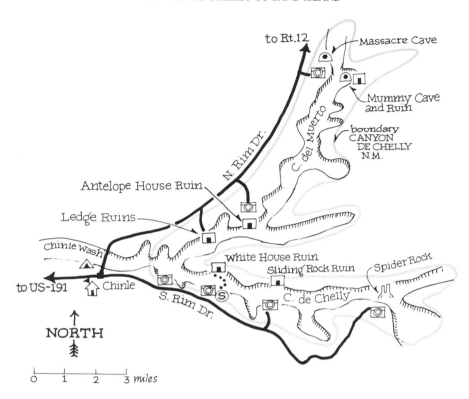

each new angle, these formations are all that remain of a high plateau sub-
jected to millions of years of erosion. Unfortunately, the road does not give
visitors a glimpse of the area's many arches. For that, you must take a
guided tour, which typically includes a stop at a "hogan," or traditional
one-room earthen dwelling made of mud and wood. Hiking is not allowed
in Monument Valley without an official guide.

From Monument Valley, continue north 19 miles on US-163 to Mexican Hat, on the banks of the San Juan River. Visit nearby Goosenecks
Overlook and Valley of the Gods (see Chapter 4, Cedar Mesa Loop, Day
5). About 22 miles farther north on US-163, just short of Bluff, is **Sand Island Recreation Area.** A few hundred yards downstream from the campground is a nice wall of pictographs, containing drawings from both the
early Basket Maker and later Pueblo stages of Anasazi cultural history.

You can camp tonight at Sand Island, which has pit toilets but no water. However, during the summer mosquito season, it would be prudent to
stay instead in Valley of the Gods, planning a brief visit to Sand Island in
the morning.

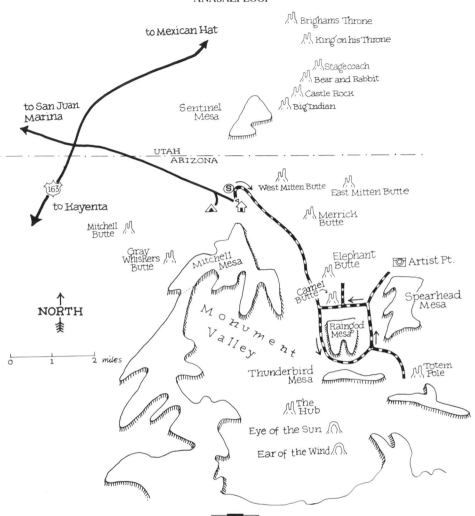

Optional River Trip: Rafting the San Juan River

Distance: 28 (or 84) miles
Time: 1 (or 4) days

Many float trips originate at Sand Island Recreation Area, concluding either at the Mexican Hat Bridge (28 miles) or Clay Hills Crossing, opposite Piute Farms at the tip of Lake Powell (84 miles). This delightful run passes through the Monument Upwarp, giving access to several washes and the rock art, ruins, and historical sites they contain. Beyond the bridge at Mexican Hat are the tortuous Goosenecks, a bowknot bend where the river repeatedly doubles back on itself. Slickhorn Canyon and Grand Gulch, both with numerous Anasazi ruins, join the river. There are moderate rapids as well as "sand waves," which boil up from the bottom at higher water levels.

The stretch from Sand Island to Mexican Hat makes an easy daylong float. From Sand Island to Clay Hills allow at least three days, plus five hours on each end for shuttling. Permits, which are required, can be obtained at the BLM office, P.O. Box 7, Monticello, UT 84535. Alternatively, you can raft the San Juan with an organized group; companies based in Bluff and Mexican Hat sponsor trips and also provide shuttle services.

DAY 4: SAND ISLAND TO HOVENWEEP

- **Locating a seldom-visited cliff dwelling**
- **Camping and hiking at Hovenweep National Monument**
- **Gas and groceries available in Bluff**

Buy two days' worth of supplies before leaving Bluff this morning for points east. Hovenweep National Monument is your ultimate destination today, but before setting out, do not miss a short hike to Seventeen Room House (see below).

Day Hike: Seventeen Room House (aka Casa de Eco)

> **Distance: 2 miles, round-trip**
> **Time: 1.5 hours**
> **Map: USGS quad for Bluff**
> **Difficulty: easy**

Immediately north of Bluff, turn right on US-163, which parallels the river. Drive about 3.5 miles, passing St. Christopher's Mission, to a dirt road on the right which descends 0.5 mile to a parking area on the river. From here take the short hike to the cliff dwelling.

This large Anasazi structure is little publicized because of its location on the Navajo Reservation, but visitors are welcome as long as they do not trespass on private land. Cross the river on the swinging footbridge. On the other side, walk a short distance down a gravel road. Where the road forks, turn left to circle around privately owned fields. In about 0.25 mile, the road bends to the right, then intersects another road that runs along the base of the cliff. Turn right here, following signs to the bottom of the shady alcove that contains the ruin. You can scramble to the top without much trouble. Notice the handprints decorating the cliff, and the hand- and foot-

A suspension footbridge bears visitors across the San Juan River, Utah

holds that the Anasazi carved out of the sandstone to gain access to their homes.

———

To reach **Hovenweep National Monument,** which offers camping and a day hike, travel east for 19.5 miles farther on US-163, passing through the town of Montezuma Creek on the way to Aneth. In Montezuma Creek the route number changes to UT-262. Just short of Aneth, turn left onto an unpaved road along the bank of McElmo Creek and follow signs to Hovenweep, 20 miles distant.

Situated in pinyon and juniper country in the shadow of Sleeping Ute Mountain, Hovenweep—meaning "deserted valley" in Ute—consists of six prehistoric Anasazi complexes, first discovered by white settlers in 1850 (see map, p. 159). The Hovenweep Anasazi, closely related to the residents of Mesa Verde, excelled in the construction of stone and mud towers. Two complexes are in Utah (Square Tower and Cajon Mesa); the others (Holly, Horseshoe/Hackberry, Goodman Point, and Cutthroat Castle) are just across the border in Colorado. The campground and visitor center are near the Square Tower Complex, the most extensive and interesting of the ruin groups.

Select a spot in the campground, then proceed to the visitor center and begin the short hike to the Square Tower Complex (see below). Afterwards, you may want to visit the **Cajon Canyon** site, about 9 miles southeast of the Square Tower group. (Ask the ranger for directions.) Among the buildings in this complex are structures that apparently served as an astronomical observatory. Unfortunately, looters have done considerable damage on Cajon Mesa.

For more information, contact the Superintendent, Mesa Verde National Park, CO 81330.

———

Day Hike: Square Tower Complex

> **Distance: 2 miles, round-trip**
> **Time: 3 hours**
> **Difficulty: easy**

Three short, loop trails, all originating from the visitor center (see map, p. 159), explore the masonry ruins found in shallow Little Ruin Canyon (formed of Dakota sandstone); these trails can be combined for a total distance of 2 miles, round-trip. Square Tower Loop dips into the canyon for a close examination of **Hovenweep Castle** and **Square Tower Ruin.** Tower Point Loop stays on the mesa top, providing views of many buildings and doubling as a nature trail, introducing visitors to local plants and shrubs. The interesting Twin Towers Loop, 1 mile in length, is somewhat more challenging, passing through a natural tunnel in the rock and climbing a short ladder to **Twin Towers Ruin.** It visits Round Tower, Eroded Boulder House, Rimrock House, and Stronghold House along the way. Spiral, bird, and snake petroglyphs are near the start of the trail.

<u>DAY 5:</u> HOVENWEEP TO MESA VERDE

- **Holly Ruins day hike**
- **Camping, showers, and laundry available at Mesa Verde National Park**
- **Gas and groceries available in Cortez**

Take advantage of the cool morning temperatures to complete the Holly Ruins Trail in Hovenweep before setting off for Mesa Verde.

Day Hike: Holly Ruins Trail

Distance: 4 miles, one way
Time: 2 hours
Map: USGS quad for Cajon Mesa
Difficulty: easy

This trail begins at the lower end of Hovenweep campground and leads up Keeley Canyon to the mesa top commanded by Holly Ruins (see map, p. 159). To make this a one-way hike, set up a car shuttle, or make some similar arrangement.

The trail descends to the canyon floor through a small joint (the only place you might get lost on the well-marked route). The waterless route sometimes follows the wash, and sometimes goes up onto the bank in its gentle progress toward the head of the canyon. In about 3 miles, you come to a small ruin located on private land. Soon, the trail ascends to the left, passing through another slot on its way to the mesa top. Once it levels out, it turns right and proceeds directly to Holly Ruins, whose major buildings include Great House, Boulder House, and Tilted Tower. Notice how the Anasazi here, without alcoves to build in, made creative use of enormous boulders to anchor their structures.

To reach Mesa Verde, return to UT-262 and drive southeast on this road, which becomes CO-41 at the border, for 19.5 miles. Intersecting US-

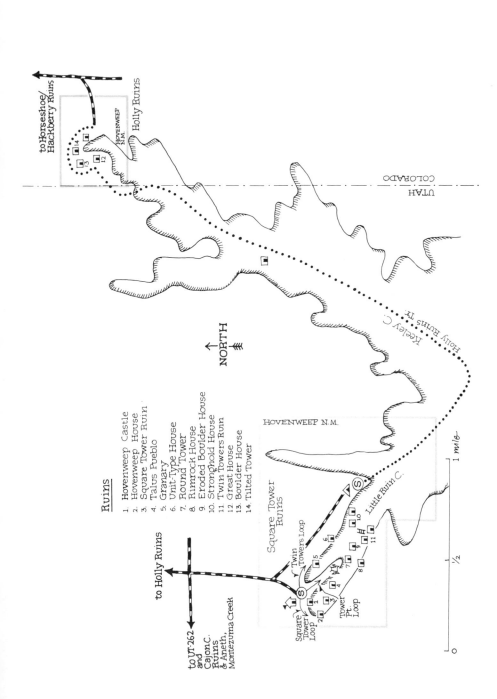

to Horseshoe/Hackberry Ruins

Holly Ruins

HOVENWEEP N.M.

14
3
12

COLORADO
UTAH

Holly Ruins Tr.

Keeley C.

NORTH

Ruins

1. Hovenweep Castle
2. Hovenweep House
3. Square Tower Ruin
4. Talus Pueblo
5. Granary
6. Unit-Type House
7. Round Tower
8. Rimrock House
9. Eroded Boulder House
10. Stronghold House
11. Twin Towers Ruin
12. Great House
13. Boulder House
14. Tilted Tower

HOVENWEEP N.M.

Square Tower Ruins

Twin Towers Loop

Little Ruin C.

Square Tower Loop

to Holly Ruins

to UT.262
and
Cajon C.
Ruins
& Aneth,
Montezuma Creek

Tower Pt. Loop

15
6
9
10
11
8
7
4
1
2
3

0   ½   1 mile

160, go left, reaching US-666 in 13 miles. Turn left onto US-666 and proceed 19.5 miles to Cortez. In the distance, watch for Shiprock across the New Mexico border—a black volcanic plug almost 2000 feet high, known to Navajo as the "rock with wings." Poised on the cusp where deserts meet mountains, Cortez (population 7000) provides all the services you will need in preparation for your trip to Mesa Verde National Park. Buy provisions for today and tomorrow.

Mesa Verde ("green table" in Spanish) is 9.5 miles farther, located about halfway between Cortez and Mancos off US-160. Turn right to the park entrance and begin the climb to the undulating, forested country 2000 feet above the valley. Make selecting a campsite your first priority.

In spite of the crowds, this internationally celebrated park is a treat to visit, for concentrated within its 52,000 acres are many of the largest, best-preserved, and most thoroughly excavated cliff dwellings in the United States. The dominant rock stratum here is Cliff House sandstone, which weathered to produce the alcoves that the Anasazi found so suitable for home-building. To date almost 600 cliff dwellings have been identified on these mesas. Because of the large number of park visitors and the fragile nature of the archaeological sites, you can expect to be regimented here to a much greater extent than elsewhere. At the cliff dwellings, everyone must be accompanied by a ranger.

The park's ruins are clustered on two mesas (see map, p. 163). Chapin Mesa stays open year-round, with drastically curtailed services from mid-October to mid-May, while Wetherill Mesa is open only in the summer months. Once accessible only by special park buses, Wetherill Mesa can now be reached by car.

Mesa Verde is not really a hiker's park, but a few short trails are open to visitors. Two of these—the Petroglyph Point and Spruce Canyon trails—start near Spruce Tree House on Chapin Mesa; hiking either of these requires official permission. Three others—Knife Edge, Prater Ridge, and Point Lookout—commence at the campground and are open to the public without restrictions.

Compared to Hovenweep, Chaco, and other ruin complexes that you will visit in this circuit, Mesa Verde—inhabited beginning about A.D. 500 and abandoned (for reasons that probably included drought, overuse of resources, and other environmental problems) before A.D. 1300—is now a bustling tourist center, complete with snack bars, showers, church services, a museum, shuttle buses, and a colossal campground. In addition to the thirteenth-century cliff dwellings for which the park is most renowned, there are two other types of Anasazi structures here: earthen pit houses dating back to the Basket Maker culture that prevailed prior to the mid-eighth century, and mesa top masonry dwellings. During most of their period of occupancy, the Mesa Verde Anasazi lived on the mesa tops, utilizing the alcoves in the cliffs below the canyon rims very early and very late in their residency. According to the current consensus, construction of the cliff dwellings was not a defensive measure taken against actual enemies, since no evidence suggests that any warfare occurred during the time when Mesa Verde was inhabited. (Indeed, the modern Hopi—who, with the Rio Grande Pueblo, are the closest living relatives of the Anasazi—are such a pacific people that their language doesn't even contain a word for war.) Anthropologists have also established fairly conclusively that building the cliff dwellings was a community effort involving men, women, and children.

To learn more about these structures and the people who built them, plan to spend some time at the visitor center and also the park museum near Spruce Tree House. If time permits, visit **Spruce Tree House** today, saving other sites for tomorrow, and hike the Petroglyph Point Trail (see below). Of the cliff dwellings in the park, Spruce Tree House (the third largest, after Cliff Palace and Long House) is the most accessible, reached by a paved, switchbacking trail from the Mesa Verde museum. Visitors to this crescent-shaped, 115-room ruin can enter a reconstructed kiva.

For further information, write to the Superintendent, Mesa Verde Na-

T-shaped doorways characterize many Mesa Verde National Park ruins

tional Park, CO 81330. For a fee, tours of sites on the Ute Mountain Reservation, adjacent to the park, can be arranged. For information, call 303-565-4684 in Towaoc, CO, on weekdays.

———

Day Hike: Petroglyph Point Trail

Distance: 2.75 miles, round-trip
Time: 2 hours
Difficulty: moderate

You must register for this pleasant and varied hike at the Chief Ranger's Office, next to the Chapin Mesa museum. A booklet with text corresponding to numbers along the route can be purchased for a modest sum. The well-marked trail begins just off one of the switchbacks down to Spruce Tree House (see map, p. 163). Go right here, and when the trail splits almost immediately, take the left fork. The first half of the trail stays one level below the canyon rim, arriving at an excellent rock art panel. It then climbs steep stairs to the mesa top—a good rest or lunch place. From an overlook on the way up, look for Echo House, a cliff dwelling in an alcove across the canyon. The trail follows the rim of Chapin Mesa, passing directly above Spruce Tree House before looping back to the museum.

DAY 6: MESA VERDE

- **Admiring America's finest cliff dwellings**
- **Ridgetop day hiking**
- **Camping, gas, groceries, showers, and laundry available at Mesa Verde**

Today's recommended itinerary includes stops at ruin sites on Chapin Mesa and, if it is open to the public, Wetherill Mesa as well.

Begin your tour by visiting Chapin Mesa's spectacular **Cliff Palace,** in the southeastern sector of the park. This ruin—discovered and named in 1888 by two local ranchers, Richard Wetherill and Charles Mason, while they were looking for stray cattle during a snowstorm—is the largest dwelling of its kind on the continent. Containing 217 rooms and 23 kivas, it is believed to have housed between 200 and 250 people. Access to the ruin is gained by steps and ladders. Near the far end of the alcove, where you exit, look for wall paintings inside one of the rooms.

Farther along on the same loop road is the relatively small but most unusual **Balcony House,** reachable by guided tour only. This cliff dwelling

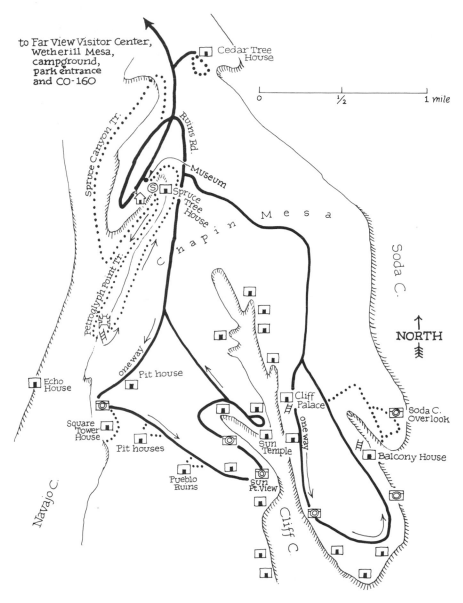

to Far View Visitor Center, Wetherill Mesa, campground, park entrance and CO-160

Cedar Tree House

Spruce Canyon Tr.

Ruins Rd.

Museum

Spruce Tree House

Petroglyph Point Tr.

Chapin Mesa

Soda C.

NORTH

one way

Pit house

Echo House

Cliff Palace

Soda C. Overlook

Square Tower House

Pit houses

Sun Temple

one way

Balcony House

Pueblo Ruins

Sun Pt. View

Navajo C.

Cliff C.

may once have served as an Anasazi nursery, according to some archaeologists; visitors must ascend a 32-foot ladder and crawl through a 12-foot tunnel.

Adjacent to the loop road off which Cliff Palace and Balcony House are situated is another loop enabling visitors to view Square Tower House and Sun Temple, and to examine pit house ruins.

Your next destination is Wetherill Mesa. To drive there, return to the Far View area and turn left at a junction just before reaching the visitor center. The Wetherill Mesa parking area is 12 miles down this road. Near the parking area, a trail descends the cliff to **Step House,** named for a set of stairs built by the Anasazi to connect the pueblo to the mesa top. Some pit house ruins are adjacent to the cliff dwelling.

A mini-bus ride from the parking lot takes visitors to the **Long House** trailhead, from which guided tours of the cliff dwelling depart. This beautiful ruin, with 150 rooms and 21 kivas, features an exceptionally large central plaza. The mini-bus also stops at a 0.75-mile trail to the Badger House Community and other pit house complexes.

When finished on Wetherill Mesa, return to the Far View area. If time allows, turn right at the intersection with the main park road and drive 1.25 miles back toward Chapin Mesa, stopping at **Far View Ruin.** Unlike the cliff dwellings, which must be approached with extreme care because of their fragility, this once densely populated site is a more "hands-on" sort of building whose walls were stabilized with cement earlier in the century. Like many pueblos here, Far View is a surface apartment, located on the mesa top rather than on the canyon cliffs. In fact, most of the Anasazi in the area lived on the mesas, which they farmed (in contrast to other Anasazi communities, where the general practice was to grow beans, squash, and corn in the canyon bottoms).

Back at the campground, before or after dinner, take a walk up the Knife Edge Trail.

Day Hike: Knife Edge Trail

Distance: 2 miles, round-trip
Time: 1 hour
Difficulty: very easy

Originating at the north end of the campground near the Lone Cone formation, this well-trod trail follows the bed of the original road through the park. Level nearly all the way, it stays very near the rim of a cliff for its entire route, affording gorgeous, unobstructed vistas of Sleeping Ute Mountain and the high snow peaks of the southern Rockies, as well as of the Knife Edge ridge itself. Unfortunately, erosion has eaten away at the old roadbed, closing the last half mile of the trail, which used to terminate at the Montezuma Valley Overlook. Until the route is repaired, hikers must double back when they reach the sign indicating that it is dangerous to proceed farther. Look for deer grazing in the meadow near the trailhead; Mesa Verde boasts hundreds, and they are drawn to the clearings around the campground.

Aztec Ruins National Monument in New Mexico boasts restored walls and kiva

DAY 7: MESA VERDE TO CHACO

- **Viewing Aztec Ruins**
- **Camping at Chaco Canyon**
- **Gas, groceries, showers, and laundry available in Durango**

Leave Mesa Verde today and drive east 35 miles on US-160, crossing a pass and dropping into Durango. Located in the Animas River valley, conveniently close to the ski areas and hiking trails of the San Juan Mountains, this small city (population 11,400) constitutes an all-season resort and proudly displays its historic past as a railroad boomtown. Tourists can ride the narrow-gauge passenger train through the mountains to Silverton, a daylong round-trip, or tour the city's restored Victorian neighborhoods. Buy gas, ice, and groceries here for the next two days.

US-550 follows the Animas valley south 35 miles to the town of Aztec in New Mexico, the location of **Aztec Ruins National Monument.** The ruins are near the junction of US-550 and NM-544. Turn north onto Ruins Road, where a sign will direct you to the national monument. The names of both the monument and the town derive from the mistaken impression of nineteenth-century settlers that the ruins were Mesoamerican in origin.

In the thirteenth century, Aztec was one of the major Anasazi communities of the Southwest, possibly housing an estimated 700 people. A very easy 0.25-mile trail acquaints you with this 500-room complex. Because building and pottery styles identified with both Chaco and Mesa Verde were replicated here in consecutive historical periods, archaeologists believe that the pueblo may have been occupied first by Chacoan Anasazi, then abandoned and later reoccupied by people influenced culturally by Mesa Verde. Of special interest is an enormous, painstakingly reconstructed kiva, into which native music is piped. The kiva occupies a portion of the plaza once used for various communal activities.

For additional information, write to the Superintendent, Aztec Ruins National Monument, P.O. Box 640, Aztec, NM 87410.

To drive to Chaco Culture National Historical Park, Mesa Verde's chief aesthetic rival, go south 8.5 miles on NM-544 to Bloomfield, an oil and gas refining center, where you pick up NM-44 south. At Blanco Trading Post, about 22.5 miles away, turn right on an unpaved road, as indicated by a highway sign. It is 23 washboardy, rutted miles to the Chaco entrance, then another 7 paved miles to the visitor center. Under rainy conditions, opt instead for the all-weather road to Chaco that begins at Nageezi, about 7 miles past Blanco Trading Post on NM-44. Find a spot in Chaco's shadeless, no-fee campground.

DAY 8: CHACO CANYON

- **Inspecting pueblos on the canyon floor**
- **Day hikes to mesa-top sites**
- **Camping at Chaco Culture National Historical Park**

Once the center of a thriving civilization, **Chaco Culture National Historical Park** contains over 400 Anasazi ruins, including 12 major sites (see map, p. 169). The canyon walls are far apart, and the Anasazi, who left the area in the late twelfth century, built out in the open instead of hugging the cliffs as they so often did elsewhere. Their masonry work is arguably the finest in all the Southwest. Residents of the canyon—which may have supported a population as large as 5000 in its heyday—established over seventy outlying pueblos throughout the San Juan Basin, whether to ease population pressure or as insurance against drought. Well-constructed, poker-straight roads led from Chaco to these various "colonies" (including the Aztec and Salmon ruin complexes to the north); these roads, some 300 miles of them, are still visible from the air. Water control systems, including irrigation, enabled the communities of the Chaco Plateau to wrest a better living from an often harsh environment. The construction of roads, water systems, and large masonry structures required a

The "great houses" in New Mexico's Chaco Canyon are set against low cliffs

rather elaborate social structure, complete with a bureaucracy to collect information, make decisions, and respond to contingencies. In fact, one of the ruin clusters here—the illustrious Pueblo Bonito—may have evolved into an administrative and religious center for the confederation, with Pueblo Alto above it serving as a commercial entrepot. Most of the so-called "great houses" are located on the north side of the canyon, with the south side supporting much smaller communities.

Although rangers conduct tours of the various sites on a daily basis between Memorial and Labor Day weekends, most visitors opt for self-guided walks through the ruins, which start from the park road. Pueblo Bonito, Chetro Ketl, and Casa Rinconada, in particular, should not be missed. Allow approximately an hour at each of the major sites.

Pueblo Bonito (meaning "beautiful town" in Spanish) is the best known of the ruins here, as well as the largest, with between 600 and 800 rooms and 33 kivas. Completed in the mid-eleventh century, this D-shaped complex housed up to 1000 people. The trail winding through this impressive ruin is under 0.5 mile. **Chetro Ketl,** next to Pueblo Bonito, is note-worthy for its uplifted platform plaza. A 0.5-mile trail introduces visitors to this 500-room ruin. In ancient times, Pueblo Bonito and Chetro Ketl were connected to the mesa top by a set of toe- and hand-holds, or Moki steps. The 280-room **Pueblo del Arroyo,** across the canyon from Pueblo Bonito, also contains a large plaza. **Casa Rinconada** ("house in a box canyon") is located among a number of small ruins on the south side of Chaco Wash linked together by a 0.5-mile trail. Built around A.D. 1100, it is a restored "great kiva" that visitors may enter. The size and location of the ceremonial chamber suggest that it serviced the community as a whole rather than belonging to any particular clan. Finally, **Una Vida** ("a life"), behind the visitor center, is a smaller, older, partially excavated ruin of about 150 rooms. The remains of a hogan and corral here indicate subsequent Navajo occupation. From the number 5 marker on the 0.25-mile loop trail, a steep path leads to an astonishing petroglyph panel near the canyon rim.

After you have viewed the major ruin sites, hike one of the trails described below, registering at the trailhead. Each of the backcountry trails in Chaco is well designed and popular with tourists, despite lacking shade and water. If the weather is hot, the trails are best hiked in the early morning or evening hours.

Remember, when you visit backcountry ruins, do not lean on their fragile ruins or take anything (including potsherds) from the sites.

For more information, write to the Superintendent, Chaco Culture National Historical Park, Star Route 4, Box 6500, Bloomfield, NM 87413.

Day Hike 1: Tsin Kletsin Ruin

> **Distance: 3 miles, round-trip**
> **Time: 1.5 hours**
> **Difficulty: easy**

Tsin Kletsin, a ruin complex on South Mesa, once commanded a panoramic view of six other major buildings from the second story of one of its kivas, and thus may have served as a communications center or relay station. Reach the trailhead from marker number 9 of the Casa Rinconada loop, near the great kiva (see map, p. 169). After ascending on switch-backs to a point just below the rim, the trail climbs through a short chimney, swings widely to the left, and levels out. It bends to the right and then goes straight to the ruin, visible from afar. From the windswept mesa top, Pueblo Bonito, Chetro Ketl, Casa Rinconada, and Pueblo del Arroyo are clearly discernible; this is arguably the best view in the park. Since the trail is not a loop, just double back to return.

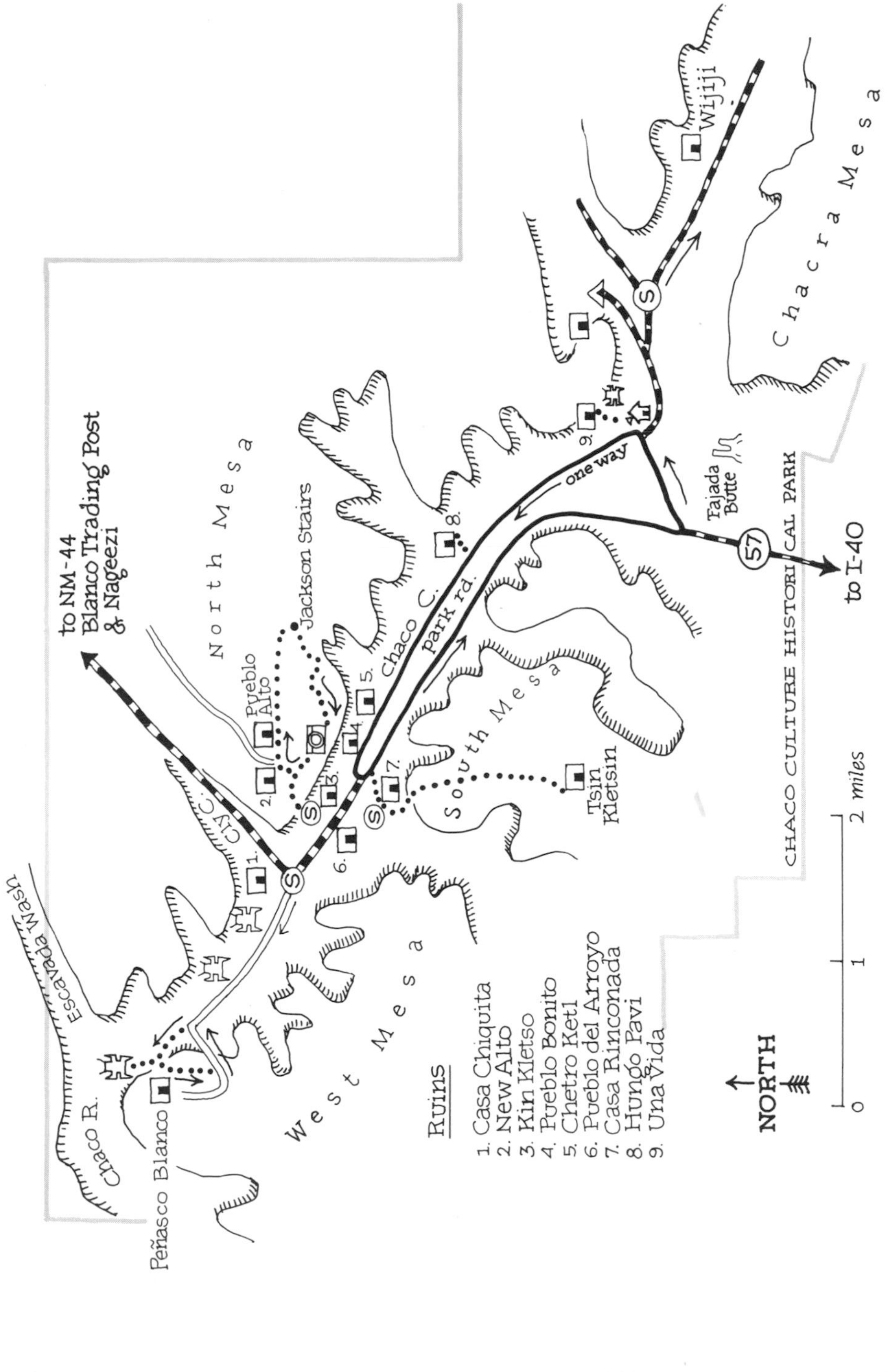

NORTH

CHACO CULTURE HISTORICAL PARK

to I-40

to NM-44
Blanco Trading Post
& Nageezi

Chacra Mesa

North Mesa

South Mesa

West Mesa

Escavada Wash

Chaco R.

Peñasco Blanco

Pueblo Alto

Jackson Stairs

Chaco C.

Park rd.

one way

Fajada Butte

Wijiji

Tsin Kletsin

57

0   1   2 miles

Ruins

1. Casa Chiquita
2. New Alto
3. Kin Kletso
4. Pueblo Bonito
5. Chetro Ketl
6. Pueblo del Arroyo
7. Casa Rinconada
8. Hungo Pavi
9. Una Vida

Day Hike 2: Wijiji Ruin

Distance: 3 miles, round-trip
Time: 1.5 hours
Difficulty: very easy

Of the backcountry ruins in Chaco Canyon that are open to the public, **Wijiji** is the best preserved and most easily reached. Driving from the campgound, turn left at the first fork in the road and proceed about 100 yards to the parking area. The route, which bicyclists can also use, follows a level service road. Wijiji, up against the left wall of the canyon, once contained 100 rooms and rose three stories. Built early in the twelfth century, it was one of the last of the "great houses."

On the return trip, you face **Fajada Butte,** where an ancient astronomical marker known as a "sun dagger" was discovered in the late 1970s. In combination with three carefully positioned rock slabs, this petroglyph enabled the Anasazi to determine the exact dates of solstices and equinoxes—information that must have been invaluable to their society for both agricultural and religious reasons. The fragility of the marker led the Park Service to close Fajada Butte to tourists, but a short film shown at the visitor center focuses on its role in Anasazi culture.

DAY 9: CHACO TO BANDELIER

- **Another Chaco day hike**
- **Driving through the Jemez Mountains**
- **Camping at Bandelier National Monument**
- **Gas, groceries, showers, and laundry available in Los Alamos**

Today's itinerary includes day hike options in Chaco (see below) before setting out on a long but beautiful car ride to Bandelier National Monument.

Day Hike 1: Pueblo Alto Loop

Distance: 4.75 miles, round-trip
Time: 3 hours
Difficulty: moderate

This is a wonderful hike, which visits two major ruins and leads to excellent vantage points on several others. Beginning at Kin Kletso ruin, the

Masonry wall detail, Chaco Canyon, New Mexico

trail ascends improbably through a sort of couloir in the Cliff House sandstone (see map, p. 169). At the top, the trail veers to the right, hugging the rim. About 0.75 mile of walking over slickrock on the cairned trail brings you to the Pueblo Bonito overlook. Here the trail forks. Turn left, climbing slowly and steadily for 0.5 mile through the Lewis shale formation and onto the Pictured Cliffs sandstone, reaching the **Pueblo Alto** ("high town") and New Alto ruins atop North Mesa. Of these, the 35-room New Alto, on the left, is better preserved, though the partially excavated, one-story-high Pueblo Alto is much larger, with 135 rooms. The trail continues on in front of Pueblo Alto, marked by a sign. From here it is 2.75 miles back to the Pueblo Bonito overlook to close the loop. The trail heads a side-canyon, revealing the so-called **Jackson Stairs,** a set of Moki steps by which Anasazi living on the mesa top gained access to the farming terraces below. Don't worry—the trail doesn't use these steps! It simply continues on the slickrock bench, eventually descending through another crack, which returns you to the level of the Pueblo Bonito overlook. As the loop closes, it offers outstanding views of Chetro Ketl directly below and Pueblo del Arroyo across the canyon.

Day Hike 2: Peñasco Blanco Ruin

Distance: 4.5 miles, round-trip
Time: 3 hours
Difficulty: easy

Handsome **Peñasco Blanco** ("white rock") perches atop West Mesa (see map, p. 169). The trail winds through a section of Chaco Wash that abounds in rock art, most notably a pictograph archaeologists believe represents the supernova of A.D. 1054. Start this hike at Casa Chiquita near the west end of the park. On the left is a service road that the route follows for about 1.75 level miles. Look for petroglyphs along the cliffs, especially at the mouth of the first significant side-canyon on the right. Opposite the second side-canyon, the road makes a big swing to the left. Before long, the trail to the supernova pictograph leaves the road, taking off to the right. Crossing the wash, it heads toward the base of the cliff of West Mesa, following it for several hundred yards to the pictograph panel, marked by a large cairn. If you backtrack a short distance, you will meet a shortcut trail that connects with the service road and ascends to the ruin. Overlooking the confluence of the Chaco River and Escavada Wash, Peñasco Blanco is a very extensive building that originally had three stories. When you finish exploring the site, you can return to your car via the service road.

To reach Bandelier National Monument, go about 6.5 miles past the Chaco Entrance Station to a fork, where you turn right toward the small Navajo settlement of Nageezi. The road passes through a scenic badlands region for much of its length. At Nageezi, turn right, rejoining NM-44 south—a spectacular route. Between here and San Ysidro, 92 miles away, colorful breaks give way to distant mesas and buttes and finally to the mountainous highlands of central New Mexico.

At San Ysidro, on the Jemez Indian Reservation, go left on NM-4, an equally beautiful drive. From here, it is 55 miles to Bandelier. The highway passes through Jemez Pueblo as it follows the narrow Jemez River Valley to its head in the mountains and crosses a divide into the Rio Grande drainage. Jemez Falls Campground has a 0.25-mile trail to a 50-foot waterfall; an 80-foot waterfall is in Battleship Rock Campground on San Antonio Creek. On the other side of the divide, you soon pass the **Valle Grande** depression, a seemingly endless green meadow that forms part of the caldera of an ancient volcano—one of the largest calderas in the world.

Before long, Bandelier's Ponderosa Campground (intended for large groups) appears on the right. A sign a few miles farther directs you to the Bandelier Entrance Station. Just beyond the pay booth, a spur to the right leads to Juniper Campground, where you should choose a campsite. Limited groceries are available in White Rock, 10 miles east on NM-4; purchase supplies for three nights. Or you can backtrack on NM-4 west to the turnoff for equidistant Los Alamos, where there are excellent supermarkets and restaurants, plus shower and laundry facilities. Many tourists rave about Los Alamos's scientific museum, which focuses on nuclear and other high technologies.

DAY 10: BANDELIER

- Peering into cave dwellings
- Hiking past waterfalls to the Rio Grande
- Camping at Bandelier
- Gas, groceries, showers, and laundry available in Los Alamos

Bandelier National Monument, adjacent to the Rio Grande, is located on the forested Pajarito ("little bird") Plateau, an area composed mainly of volcanic rock. Its 50 square miles are geographically diverse, ranging from 5300-foot elevation near the river to over 10,000 feet in the Jemez Mountains. Decisive in the park's natural history was the eruption, over a million years ago, of the Jemez volcano, which blanketed the area with white volcanic ash, or "tuff." Subsequently, streams like the Alamo and Frijoles cut deep canyons through this material, exposing the underlying basalt—a dark, dense rock left over from previous volcanic activity. One unusual aspect of the park's geology is the presence of pyramidal formations called "tent rocks." Composed of tuff, some tent rocks exist because hard caps enabled them to resist erosion; others were produced by subsurface geothermal activity. After the volcano expelled huge quantities of ash and lava, its center collapsed, producing the circular caldera occupied in part by Valle Grande.

Another important legacy of the vulcanism was that the land became very fertile. This helps explain why Bandelier contains the greatest aggregation of prehistoric ruins found anywhere in our national park system. Members of the large Anasazi farming colony, which flourished here until about A.D. 1550, built multistory apartments along the base of cliffs, enlarging caves in the soft volcanic rock with the aid of stone implements. The excavated ruin sites are concentrated in Frijoles Canyon, which is honeycombed with trails.

The adventurous backpacker can explore over 70 miles of trails leading to mesa tops with panoramic vistas and archaeological sites in nearby canyons. Today's recommended itinerary, however, includes three of the shorter and more popular trails, which can easily be combined into one trip

Backpackers enjoy cool, forested uplands in Bandelier National Monument, New Mexico

beginning at the campground. At the visitor center today, make arrangements for the upcoming overnight backpacking trip to the Stone Lions archaeological site (see Days 11 and 12), securing a permit to camp in Capulin Canyon.

For further information, contact the Superintendent, Bandelier National Monument, Los Alamos, NM 87544.

———

Day Hike 1: Frey Trail

Distance: 1.5 miles, one way
Time: 1 hour
Map: USGS topo for Bandelier
Difficulty: moderate

This well-designed trail, once the sole route into Frijoles Canyon, starts near the amphitheater in Juniper Campground (see map, p. 176). After a short distance the trail crosses two service roads. At the second road, turn left and walk about 50 feet in that direction to continue the route again on the other side. As you reach the rim, sweeping views up and down the canyon greet you. The trail contours around to the right and abruptly descends 400 feet on an excellent set of switchbacks past some tent rocks to the canyon floor. Tyuonyi Ruin, a large, circular apartment house, is visible from above for much of the way. At the base of the cliff, the trail intersects with the Frijoles Canyon loop very near Talus House, on your left.

Day Hike 2: Frijoles Canyon Loop

Distance: 2 miles, round-trip (or 1.5 miles one way from
Frey Trail junction to visitor center)
Time: 1.5 hours
Map: USGS topo for Bandelier
Difficulty: easy

This walk is a must for all visitors to Bandelier, for it loops around the New Stone Age cave, cliff, and surface dwellings of lovely Frijoles Canyon, which was inhabited from the eleventh to the sixteenth centuries. For much of its length, it is a shady trail, fairly cool even in midsummer.

Assuming you have just descended the Frey Trail from the campground (see map, p. 176), turn left at the first trail junction to examine **Talus House,** a restored cliff dwelling, and the nearby caves that the Rio Grande Anasazi enlarged out of the soft volcanic tuff to serve as living and storage rooms. Pass Talus House and stop to visit **Tyuonyi Ruin** (possibly

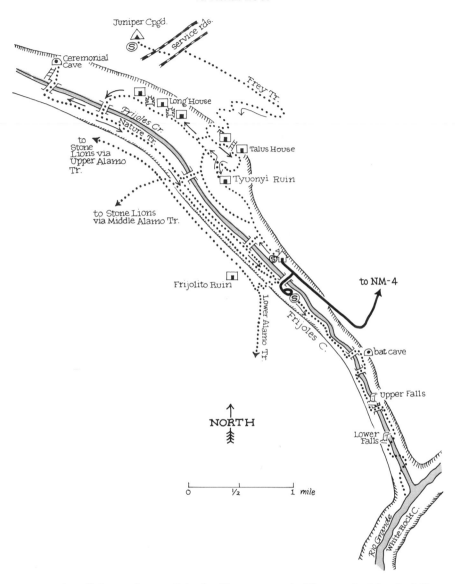

meaning "place of treaty" in the Keres tongue). The nearby kiva is fully excavated.

Continuing northwest up the canyon, away from the visitor center, you soon pass a second set of foundations and cave dwellings, collectively known as **Long House**, set against the cliff. There are petroglyphs and a pictograph here. Notice the branching cholla plants that seem to favor this location. Cross Frijoles Creek, then go right to walk through the woods along the creek 0.5 mile, which brings you to **Ceremonial Cave**, 150 feet above the canyon floor. Reached by a series of ladders, it contains a reconstructed kiva.

Retracing your steps, you can go straight ahead at the first trail junction, following the Nature Trail. At the second junction, cross Frijoles Creek on a small bridge, then turn right below Tyuonyi and continue on toward the visitor center.

Day Hike 3: Falls Trail

Distance: 5 miles, round-trip
Time: 3 hours
Map: USGS topo for Bandelier
Difficulty: easy to Upper Falls, moderate thereafter

Because of its suitability for family outings, this delightful trail can be congested all the way down to the Rio Grande, but especially to Upper and Lower Falls (see map, p. 176). The hike can be hot, especially at the top and bottom where little shade is available. Be sure to bring along water.

Beginning at the far end of the hikers' parking lot past the visitor center, the trail crosses Frijoles Creek twice on wooden bridges, descending gradually. It stays somewhat above the creekbed as the stream becomes entrenched, diving deeply into the earth. Soon it reaches an overlook of lovely 140-foot **Upper Falls,** 1.25 miles from the trailhead.

Past this point the trail becomes a bit rougher. Descending on switchbacks, it recrosses the creek on a bridge immediately above some small wading pools before swinging down to a viewpoint for the (less dramatic) **Lower Falls,** 80 feet high. Crossing the stream three times on stones and logs, the trail enters open, deserty country, where it meets the **Rio Grande.** The canyon banks are littered with dead cottonwoods, a bleak legacy of a flood that backed Cochiti Reservoir up some 200 feet above its normal level.

The river, at mile 2.5, represents a 700-foot descent from the trailhead. The Cerros del Rio mesas are visible on the other side. The trail past this point is not maintained, so you must double back to the visitor center.

DAYS 11 AND 12: STONE LIONS

- ■ **Stunning views of mountains and canyons**
- ■ **Visiting a sacred shrine**
- ■ **Camping at Capulin and Juniper campgrounds**

The Shrine of the Stone Lions is a small, ancient religious site that still draws Pueblo Indians from all over northern New Mexico. Probably erected originally to promote good hunting, it consists of two side-by-side figures of crouching mountain lions carved out of volcanic rock and ringed by antlers and boulders. Offerings of pottery and semiprecious stones such as amber and turquoise are traditionally placed next to the eroded carvings. There are several approach routes to the shrine, the shortest and most popular being the Middle Alamo Trail, but the route described below gives the hiker more of a feel for Bandelier's backcountry. It does require a short car shuttle or some equivalent, however. One non-shuttle option is to return to your car from the visitor center via Frijoles Creek, which would add 7.75 miles (an extra day) to the trip.

Backpack: The Stone Lions

Distance: 18.75 miles, one way
Time: 2 days
Map: USGS topo for Bandelier
Difficulty: moderate

To get to the trailhead, drive to the entrance station, and then go left on NM-4, reaching the turnoff for Ponderosa Campground on the left in about 5.5 miles (see map, p. 179). Park here. Your trailhead into upper Frijoles Canyon is to the right of the campground.

For over a mile, follow a jeep road, which turns into an excellent trail for the 400-foot (in 1.0 mile) descent to **Upper Crossing** at mile 1.75. (This point can also be reached by hiking 6 easy miles up-canyon from the visitor center.) Cross Frijoles Canyon on a log bridge and ascend 400 feet to a windswept mesa top. Magnificent 360-degree views of the surrounding peaks can be enjoyed from this high vantage point, especially since a major forest fire in the late 1970s leveled most obstructions.

At about mile 3 your trail will intersect the trail to lower Frijoles Canyon, and then the trail into Alamo Canyon. Go right at each of these Y intersections, heading south and dropping into narrow Alamo Canyon at mile 4. This involves another 400-foot descent on a good trail as well as another stream crossing. Follow the canyon downstream for a short distance before starting the gradual climb out past some tent rocks. Again you arrive at a high plateau at mile 5. Turning right at the trail junction (away from the Stone Lions, which are lower down on this same mesa), you soon reach the lip of the **Capulin** ("chokecherry") **Canyon,** where you begin your third and most precipitous descent (600 feet). The trail deteriorates here, but views of the mountains on the other side provide ample compensation. You reach the floor of Capulin Canyon at mile 6. Turn left and proceed down the canyon through heavy timber for 2 miles until you reach the back-country ranger's cabin and the numbered campsites just beyond it. Except

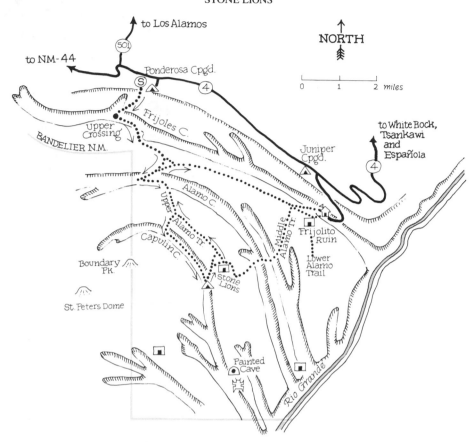

in times of severe fire danger, there should be wood provided in the individual sites along the creek. Those with extra time will find it worthwhile to hike down-canyon to **Painted Cave** (5 miles round-trip), with its colorful pictographs.

At the campground, find the junction with the Stone Lions (Middle Alamo) Trail. Go north on that trail and climb out of Capulin Canyon. In less than 1.5 miles you will reach a set of Y-type trail junctions. Turn right at the first one; the **Shrine of the Stone Lions** is immediately to the right of the second. After visiting the shrine, head northwest and climb back to the mesa top between Capulin and Alamo canyons. In about 2 miles you will arrive at an intersection; turn right here for the drop into Alamo Canyon. This is the same trail you were on before. Continue down to the canyon floor (3.5 miles past the Stone Lions) and then back up to the mesa on the other side. A mile past the floor of Alamo Canyon you come to the familiar Y where your trail joins the ones to Upper Crossing/Ponderosa Campground and Lower Frijoles Canyon. Turn right at each intersection to head east along the sloping mesa top toward the visitor center.

Pueblo Indians still visit the ancient Stone Lions shrine in Bandelier National Monument, New Mexico

The next 4 miles are very easy and beautiful, paralleling the right lip of Frijoles Canyon. After about 3 miles, you arrive at a trail junction; the left fork drops directly down to Frijoles Creek, while the right (the Middle Alamo Trail) returns to Alamo Canyon. Instead of turning here, continue straight ahead along the rim. Near the end, as you undertake a rapid 500-foot (in 0.75 mile) descent on switchbacks into Frijoles Canyon, you command a bird's-eye view of the ancient ruin sites in Frijoles Canyon itself, and you also pass Frijolito Ruin at its rim, where the Lower Alamo Trail branches off to the south. After some refreshments at the snack bar, all that remains is to pick up your vehicle and claim a spot for the night in Juniper Campground.

DAY 13: BANDELIER TO TAOS

- **Day-hiking to Tsankawi Ruin**
- **Stopping at magnificently situated pueblos**
- **Camping and showers available at Rio Grande Gorge State Park**
- **Gas, groceries, and laundry available in Española**

Your first stop today is **Tsankawi** (san-kuh-WEE), a detached unit of Bandelier, located 11 miles to the northeast on NM-4. The entrance gate, very unobtrusive, stands directly opposite the start of the truck route to Los Alamos. Park here and prepare yourself for an interesting early-morning hike.

───■───

Day Hike: Tsankawi Ruin

Distance: 2 miles, round-trip
Time: 2 hours
Map: USGS topo for Bandelier
Difficulty: easy

The ostensible attraction here is an unexcavated 350-room pueblo, built in the fifteenth century, that looks like a heap of rubble to the untrained eye. Nevertheless, this section of the park (its name derived from a Tewa phrase meaning "village between two canyons at the clump of sharp, round cacti") deserves a visit, both for its glorious views of the surrounding canyons and high country and for other attractions along the self-guiding trail.

The trail starts near the ranger station a level below the mesa top where the ruin, once two or three stories tall, is situated (see map, p. 182). It soon forks; go left here, proceeding to the top with the aid of a short ladder. Look for petroglyphs here at marker number 6. After visiting the main ruin, a masonry surface site, the trail drops back down to the lower level by means of another ladder. Petroglyphs and cave dwellings abound in this area; look for rock art especially around stake number 18. The trail follows for some distance an Anasazi footpath worn nearly a foot deep into the soft tuff. It then rejoins the other section of the trail, closing the loop and going back to the parking area.

───■───

Once you have returned from Tsankawi, devote the rest of the day to visiting pueblos. Several interesting ones lie north and east of Bandelier, near Española, which can be reached via either NM-30 or NM-502 and US-84/285. **San Ildefonso,** a left turn off NM-502, is an attractive village set dramatically under pink mesas and blue mountains. Famous for black matte pottery, it also takes pride in its impressive above-ground kiva, located in the center of the town's treeless plaza. The residents here, like those at Cochiti pueblo, claim that their forebears inhabited Tsankawi and other sites in Bandelier. An exact replica of the original Spanish colonial mission was completed in 1968. **Santa Clara Pueblo** nearby, a left turn off NM-30, is a black-on-black pottery center too; on the reservation you

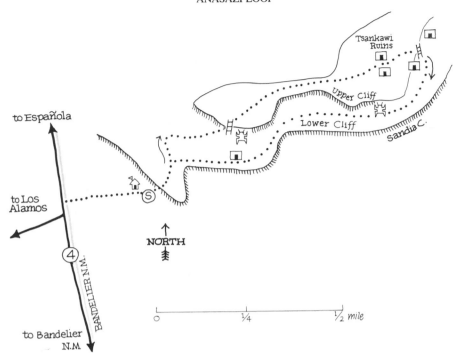

can visit Puye Cliff Dwellings, which the Santa Clarans regard as another ancestral home. **Nambe Pueblo,** also near Española, boasts sacred Nambe Falls, one of only a few large waterfalls in the entire state. If Nambe is the oldest of the northern Rio Grande pueblos, tiny **Pojoaque** (a right turn off US-84/285) is the youngest, constructed in the 1940s by the members of a tribe whose ancestors were nearly wiped out by a smallpox epidemic.

Driving north from Española on NM-68, look for a campsite in **Rio Grande Gorge State Park** near Pilar. If all sites are taken, there are other campgrounds nearby on NM-567 along the river, and even more in the mountains above Taos.

Approximately 47 miles north of Española on NM-68 is **Taos Pueblo** ("place of the red willows") on the outskirts of the Hispanic and Anglo town of the same name. Tucked comfortably between the Rio Grande Gorge and the Sangre de Cristo Mountains, Taos's charming adobe dwellings—all interconnected, Anasazi style—house 1800 Tewa-speaking residents. Take special note of the traditional beehive ovens, or "hornos," in which bread is baked, and the plaza's handsome Catholic church, dating from the mid-nineteenth century.

The town of Taos, cool in summer because of its high elevation, has been a haven for writers and artists at least since the time of D. H. Lawrence and Georgia O'Keeffe. Indeed, its plaza district appears to support even more art galleries, craft shops, and bookstores per capita than its larger counterpart, Santa Fe. And it contains fine restaurants and hotels, as well as historic attractions like the Kit Carson Home, just off the plaza. Only a few miles south of here in Ranchos de Taos is the St. Francis of Assisi Mission, an enduring subject for generations of painters, most notably O'Keeffe.

By now you may be ready to return to your campsite on the Rio Grande Gorge. The impressive 1000-foot-deep gorge, with its black volcanic walls, contains celebrated white-water rafting opportunities (among them the wild Taos Box, a full-day run). Look for petroglyphs along the river bank.

DAY 14: TAOS TO ALBUQUERQUE

- **Taking the High Road through Spanish Rio Grande country**
- **Romancing elegant, cultured Santa Fe**
- **Camping and showers at Coronado State Park**
- **Gas, groceries, and laundry available in Española or Santa Fe**

From Taos return to Española via NM-518, -75, and -76, the so-called "High Road" through the pine and aspen uplands of the Carson National Forest. This 52-mile route connects a series of poor but intriguing Spanish-speaking villages celebrated for their weaving, their strings of fiery red chiles, and their piety. The **Spanish Rio Grande** region, with its exquisite mission churches, such as the ones at Chimayo and Las Trampas, is the center of the waning Penitente movement, a heretical Christian sect whose members practice rites of physical self-mortification, particularly during the Easter season.

In Española, pick up US-84/285, the expressway to historic **Santa Fe,** which ranks among America's most beautiful cities. It owes its charm to its unique amalgamation of three cultures: Pueblo, Hispanic, and Anglo. A regulation promulgated here decades ago stipulated that all new construction be faced with adobe or some look-alike material, and as a result the city exhibits a wonderful unity of style. The capital of New Mexico, Santa Fe is renowned for the fashionable shops and restaurants of its central plaza district, its opera and symphony orchestra, its Canyon Road art galleries, its Wheelwright and Fine Arts museums (dedicated to showcasing, respectively, contemporary Native American culture and the painting and photography of Southwestern masters), and its Palace of Governors, dating from colonial times, in front of which local Indians sell handmade jewelry spread on blankets and mats.

When finished in Santa Fe, take US-84/285 south 5.5 miles to I-25, and I-25 for 35.6 miles to Bernalillo, near Albuquerque. Along the way

Spanish padres built Chimayo's Santuario mission to last

you pass more pueblos, including **Santo Domingo** on the Rio Grande, noted for its jewelry, and **Tesuque,** which contains a strange butte named Camel Rock.

Exiting at Bernalillo, follow signs to **Coronado State Park.** Located on the west bank of the Rio Grande, it offers commanding views of the Sandia Mountains. It has extensive low-walled ruins and an interesting museum filled with Spanish artifacts from the colonial period, which began with Coronado's failed 1640 expedition in search of the Seven Cities of Cibola. But the star attraction here is the restored kiva in which archaeologists found several layers of colorful murals, dating from the fourteenth to the sixteenth centuries. The originals have been removed to the museum for their protection, but exact reproductions now line the kiva interior, accessible by ladder. You can camp tonight at the state park in preparation for tomorrow's trip home.

Chapter 6

PAINTED DESERT LOOP

Arizona, Utah

Focusing on northeastern Arizona, this diverse loop roughly circumscribes the Navajo Reservation. It features day trips to prehistoric ruins and modern pueblos, short walks along canyon streams or on mesas covered with petrified wood, and two rugged backpacking opportunities, one to Rainbow Bridge on the shoulder of Navajo Mountain and the other to the floor of the Grand Canyon. Alternatives are suggested for readers preferring less strenuous activities.

DAY 1: FLAGSTAFF AND SEDONA

- **Walking up Oak Creek Canyon**
- **Playing on natural water slides**
- **Touring Sinagua ruins at Tuzigoot**
- **Camping at Dead Horse Ranch State Park**
- **Gas, groceries, showers, and laundry available in Flagstaff**

Flagstaff (population 34,650), one of the biggest cities in the high desert region, is positioned on the slope of the San Francisco Peaks, volcanic mountains sacred to the Hopi and Navajo. Its high altitude makes it quite comfortable even in summer, and its first-rate **Museum of Northern Arizona,** dedicated to the perpetuation and promotion of the Southwest's Native American cultures, should not be missed. Purchase a day's worth of gas, food, and ice in the city, then drive to the museum, 2 miles north of town on US-89.

After visiting the museum, return to Flagstaff and pick up US-89A going south. The 29-mile drive through national forest land to the resort town of Sedona is uncommonly lovely, following the main drainage of **Oak Creek** for much of the way. This 16-mile-long stream, adjacent to the Secret Mountain Wilderness, cuts a watery canyon up to 2500 feet deep through the dramatic sandstone and limestone cliffs of the Coconino Plateau. Coconino sandstone is the dominant stratum here. The day hike

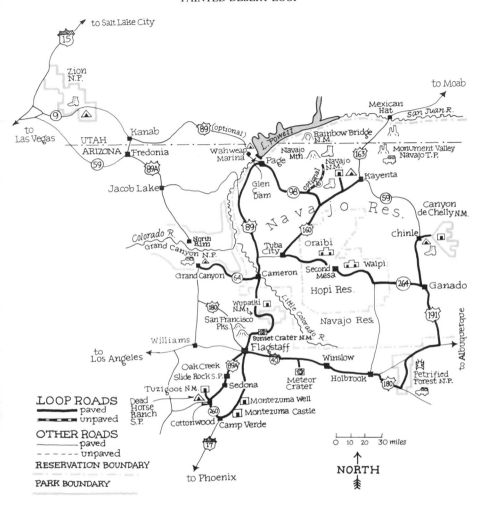

LOOP ROADS
—— paved
▪▪▪▪▪ unpaved
OTHER ROADS
—— paved
- - - - - unpaved
RESERVATION BOUNDARY
PARK BOUNDARY

0 10 20   30 miles

↑
NORTH

described below is just one of the many excellent hiking possibilities along the West Fork of Oak Creek, open only to foot traffic.

To reach the confluence of Oak Creek and West Fork, where the hike begins, drive about 18.5 miles south of Flagstaff on US-89A, or 0.75 miles south of Cave Springs Campground. (If you reach Bootlegger Campground, you have driven about 1.25 miles too far.) Although no highway signs mark the trailhead, this short day hike is very popular, so look for other cars parked along the road. A trail map is not really necessary, but don't attempt the hike during high-water periods, such as the spring run-off, or when flooding threatens from up-canyon storms. Camping and campfires are not allowed along this trail.

Day Hike: West Fork of Oak Creek

Distance: 4.5 miles, round-trip
Time: 3 hours
Maps: USGS quads for Munds Park and Wilson
Mtn.
Difficulty: easy

Park by the side of the road and look for a paved path on the right between two private driveways. A sign that may be partially obscured by brush will indicate that you are entering public land. Descend slightly to Oak Creek, crossing on a small footbridge near burned-out Mayhew Lodge and its surrounding apple orchard. Past this meadow, cross the **West Fork** near a shallow pool, and enter the narrow, orange and white gorge lined with evergreens and deciduous trees.

The trail is easy, with frequent stream crossings but virtually no elevation gain. Distance markers have been erected every 0.5 mile. Many exotic bird species, including the painted redstart and the red-faced warbler, make their home here. In about 2.25 miles, at a rock ledge overhanging the creek's right bank, stop for lunch and some bird-watching before retracing your steps to your car. Past this point the trail becomes very brushy and difficult to follow.

For additional information, contact the Sedona Ranger District, P.O. Box 300, Sedona, AZ 86336.

Down US-89A just south of the trailhead, about 8 miles north of Sedona, look for **Slide Rock State Park** on the right. Small, erosion-sculpted chutes make delightful water slides at this swimming area. Also visit Sedona, with its fashionable shops and restaurants and a spectacular setting that's made it a favorite location for films. See if you can identify some of the local monoliths, such as Coffee Pot, Bell, Castle, and Court House rocks. Although the drive from Flagstaff to Sedona along Oak Creek is justly famous for its scenic beauty, the redrock country south of Sedona is equally remarkable, offering views of the Sycamore Canyon system.

Near Clarkdale and Cottonwood, adjacent towns farther south on US-89A, is **Tuzigoot National Monument** (from the Apache word meaning "crooked water"), located just past Dead Horse Ranch State Park, where you will spend the night. This substantial freestanding ruin and six others were built around A.D. 1200 by skilled masons from the Sinagua culture. In pre-Columbian times, the Sinagua and Hohokam tribes coexisted peacefully in the fertile Verde Valley, the Sinagua sharing their masonry skills (borrowed from the Anasazi) and the Hohokam teaching the Sinagua about

Montezuma Castle National Monument guards the valley of Beaver Creek, Arizona

irrigation. Take a short, self-guided tour of this impressive structure, which once housed over 200 people. Don't miss the outstanding exhibits inside the visitor center.

For more information, contact the Superintendent, Tuzigoot National Monument, P.O. Box 219, Camp Verde, AZ 86322.

<u>DAY 2:</u> SINAGUA COUNTRY TO THE PETRIFIED FOREST

- **Visiting Montezuma Castle**
- **Gazing into a gigantic meteor crater**
- **Camping in the Petrified Forest backcountry**
- **Gas, groceries, showers, and laundry available in Holbrook**

In Cottonwood, pick up AZ-260 south, which intersects I-17 in 12.5 miles. Follow signs to another Sinagua site, **Montezuma Castle,** just north of Camp Verde. Early settlers believed the well-preserved dwelling was erected by Aztecs from Mexico. One of the Southwest's most amazing archaeological discoveries, Montezuma Castle was fashioned of limestone blocks and river stones in the thirteenth century. Fifty people once lived in this five-story, seventeen-room structure, encased like a jewel in the cliff. It is too fragile to enter but can be seen from a dramatic overlook a short distance from the visitor center. Past the overlook, the very easy 0.25-mile round-trip trail visits another ruin before looping back to the parking lot by way of Beaver Creek, where the Sinagua farmed.

Located north of Montezuma Castle, a few miles on a dirt road from I-17's McGuireville exit, is **Montezuma Well,** part of the national monument. An easy 0.5-mile loop trail begins at the parking lot. The well, formed when the roof of a large limestone cavern collapsed, is fed by perennial springs. Both the Hohokam and Sinagua tribes utilized this reliable water source in their irrigation systems, and ruins of ancient dwellings still ring the well.

For additional information, contact the Superintendent, Montezuma Castle National Monument, P.O. Box 219, Camp Verde, AZ 86322.

Continue north on I-17 for 40.5 miles to I-40 and turn east. About 35 miles past Flagstaff is an exit for **Meteor Crater,** a privately run national landmark 5 miles to the south. This impact site, at 560 feet deep and almost a mile across, is one of the world's largest. Films and exhibits at the Astrogeological Museum on the crater's rim detail how and why the collision occurred nearly 50,000 years ago, while the Astronaut Hall of Fame demonstrates the crater's use as a mock moon surface for Apollo astronaut training. A 3.5-mile Rim Trail encircles the crater, but entry into the depression is not allowed.

For more information, write to Meteor Crater Enterprises, 603 North Beaver Street, Flagstaff, AZ 86001.

Go eastward on I-40 through Winslow and its neighbor Holbrook; both towns contain campgrounds with shower and laundry facilities. For backcountry camping, take US-180 south from Holbrook to the lower end of the Petrified Forest National Park. Obtain a backcountry camping permit from the ranger at the Rainbow Forest Museum (located just inside the entrance). The Flattops area makes a good overnight destination. You will need to walk at least 0.5 mile from and out of sight of all roads and trails.

DAY 3: PETRIFIED FOREST TO CANYON DE CHELLY

- ▪ **Seeing petrified logs and Anasazi rock art**
- ▪ **Admiring handicrafts at Hubbell Trading Post**
- ▪ **Camping at Canyon de Chelly National Monument**
- ▪ **Gas and groceries available in Ganado and Chinle**

The **Petrified Forest** and **Painted Desert,** combined in one national park, straddle I-40 east of Holbrook (see map, p. 191). Although the main attraction is the abundance of petrified wood, prehistoric Indian ruins and rock art are also scattered through these gray, pink, and orange Chinle formation badlands. Petrified wood develops when dead trees somehow saved from normal processes of decay are invaded by mineral-bearing waters that gradually replace the trees' cellular material with cryptocrystalline structures such as those found in agate or jasper. Please don't take pieces of petrified wood as souvenirs; the Park Service estimates that over ten tons of it is illegally pilfered annually.

Scenic Drive: Petrified Forest/Painted Desert

> **Distance: 28 miles, one way**
> **Time: 4 hours or more, with stops**

Numerous short trails, all easy or very easy, branch off from the scenic drive. At the southern end, where the petrified wood is concentrated, the Rainbow Forest Museum explains the process of petrification. The **Giant Logs Loop** (0.5 mile), which originates here, displays some outstanding specimens, including Old Faithful Log. Up the road, the paved **Long Logs Loop** (0.5 mile) visits the park's largest collection of petrified logs; from the same parking lot a 1-mile round-trip trail departs for **Agate House,** an Anasazi dwelling constructed of petrified wood.

Farther north, past the Flattops (low mesas that provide sweeping views of the Rainbow Forest), is the **Crystal Forest,** where a 0.75-mile loop trail traverses an area of petrified logs filled with amethyst quartz crystals. From the **Jasper Forest Overlook,** the next stop along the scenic drive, visitors can observe huge numbers of petrified logs strewn throughout the valley below. The next stop on the right is **Agate Bridge,** a long, low span created when both ends of a petrified log became embedded in sandstone. Off a spur road to **Blue Mesa,** a 1-mile loop trail descends steeply into some erosion-scoured, sedimentary badlands. Closer to the highway, and just opposite each other, are Newspaper Rock and Puerco Ruin. An overlook permits views of **Newspaper Rock,** with its vast array of memorable petroglyphs, probably left by peoples who later migrated east to Zuni and west to the Hopi mesas. **Puerco Ruin,** overlooking the river of the same name, is a largely unexcavated 75-room Anasazi site with more petroglyphs below it.

North of the interstate, in the true Painted Desert region, the loop road leads to numerous overlooks. A very easy 1.25-mile trail connects Kachina and Tawa points. Past **Kachina Point** is the visitor center. Kachina Point is a favorite departure place for backpackers. Although no wilderness hiking trails exist in the park, limitless cross-country opportunities beckon. Destinations include the dark petrified stumps of the Black Forest, including a

PETRIFIED FOREST TO CANYON DE CHELLY

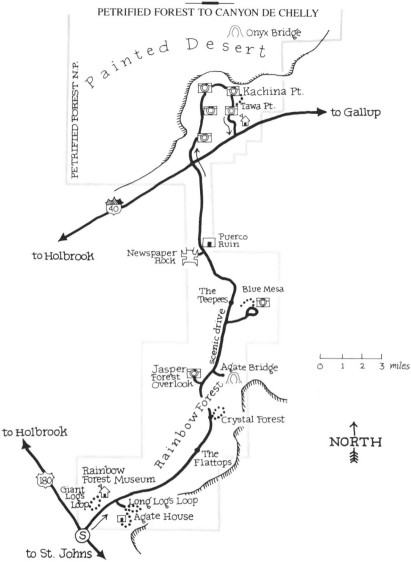

standing stump; Pilot Rock, a volcanic butte; and Wildhorse Wash.

For further information, write to the Superintendent, Petrified Forest National Park, AZ 86028.

———

When your tour of the park is over, travel east on I-40 for 23 miles to Chambers. Turning north on US-191, drive 73.5 miles to Chinle, on the outskirts of Canyon de Chelly, and pitch your tent at lovely Cottonwood Campground. Along the way, make a stop at **Hubbell National Historic**

Site and trading post in Ganado; for details, see Chapter 5, the Anasazi Loop, Day 2.

DAY 4: CANYON DE CHELLY TO NAVAJO NATIONAL MONUMENT

- **Anasazi cliff dwellings**
- **Ancient Hopi villages**
- **Camping at Navajo National Monument**
- **Gas, groceries, showers, and laundry available in Tuba City**

Devote this morning to **Canyon de Chelly,** stopping at overlooks and hiking 2.5 miles round-trip to **White House Ruin.** See Day 2 of Chapter 5, the Anasazi Loop, for a full description.

After Canyon de Chelly, proceed to the **Hopi Reservation** by backtracking 30 miles on US-191 to AZ-264 and heading west toward Tuba City. The Hopi population of about 10,000 is concentrated on three mesatop projections of Black Mesa, named First, Second, and Third. A visitor center on Second Mesa (57.5 miles down AZ-264) acquaints tourists with Hopi history and crafts.

The Hopi, a very traditional people, do not normally charge an admission fee, but neither do they normally allow photography in their villages. Third Mesa's **Shungopavi** and some of the other twelve Hopi towns discourage contacts with outsiders; for a while, in fact, the ancient pueblo of **Oraibi**—the oldest continuously inhabited settlement in the United States (dating back to A.D. 1150)—was off-limits to visitors. But others will welcome you, even during some of their fascinating sacred dances, as long as you observe the rituals respectfully and do not attempt to record them in any manner. Check at the Hopi Cultural Center for dates and times. From January through July, the dances feature "kachinas"—men dressed in colorful costumes to represent the nature deities of the Hopi religion, who reside in the San Francisco Peaks. The Spanish had even less luck Christianizing the Hopi than they had with the Pueblos; in the late seventeenth century the ordinarily peace-loving Hopi rose up violently against their conquerors, and Spanish colonial efforts here never recovered.

One particularly interesting Hopi community is First Mesa's **Walpi,** situated on a finger of land so narrow that only two rows of houses will fit on it. To visit Walpi you may need a guide; check at the village information booth. First Mesa, incidentally, is known as the pottery-making capital of the reservation.

For more information on the Hopi, contact the Hopi Cultural Center, P.O. Box 67, Second Mesa, AZ 86043.

Tuba City, one of the larger communities on the Navajo lands surrounding the Hopi Reservation, is a good place to purchase three days' worth of food before turning right (north) on US-160. At tiny Black Mesa, a coal mining center 51.5 miles distant, go left onto AZ-564, winding through a slickrock wilderness for 9.5 miles to Navajo National Monument. Camp here.

DAY 5: BETATAKIN

- **Day-hiking to a marvelously well-preserved ruin**
- **Camping at Navajo National Monument**

If you want to visit some major Anasazi cliff dwellings but the crowds at Mesa Verde leave you cold, **Navajo National Monument** may be your kind of place. In addition to countless smaller sites, it contains three ruins of real significance: Keet Seel (the largest in Arizona), Betatakin, and Inscription House (presently closed to the public). As mentioned previously, the Navajo are culturally and genetically unrelated to the Anasazi; the national monument's name refers to the surrounding reservation.

Be at the visitor center when it opens to register for today's hike to Betatakin and tomorrow's backpack to Keet Seel. Since only a limited number of backcountry permits to tour Keet Seel are available, it is strongly recommended that you make reservations up to two months in advance, reconfirming them a week before your visit. The ruin is currently open to authorized visitors on weekends between Memorial Day and Labor Day.

For more information, write to the Superintendent, Navajo National Monument, Tonalea, AZ 86044.

Day Hike: Betatakin Ruin (ranger-led only)

Distance: 5 miles, round-trip
Time: 5 to 6 hours
Difficulty: moderate

During the summer months, ranger-guided tours, filled on a first-come, first-served basis, leave twice daily for **Betatakin** (a Navajo word for "ledge house"). After walking to the rim of Tsegi Canyon, you descend about 700 feet to the 135-room apartment building, located in the forest in a magnificent, vaulting amphitheater. Erected in the late thirteenth century, this multilevel dwelling was first seen by non-Indians (John

Steps leading to unforgettable Betatakin Ruin, Arizona

Wetherill's party) in 1909. Take special note of the rock art to the right of the ruin. Betatakin is also visible from an overlook at the end of the easy **Sandal Trail**, a 1-mile round trip, that originates at the visitor center.

DAYS 6 AND 7: KEET SEEL

- Hiking past waterfalls in deep desert canyons
- Admiring a superlative ruin
- Camping at Keet Seel and Monument Valley
- Gas, groceries, showers, and laundry available in Kayenta

Unlike the Betatakin trip, the 8-mile hike to Keet Seel is unguided (though some people hire horses and local Navajo escorts through the monument headquarters). A ranger is stationed at Keet Seel at all times, however, to accompany visitors inside the ruin. At the visitor center, obtain a hiking permit, a trail map, and instructions for finding the trailhead. The proximity of a usually reliable spring enables you to carry just a half gallon of water apiece to the ruin and camping area.

At the conclusion of your hike, you will drive back to US-160, the main road through the northern part of the Navajo Reservation, and turn left toward Kayenta. The highway will take you past the mouth of Tsegi Canyon through a dramatic desert landscape. In Kayenta, head north on US-163 past Owl Rock on the left and Agathla Peak (aka El Capitan), a volcanic plug, on the right. Your destination will be Monument Valley, which straddles the Utah–Arizona border. Turn right into this Navajo tribal park and set up camp for the night of Day 7.

———

Backpack: Keet Seel Ruin

Distance: 16 miles, round-trip
Time: 2 days
Difficulty: moderate

The only hard part of the hike to Keet Seel is a 1000-foot descent into (and subsequent climb out of) the canyon system in which the ruin is located. Don't drink any water found in these canyons without treating it, for it has been polluted by grazing livestock. Waterfalls and interesting rock formations are encountered along the way to the campground, which is just short of the ruin.

Drop your gear at the campground and approach the ranger's cabin for an extensive tour of **Keet Seel**, situated under a cavernous Navajo sandstone overhang where the canyon opens up. This unforgettable ruin, with its 165 rooms, was "discovered" by Richard Wetherill; its name is from the Navajo word for "broken pottery." To prevent damage to the fragile cliff dwelling, ranger-guided tours—which last about an hour—are limited to five people. The ranger can also direct you to the ground-level spring. Plan on an early start tomorrow for the return to your car.

DAY 8: MONUMENT VALLEY

- **Touring spectacular desert landscape**
- **Setting up a boat or backpack trip**
- **Camping near Navajo Mountain or Lake Powell**
- **Gas, groceries, showers, and laundry available in Kayenta**

Today's uncrowded itinerary allows you to enjoy a leisurely swing through **Monument Valley** (see Chapter 5, Anasazi Loop, Day 3, for description and directions) before making preparations for the upcoming trip to Rainbow Bridge. You will have to decide whether to visit Rainbow Bridge on foot or by boat, so that you can make the necessary arrangements. At the conclusion of your Monument Valley tour, backtrack to Kayenta. If you are planning to hike to Rainbow Bridge, buy groceries here for four nights and fill all available canteens.

In Kayenta, go west on US-160 for 31.5 miles, until you reach AZ-98. Turn right onto this spectacular road, which crosses a high plateau before dropping down to Lake Powell.

Only those taking a boat trip to Rainbow Bridge should continue on AZ-98 all the way to Page. Make arrangements for tomorrow's full-day excursion at the lodge at **Wahweap Marina,** northwest of town on US-89, where it may also be convenient to camp both tonight and tomorrow. On Day 10, plan to drive 110 miles from Wahweap to **Zion National Park** on US-89 West and UT-9. Consult Chapter 7, Canyons Loop, Days 1 through 3, for hiking suggestions. Return to Page on the morning of Day 13, and head as directed to the South Rim of the Grand Canyon.

Those who are backpacking to Rainbow Bridge should go about 12.25 miles northwest on AZ-98 from the US-160 junction. Turn right onto the unpaved Navajo Mountain Road (Route 16), whose condition varies from year to year and even from day to day. Drive northeast on this road for about 35 miles, past Inscription House Trading Post. The road will then fork.

Which way you should go at the fork depends on whether you want to combine the North and South Rainbow trails for a 27.5-mile one-way trip, or hike to the bridge on one trail and double back. (The North Rainbow

Thumb-shaped monolith, Monument Valley, Arizona/Utah

Trail is 28.5 miles round-trip, the South is 26.5.) Combining the two trails requires a car shuttle; hikers without two cars may be able to arrange a shuttle at a local trading post (see below). If you hike both trails, it is better to start on the South Rainbow Trail and end on the North.

To reach the South Rainbow Trail, turn left at the big fork mentioned above. Drive for about 5 miles, passing a barn to the left and a house on the right. Turn right just before a large sandstone dome. The road gets very rough, and it might be best to walk these last 2.5 miles to the trailhead at Rainbow Lodge.

To get to the North Rainbow Trail, turn right at the fork mentioned above and proceed to the Navajo Mountain School and Trading Post, 6 miles away. About 4 miles past the trading post is a four-way intersection with another dirt road near a butte named Navajo Begay. There are several buildings at this junction. Continue straight ahead for about 3 miles to a Y in the road. Turn left here. Where the road descends a slope, it deteriorates badly and should be attempted only in a 4-wheel drive vehicle. The small Cha Canyon parking lot, 2 miles from the Y, is where the North Rainbow Trail begins.

Camp tonight near whichever trailhead you have selected, planning on an early start in the morning.

DAYS 9 THROUGH 12: RAINBOW BRIDGE

- **Unexcelled desert scenery**
- **A world-famous natural span**
- **Camping in watery canyons along the trail**

This backpack trip would be well worth the effort even without the opportunity to savor Rainbow Bridge, 275 feet across. Together, the South and North Rainbow trails nearly encircle 10,400-foot-high Navajo Mountain, considered sacred by traditional Indians. At the base of this isolated peak lies some of the most rugged and magnificent redrock wilderness in the United States.

Because this hike is on the Navajo Reservation, a permit is required. Obtain one in person or by mail from the Navajo Tourism Office, P.O. Box 308, Window Rock, AZ 86515, where the tribal headquarters is located. Bring along enough canteens (at least a 1-gallon capacity per person) and some way to purify water, since this is grazing country.

When your hike is over, drive to Page on US-98 for supplies, and then camp at Wahweap Marina, where showers are available.

For more information, contact the Superintendent, Glen Canyon National Recreation Area, Box 1507, Page, AZ 86040.

Backpack: South and North Rainbow Trails

Distance: 27.5 miles, one way
Time: 4 days
Map: USGS quad for Navajo Mountain
Difficulty: very strenuous

The **South Rainbow Trail** begins at Rainbow Lodge, a group of dilapidated pink stone buildings (see map, p. 200). A large cairn indicates the trailhead, and red mileposts mark the entire route. In the first 5 miles, expect many tiring ups and downs as you cross the arms of First and Horse canyons. Be careful not to lose the trail as you approach Sunset (also called Yabut) Pass at mile 5, which offers astounding views into **Cliff Canyon,** 1600 feet below. The difficult 2-mile descent into Cliff is steep and rocky, but the canyon's lower reaches are uncommonly lovely. First Water Campsite, at mile 8, has flowing springs, sometimes even small pools. The more scenic campsites, however, are about a mile farther, near the junction with Redbud Pass Canyon, where deep alcoves provide shelter.

You can't miss the junction at mile 9 with the first sizable side-canyon to the right, opposite a huge alcove and not far past a slickrock dome called the Elephant. Look for Anasazi rock art 50 yards to the left of the junction. Turn right up this side-canyon, which gets progressively narrower as it climbs toward **Redbud Pass,** at mile 9.5. The pass was blasted out in 1922 by John Wetherill, who led the first party of white men to Rainbow Bridge. The trail goes through a narrow cleft to extraordinary Redbud Canyon at mile 10. Turn left and walk downstream. Near a small ruin at mile 11, Redbud Canyon meets Bridge Canyon; the South Rainbow Trail forks left, heading downstream. Just before Bridge Canyon takes a deep dive into the earth, the trail ascends slightly up to the right bank of the arroyo and remains on this shoulder the rest of the way. In about 0.25 mile you can see the bridge down the canyon. Immediately thereafter, a spur trail to the right leads to Echo Camp at mile 13—an exceptional grotto marred by the remains of a horse camp. At least two good springs are here.

It's a flat, easy walk down the main trail to **Rainbow Bridge.** Carved out of Navajo sandstone, this is among the largest formations of its kind in the world. At high-water levels, Lake Powell backs up under the span. Other tourists come to within 0.25 mile of the bridge by boat. Nearby is a plaque honoring Nasja, the Paiute guide who assisted Wetherill. Although no camping is allowed in the postage-stamp-sized national monument, you can pitch your tent within a short distance of both the bridge and the springs.

To return via the **North Rainbow Trail,** backtrack up Bridge Canyon and take the left fork at the Redbud Canyon junction. Although the next 2

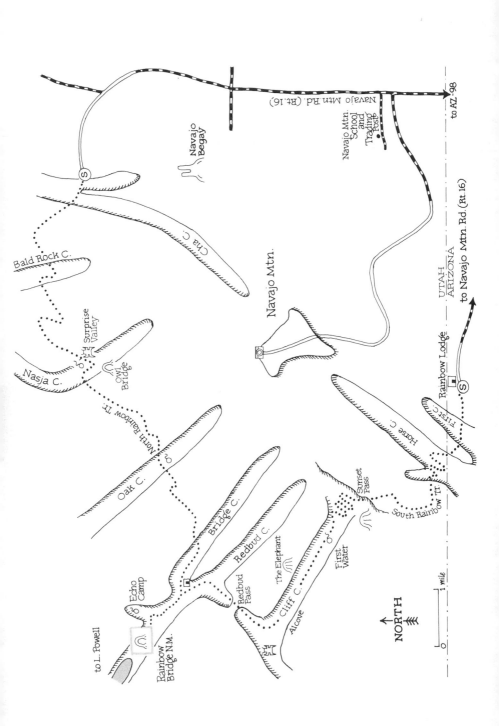

Navajo Mtn. Rd. (Rt. 16)

to AZ-98

Navajo Begay

Navajo Mtn. School and Trading Post

Cha C.

Bald Rock C.

Surprise Valley

Navajo Mtn.

Nasja C.

Owl Bridge

North Rainbow Tr.

Rainbow Lodge

UTAH
ARIZONA

to Navajo Mtn. Rd. (Rt. 16)

First C.

Horse C.

Oak C.

Bridge C.

Sunset Pass

South Rainbow Tr.

Echo Camp

Redbud C.

The Elephant

First Water

to L. Powell

Rainbow Bridge N.M.

Redbud Pass

Cliff C.

Alcove

NORTH

0   1 mile

miles are steeper than the section near the bridge, good campsites do exist in this area. Be careful not to lose the trail here. It goes up a side-canyon to the left and onto the slickrock rim above. You may find a fair amount of water in upper Bridge Canyon as well as in some or all of the canyon systems to the east: Oak, Nasja, Bald Rock, and Cha. Between these drainages you're usually walking on high benchlands, with exceptional views.

The trail to Oak Canyon (5 miles from Rainbow Bridge) is faint and hard to follow in spots. This V-shaped canyon, not as deep as the others to come, offers cold mountain water to refresh the thirsty hiker. Three miles farther is **Nasja Canyon,** the biggest and most beautiful on the North Rainbow Trail. Plentiful water makes camping excellent here. There is even a picnic table close to Owl Bridge, a natural span that will come into view. Climbing out of this canyon toward Surprise Valley, look for a Navajo drawing of a horse on the wall just above the trail.

Bald Rock Canyon, 2.5 miles past Nasja, has a small unnamed arch to your right and some good places to camp. After Bald Rock cross two arms of the Cha Canyon system in the next 3 miles. When the trail forks, about a

Navajo Mountain's slopes provide backdrop for Rainbow Bridge, Arizona/Utah

mile before it ends, go right. The second arm of Cha Canyon is shallow where you cross it, and, immediately beyond, a large rockpile marks the trail's end at the Cha Canyon parking lot.

DAY 13: PAGE TO SOUTH RIM, GRAND CANYON

- **Gazing into a staggering abyss**
- **Easy day-hiking on nature trails**
- **Camping at Grand Canyon National Park**
- **Gas, groceries, showers, and laundry available in Page**

From Page, take US-89 south 82 miles through the Navajo Reservation to Cameron. Turn west on AZ-64, a road that follows the Little Colorado River to Desert View, where you enjoy your first dizzying look into that wonder of wonders, the **Grand Canyon.**

Carved out by the Colorado River over the millennia, this 277-mile-long gorge defies description. Nothing can prepare you for how it feels to stand on the rim and contemplate this awesome abyss. Somehow your mind tends to imagine one very deep and colorful gash in the earth. What it doesn't anticipate are the magnificent side-canyons, the high desert mountains flanking the river, the sheer vastness of the space between rims, and above all, the play of light and shadow on layered cliffs. The famous naturalist and Sierra Club founder, John Muir, summed it up best: "The Grand Canyon," he said, "seems a gigantic statement for even nature to make."

Discovered by the Spanish in the mid-sixteenth century, the canyon remained virtually unexplored by white men until Major John Wesley Powell's party made its historic boat trip down the Green and Colorado rivers in 1869. But Native American artifacts (including split-twig figurines of mule deer and bighorn sheep dating back 3000 or 4000 years) have been found at its 1000 archaeological sites, and the Havasupai Indians—whose ancestors constructed a number of trails from the rim to the river—still farm in the Supai area west of the main park corridor.

Both the North and South rims of the Grand Canyon are developed, offering stores, restaurants, lodges, showers, gas stations, hotels, and (of course) campgrounds. The South Rim in particular has the feel of a miniature city, and a very cosmopolitan one, drawing visitors from every corner of the earth. In the summer months, the Park Service provides free, reliable bus service several times an hour to South Rim viewpoints between Bright Angel Lodge and Hermits Rest; you can disembark at any stop and catch a later bus to resume your tour. By contrast, the North Rim is more remote and consequently much less crowded, though perhaps no less regulated. But both rims equally offer what you came here for: awe-inspiring overlooks, rewarding nature trails, and the chance to descend thousands of feet into the canyon, reading the earth's history as you go.

Because Mather Campground at Grand Canyon Village fills up very early in the day, either make advance reservations through Ticketron or set up camp immediately upon arrival; write the Ticketron Parks Department, P.O. Box 62429, Virginia Beach, VA 23462, or call their office at (900) 370-5566. If the main campgrounds are already full, sites may still be open at Desert View, or in the Kaibab National Forest off AZ-64 South. Rooms can be rented on either rim, though they generally must be booked well ahead.

Stop along South Rim Drive at places such as Tusayan Ruins and Museum, and Lipan, Moran, Grandview, Yaki, and Yavapai points. If you want to hike to the canyon bottom, secure a backcountry use permit (required for all overnight hikes) from the ranger station. The Park Service recommends booking reservations a year in advance for popular trails, but you may luck into a cancellation.

Another option that generally requires advance planning is riding a mule to Phantom Ranch, a rustic hotel near the floor of the canyon, and spending a night there before returning to the rim. Young children and persons weighing over 200 pounds are ineligible for these rides. Other options include scenic flights over the canyon (loathed by backpackers for their noise pollution) and multiday white-water raft trips down the Colorado, beginning at Lees Ferry, Arizona.

For further information, contact the Superintendent, Grand Canyon National Park, P.O. Box 129, Grand Canyon, AZ 86023, or Grand Canyon National Park Lodges, P.O. Box 699, Grand Canyon, AZ 86023. The phone number of the Backcountry Reservation Office is (602) 638-2473; phone reservations are not accepted.

Day Hike: Rim Trail

Distance: up to 9 miles, one way
Time: up to 1 day
Map: USGS topo for Grand Canyon National Park
Difficulty: very easy

The **Rim Trail,** from Hermits Rest at the farthest west end of development to Yavapai Point where the park museum is located, has multiple accesses, thanks to the West Rim shuttle bus. You can therefore sample this incredibly scenic route in small portions. Since the bus does not run east of Yavapai Point, you'll have to walk back if you follow the trail beyond it. Probably the best sections are from Yavapai Point to the El Tovar Hotel (paved), Bright Angel Lodge to Maricopa Point (also paved),

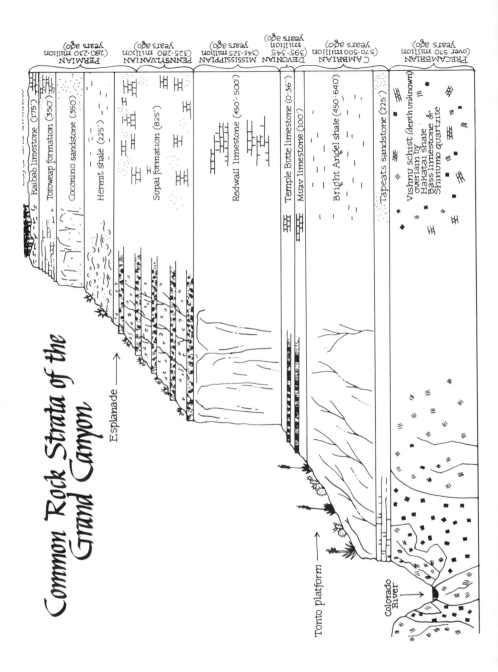

Common Rock Strata of the Grand Canyon

Esplanade →

Tonto platform →

Colorado River →

PERMIAN (280-230 million years ago)
- Kaibab limestone (175')
- Toroweap formation (350')
- Coconino sandstone (350')
- Hermit shale (225')

PENNSYLVANIAN (325-280 million years ago)
- Supai formation (825')

MISSISSIPPIAN (345-325 million years ago)
- Redwall limestone (450'-500')

DEVONIAN (395-345 million years ago)
- Temple Butte limestone (0-36')

CAMBRIAN (570-500 million years ago)
- Muav limestone (100')
- Bright Angel shale (450'-640')
- Tapeats sandstone (225')

PRECAMBRIAN (over 570 million years ago)
- Vishnu schist (depth unknown) overlain by Hakatai shale, Bass limestone & Shinumo quartzite

and the Abyss to Pima Point or Hermits Rest (unpaved); in all of these sections, the road is relatively far from the rim.

DAYS 14 THROUGH 17: INNER CANYON ADVENTURE

- **Selecting from among various backpacking options**
- **Or taking a mule trip to Phantom Ranch**
- **Camping in the canyon**
- **Gas, groceries, showers, and laundry available in Grand Canyon Village**

The park's backcountry trails vary tremendously in length and difficulty and are either maintained or unmaintained. Visitors should hike a maintained trail (either the Bright Angel or the Kaibab) before attempting any other routes; rangers question permit-seekers about prior experience and check for canteens and other essential gear.

Before venturing into the canyon, familiarize yourself with major rock strata through which you will be passing. In the vicinity of Grand Canyon Village, those layers are, from top to bottom: Kaibab limestone (gray), Toroweap formation (very narrow gray), Coconino sandstone (white and sheer), Hermit shale and Supai formations (red and sloping), Redwall limestone (red or light gray, thick and sheer), Bright Angel shale (greenish gray, narrow and sloping), Tapeats sandstone (brown and vertical, below the Tonto Rim), and Vishnu group (the black, jumbled rock of the inner gorge).

To journey into the Grand Canyon is to journey through geologic time. But it is also a journey toward the equator, because every 1000 feet of descent is equivalent to 300 miles of southward travel in terms of flora and fauna. This change is especially evident in a descent from the North Rim, which passes through several life zones: the Canadian, Transition, Upper Sonoran, and Lower Sonoran. Ecologically speaking, the Grand Canyon hiker has gone from Canada to Mexico in only 14 miles. The change is less dramatic in descents from the South Rim, where the Upper Sonoran life zone predominates.

But the most important thing about hiking the Grand Canyon is carrying enough water. This basic rule of all desert travel is even more imperative here, because of the often extreme heat and fatiguing hiking conditions (particularly on the ascent, which can take at least twice as long as the descent). A minimum of 1 gallon per person per day is essential, and it is sometimes advisable to exceed this requirement, even to double it in the summer months when hiking completely dry trails.

Whatever you might choose to do, plan to camp on the South Rim on Day 17.

Backpack 1: Bright Angel Trail

Distance: 11.5 miles, round-trip, to Plateau Point
Time: 2 days
Map: USGS topo for Grand Canyon National Park
Difficulty: strenuous

The **Bright Angel Trail,** from Bright Angel Lodge on the South Rim down to Indian Gardens Campground and the Colorado River (see map, p. 207), is the "easiest" and most popular inner canyon trail in the park. It receives heavy use not only from hikers but from mule parties on their way to Phantom Ranch, a commercial establishment on the other side of the river. Expect your senses to be assaulted by animal droppings along the way, and when you encounter mule parties, quietly step aside so they can pass. From May through September, water is available at small shelters erected by the Park Service. A year-round water source is 4.75 miles down the trail at **Indian Gardens,** a lovely creekside oasis shaded by cottonwoods, where the Havasupai once grew crops. **Plateau Point,** a gently rolling mile past Indian Gardens on the edge of the Inner Gorge, offers excellent river views.

Since the other hikes outlined below finish with an ascent of the Bright Angel, this trip will be described from the bottom up. Along the steep, wide trail from Indian Gardens, you can look forward to two huts, complete with shade, emergency telephones, and (during the summer months) water. But despite the huts, even this easiest of Grand Canyon ascents can be quite exhausting, and in hot weather it should be started before dawn. Your pack should be as light as possible for the climb, which usually takes three hours for a hiker in good condition who begins early enough. Although higher means cooler in the Grand Canyon, the sun's increased strength as the morning wears on more than offsets any advantage gained from elevation.

The trail stays to the east side of the Garden Creek drainage for most of its route. Some prominent formations visible on the ascent are Cheops Pyramid, the Battleship, Brahma Temple, and the Tower of Ra. Through the vertical Redwall formation, the trail consists of 500 feet worth of switchbacks called Jacobs Ladder. Three-Mile Resthouse beckons at the top of these switchbacks, where the Redwall meets Supai formation. At Two-Mile Corner, look up at some light-colored rocks above the trail after a series of long switchbacks in the Supai layer; you may be able to spot a panel of Havasupai pictographs. Past here is Mile-and-a-Half Resthouse, in the Hermit Shale formation, and some tight switchbacks through the Coconino Sandstone layer. Near the end of the ascent, the trail passes through two tunnels: Second Tunnel, in the Toroweap formation, and First Tunnel, in the Kaibab Limestone. Just below is more ancient rock art. At the top is the Bright Angel Lodge, where food and drink are sold.

An alternative to the round-trip Plateau Point hike is a 13-mile trip

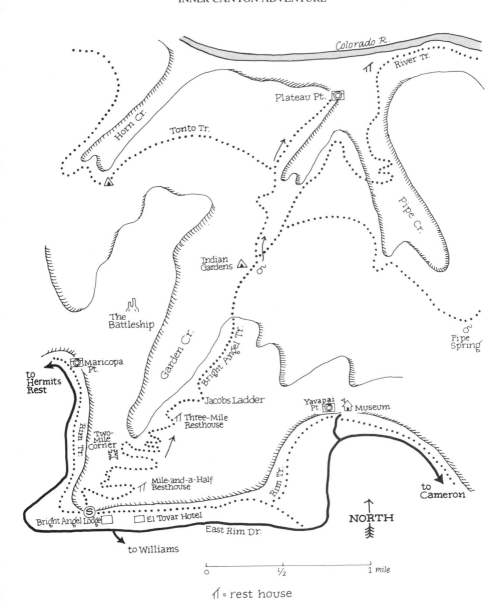

↑ = rest house

from Yaki Point, down the **South Kaibab Trail,** across the Tonto Platform, and up the Bright Angel Trail. (That is the preferred direction for the hike, since the South Kaibab is waterless, and water sources are not so vital on the descent.) To make it a three-day, 16.5-mile walk, camp the first night at Bright Angel Campground on the north side of the river, and spend the second night at Indian Gardens. Reservations are needed for both.

Backpack 2: Hermit Trail to Grand Canyon Village

Distance: 26 miles, one way, including side trip to river
Time: 4 days
Map: USGS topo for Grand Canyon National Park
Difficulty: very strenuous

The **Hermit Trail,** built for tourists by the Santa Fe Railroad Company early in this century as a commercial venture, is by far the easiest of the nonmaintained routes from the rim to the river, and also one of the most beautiful. The hike is a popular one and advance reservations with the backcountry office may be required.

To begin the trip, park your car in back of the Bright Angel Lodge and catch the free shuttle bus to the trailhead at **Hermits Rest,** 8 miles distant and the westernmost stop on the run (see map, p. 209). Take either the first bus in the morning (a hikers' express) or one in the late afternoon, to avoid hiking in the midday sun. You might want to stop at Pima Point, to enjoy a bird's-eye view of most of your route into the canyon.

At Hermits Rest, walk less than 0.25 mile down a short service road toward the rim to the trailhead sign. It is a 7.25-mile hike from here to Hermit Camp, and then another 1.5 miles to the river. Switchback through rocky terrain, bearing right at the intersection with the Waldron Trail and with the trail to the bird-lover's paradise of **Dripping Springs** (at mile 1.75). This trail connects with a difficult, unmaintained route down to the river via Boucher Creek. (Louis Boucher was the hermit for whom the trail was named; headquartered at Dripping Springs, this French Canadian prospected in the canyon for over fifteen years.)

After the trail junctions, descend to Santa Maria Spring, which has water and a small shelter. The trail skirts the eastern edge of Hermit Creek gorge. By now you have entered the Supai formation. Fourmile Spring, noted on the topo map, ran dry many years ago.

The trail switchbacks down to Lookout Point, which offers splendid views of the temples and canyons across the river. Around a bend is a long, gently sloping section of trail. Soon you come to a potentially hazardous area, where rock slides have damaged the trail; follow a cairned route through the rubble. A short distance from the rock slides is the big Redwall descent at mile 5. The steep switchbacks here, on the west side of Cope Butte, are called the Cathedral Stairs. At the bottom of yet another set of switchbacks is the **Tonto Rim** (mile 6) and the junction with the Tonto Trail. Bear left and continue for 1.25 miles until you drop into the creekbed and arrive at **Hermit Camp,** a pleasant, "improved" campground with water and a toilet.

The 1.5-mile hike from Hermit Camp to the **Colorado River** is delightful and unchallenging. This route starts a short distance back up the Hermit Trail and follows the bed of Hermit Creek down to the river. Unless

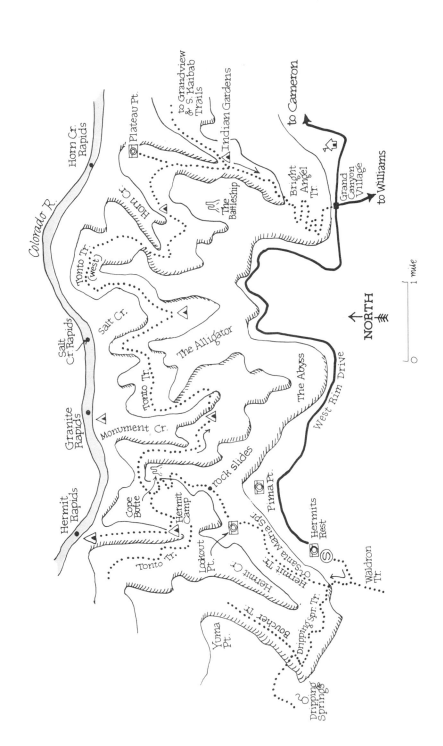

Colorado R.

Horn Cr. Rapids

Salt Cr. Rapids

Granite Rapids

Hermit Rapids

Horn Cr.

Plateau Pt.

to Grandview & S. Kaibab Trails

Indian Gardens

to Cameron

Bright Angel Tr.

The Battleship

Grand Canyon Village

to Williams

Tonto Tr. (west)

Salt Cr.

Tonto Tr.

The Alligator

Monument Cr.

The Abyss

West Rim Drive

NORTH

0   1 mile

rock slides

Cope Butte

Hermit Camp

Pima Pt.

Lookout Pt.

Hermit Cr.

Hermits Rest

Tonto Tr.

Dripping Spr. Tr.

O Santa Maria Spr.

Waldron Tr.

Yuma Pt.

Boucher Tr.

Dripping Springs

A hiker enjoys solitude and unmatched beauty along Tonto Trail, Grand Canyon National Park, Arizona

the year has been particularly dry, you'll probably find little pools along the way. The beach at the river is extremely rocky and not good for swimming, but it's fun to watch rafts negotiate the fierce Hermit Rapids formed by a boulder fan at the creek's mouth.

From Hermit Camp, backtrack to the junction with the Tonto Trail and turn left (east), heading Cope Butte rather precipitously. The trail follows the lip of **Monument Canyon** for some distance before dropping into the drainage about 3.5 miles past Hermit Camp. The scenic beauty of this part of the trip is unexcelled, affording haunting views of the inner gorge. Monument Creek is named after the tall spire that dominates its upper reaches. Excellent campsites are in the main canyon just past this spire, as well as an assured water supply and a (rather exposed) pit toilet. With care, you can reach the river from here and watch boats shoot Granite Rapids.

The Tonto Trail goes past a Sphinx-like formation and out the east arm of Monument Creek. Back on the Tonto Rim, it swings around a formation called The Alligator. Above is The Abyss, a beautiful red amphitheater. Salt Creek, the next major drainage, 3.5 miles past Monument, is a hydra-headed monster that takes a while to circumambulate. Four miles later is the similar Horn Creek system. Reaching the river from either canyon is difficult, but sometimes nearby springs are flowing; check with the ranger on this. About 1.5 miles past Horn Creek the trail forks; drop your pack and hike down the trail to the left for outstanding views of the river from Plateau Point.

Back at the fork, turn the other way and within a mile or so reach the campground at Indian Gardens, where you'll find cottonwoods, fireplaces, toilets, and crowds of people. Most hikers reserve a campsite here in preparation for the arduous climb out of the canyon. Travelers able to afford the accommodations at Phantom Ranch may wish to arrange in advance to sleep and eat there. Others may want to walk across one of the two suspension bridges over the Colorado's inner gorge and spend the night at Bright Angel Camp. This excursion adds about 10 round-trip miles to the hike, and an extra day or two should be allotted for it. It involves joining the **River Trail** in the inner gorge, which connects with the North Kaibab on the other side of the Colorado.

Backpack 3: Grandview Trail to Grand Canyon Village

> **Distance: 36 miles, one way**
> **Time: 4 days**
> **Map: USGS topo for Grand Canyon National Park**
> **Difficulty: very strenuous**

This trip begins at the Grandview Point, an overlook, reached by driving 9 miles on East Rim Drive past its junction with South Entrance Road (see map, p. 212). Only backpackers in excellent condition who have prior Grand Canyon experience should attempt this hike. The trip to Horseshoe Mesa makes a suitable day hike for most others. In the summer months, especially in dry years, hikers must carry 2 gallons (about 16.5 pounds) of water apiece over a 16-mile waterless stretch along the rolling, scrubby Tonto Rim. The rewards of this hardship, however, more than justify it. Solitude is all but guaranteed, and this is surely one of the most impressive sections of the canyon.

Built by Pete Berry, a miner in the late nineteenth century, the un-

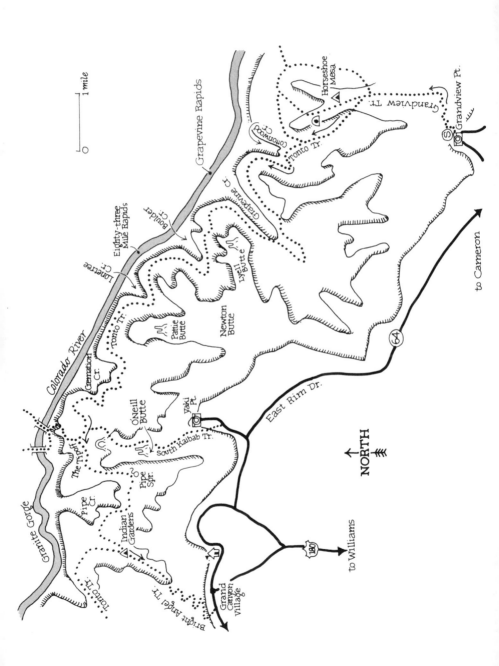

maintained **Grandview Trail** is in fair condition and is not hard to follow. Though steep, it is relatively shady, particularly toward the top. After 3 miles and 2600 vertical feet, it reaches **Horseshoe Mesa** at the start of the Redwall formation, where some abandoned mines are located. Three rocky trails descend from Horseshoe Mesa, cutting through the Redwall and eventually intersecting the Tonto Trail, which winds across the Bright Angel shale formation. Your route is the trail on the left, which heads west toward Cottonwood Creek. (The right-hand trail goes east toward Red Canyon.) Before descending the mesa, however, continue straight on the Grandview Trail past the trail junctions to a short spur trail on your left; it leads to a limestone cave complete with stalactites. Then backtrack to the trail that descends to Cottonwood Creek.

Cottonwood Creek, where you pick up the Tonto Trail, has water and shade, making it a good place to camp. With some effort, you can scramble down to the river both here and at Grapevine Creek, the next drainage to the west. This is another desirable camping spot, for it generally has water in its upper end. Boulder Creek and Lonetree Creek, about 3 miles apart, occasionally contain water, but unless informed otherwise by the backcountry ranger, you should expect to find none between Grapevine Creek and reliable Pipe Spring, about 16 miles distant. You'll therefore have to make a dry camp somewhere on the Tonto Platform. In hot weather, hike this stretch as early as possible in the morning and, after a midday siesta, as late as possible in the evening. There's no shade on the Tonto Rim, so you must seek it in the numerous canyons that the trail skirts. But the walking here is fast, and what you can endure in temperature is amply rewarded by matchless views of formations like Wotans Throne and Zoroaster Temple across the river. Occasionally, you can also peer into the innermost part of the main canyon far below, watching hawks ride the thermals and specklike rafts negotiate the Granite Gorge.

After leaving Grapevine Creek, you head Boulder, Lonetree, and Cremation canyons. **Cremation Canyon** received its name from charred human remains discovered there; cremation evidently was a traditional practice of the Havasupai tribe. The three sizable bays at Cremation Canyon take forever to get around. On the canyon's far side, near an Inner Gorge overlook called the **Tipoff,** the Tonto briefly merges with and then crosses the popular South Kaibab Trail; a natural arch is visible a short distance up the South Kaibab toward the rim. Like its easier neighbor, the Bright Angel Trail (which merges with the Tonto for a few miles after the Tipoff), the South Kaibab is used for mule train access into the canyon.

Eventually the joint Tonto-Bright Angel Trail leads to cool, brushy **Pipe Spring,** a perennial water source in Pipe Canyon. Less than 2 miles from here is Indian Gardens Campground. Plan to spend the night here (advance reservations are required) before tackling the 4.75-mile, 3100-foot climb up the Bright Angel Trail (described above).

DAY 18: WUPATKI AND HOME

- **Contemplating Sinagua ruins**
- **Visiting Sunset Crater**
- **Optional climb of Humphreys Peak**
- **Gas, groceries, showers, and laundry available in Flagstaff**

To start this last day of the travel circuit, drive east 51.5 miles on AZ-64 to Cameron and turn south on US-89. Continue for 20.5 miles, bearing left onto the 36-mile road connecting Wupatki and Sunset Crater national monuments.

The Wupatki–Sunset Crater area was once a cultural meeting-place for the Sinagua, Anasazi, and Cohonina tribes. The national monuments protect close to 2700 Neolithic ruins, a few of which can be visited by the public. Because of the fragility and historical and scientific value of these archaeological sites, the backcountry is closed to all hiking and camping without official permission from the Superintendent.

The first attraction along the northern end of the scenic drive is **Lomaki** ("beautiful house") **Ruin,** a multistory apartment building at the end of a 0.5-mile spur road. Box Canyon Ruins are nearby. A short distance farther down the main loop road, on the right, one can visit **Citadel Ruin,** a relatively large, unexcavated complex. Positioned on a knoll composed of volcanic rock, it grants fine views of the lofty San Francisco Peaks and surrounding countryside. Adjacent to Citadel Ruin is the Nalakihu site (meaning "house standing alone" in the Hopi tongue). At the visitor center, near the southern end of the monument, is the most extensive and interesting cluster, **Wupatki** ("tall house" in Hopi). This magnificent, well-preserved surface site features a large outdoor amphitheater and a smaller, elliptical structure thought to have been a ball court. Ball courts were widely used by Mesoamerican indigenous peoples like the Mayas and Toltecs; the presence of a ball court here attests to the vast reach of those peoples' cultural influence. About 0.25 mile past the visitor center, a 3-mile spur road on the left leads to **Wukoki** ("wide house") **Ruin.** All the above buildings were constructed in the early thirteenth century.

Leaving Wupatki National Monument, the loop road skirts the Kana-a Lava Flow before entering Sunset Crater National Monument. **Sunset Crater,** a black and red cinder cone, was formed almost 1000 years ago. The ash deposited during the volcanic eruption made for improved farming for the area's native peoples, and may have attracted additional immigrants. Although tourists are not allowed to scale the 1000-foot-high cone, they can hike to its base on the very easy, mile-long **Lava Flow Trail,** which includes a stop at a lava tube.

For further information, write to the Superintendent, Wupatki and

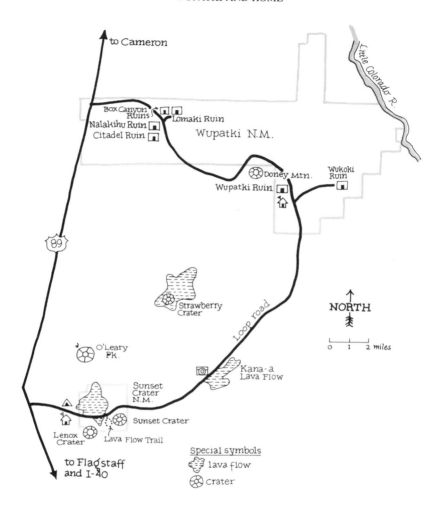

Sunset Crater National Monuments, 2717 North Steves Boulevard, Suite 3, Flagstaff, AZ 86004.

From Sunset Crater, proceed south on US-89 for 12.25 miles to Flagstaff and the highway home. If you can spare another day, consider climbing **Humphreys Peak** (elevation 12,625 feet), a member of the San Francisco chain and the highest mountain in the state. The strenuous, 9-mile round-trip trail begins near the Fairfield Snow Bowl northwest of Flagstaff, off US-180.

Chapter 7

CANYONS LOOP

Utah, Arizona

Inveterate backpackers seeking memorable wilderness adventures would find this loop especially appealing. But it contains enough day-hiking and car exploring to keep everyone else busy, too. Its star attractions are the "big three" of the western Colorado Plateau: Zion, Bryce, and Grand Canyon national parks. The ready availability of various services and facilities also recommends this loop.

DAY 1: ST. GEORGE TO ZION

- **Easy day hikes to pools, springs, and narrows**
- **Camping at Zion National Park**
- **Gas, groceries, showers, and laundry available in St. George**

St. George, population 13,500, makes a good jumping-off point for this loop. Located on I-15, in the extreme southwestern corner of Utah, this gateway community offers services disproportionate to its size. It is an attractive resort town where Brigham Young, the early Mormon leader, liked to spend his winters. (Not his summers, though; at under 3000 feet elevation, St. George can get uncomfortably hot in July and August.)

St. George is about 39 miles from Zion's South Entrance (see map, p. 217). Go north on I-15 to the exit for Hurricane on UT-9, a road that continues through the park. Just past the entrance station, pull into one of the two large campgrounds and find a spot to spend the night—preferably a sheltered spot, to avoid being sandblasted by the gusty canyon winds that regularly start up in the wee hours of the morning. Once this chore is completed, begin your tour of the park.

Zion National Park is Yosemite dressed in red, a crowded (except in winter months) but otherwise unblemished paradise that more than lives up to its name. The dominant rock strata in this 147,000-acre preserve are Navajo sandstone and the Kayenta formation. The park's main road snakes through the bottom of the lush and spectacular canyon carved into the

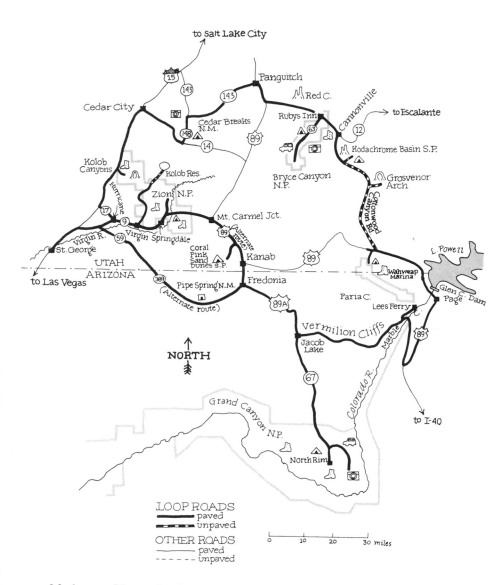

Markagunt Plateau by the North Fork of the **Virgin River,** a tributary of the Colorado. Over 150 miles of trails branch off in every direction, leading to desert waterfalls, hanging gardens, cool pools and grottoes, and dazzling overlooks. Wildlife is varied: Zion's larger mammals include bobcat, mule deer, elk, and fox. Only a portion of the Virgin's East Fork, called Parunuweap ("raging waters" in Ute), is protected within the park, but generations of backpackers have found the lure of this beautiful gorge equally irresistible.

Visitors who enter the park from the south should drive around to the East Entrance, at almost 6000 feet, just for the scenery. The section of UT-9 that takes you there switchbacks up Pine Creek past the Great Arch (really an alcove) to the top of the canyon. It then braves a dark, mile-long tunnel constructed in the 1920s, and winds among cross-bedded sandstone domes. Of these, **Checkerboard Mesa** is the best known. From the parking lot beyond the tunnel departs the easy **Canyon Overlook Trail** (1 mile round-trip); this self-guiding nature trail leads to an aerie above the Great Arch, with dramatic views of the western portion of Zion Canyon.

A possible threat to Zion is a county proposal to build dams upstream on both forks of the Virgin River. Environmentalists warn that such a project would disrupt the park's delicate ecology, by lowering water temperatures and altering stream flows.

Today's recommended itinerary involves a trip on the scenic drive through Zion Canyon (12 miles round-trip), with hiking stops at Weeping Rock, Emerald Pools, and the Gateway to the Narrows—all very popular destinations. Before the day is through, obtain a camping permit for one of tomorrow's backpacking options, the East or West Rim hikes. To back-

Trees silhouetted against Zion National Park's Navajo sandstone domes

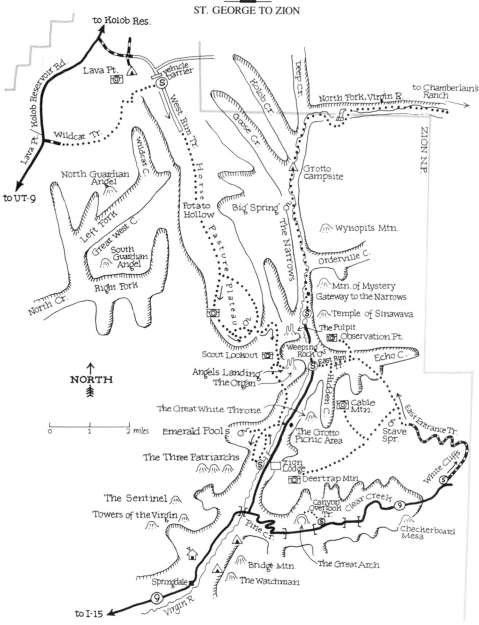

pack either comfortably, you'll need a car shuttle or some equivalent. Consult the rangers at the visitor center for suggestions.

For more information, write to the Superintendent, Zion National Park, Springdale, UT 84767.

Day Hike 1: Emerald Pools

Distance: 2.5 miles, round-trip
Time: up to 3 hours
Map: USGS topo for Zion National Park
Difficulty: very easy to Lower Pool, moderate to Upper Pool

Trails originating from either Zion Lodge or the Grotto Picnic Area lead to two idyllic pools (see map, p. 219). The first of these, **Lower Pool,** is only 0.5 mile from the Zion Lodge. Cross a footbridge over the Virgin River and turn right, following a paved path. At Lower Pool, you will pass under some gossamer waterfalls that drip cool water on your head. The **Upper Pool,** involving a picturesque but somewhat rocky 350-foot ascent, lies 0.5 mile farther on. It rewards you with a small beach, where you can swim and relax. But take care not to injure yourself on the uneven, sometimes slippery terrain. On your descent, look for an alternate 1-mile trail beginning 0.25 mile below Upper Pool on the right for the return to the lodge.

Day Hike 2: Weeping Rock

Distance: 0.5 mile, round-trip
Time: 0.5 hour or less
Map: USGS topo for Zion National Park
Difficulty: easy

This trail to a gushing spring surrounded by hanging gardens begins about 2 miles up the road from Zion Lodge at a designated parking area on the right (see map, p. 219). Initially, the paved route is concurrent with the East Rim Trail (see below), but then it immediately veers off to the left and wends its way over to the cliff that houses the spring, climbing steadily. The water here is unrivaled for purity, having just been filtered through hundreds of feet of sandstone.

Day Hike 3: Gateway to the Narrows

Distance: 2 miles, round-trip
Time: 1.5 hours
Map: USGS topo for Zion National Park
Difficulty: very easy

The walk on this paved, level trail begins from the Temple of Sinawava parking lot at the end of the scenic drive (see map, p. 219). It follows the right bank of the Virgin River as its cliffs progressively close in. This lush gorge teems with life: dark green ferns, babbling springs, and miniature gardens of wildflowers. Most people turn back at a rocky viewpoint beyond which the canyon becomes too constricted to accommodate a trail. But the intrepid continue upstream by wading through the rushing river—a safe practice as long as the water remains fairly shallow and no flash flood danger exists. Walking sticks are recommended. Check at the visitor center or at the trailhead for the posted danger level.

<u>DAYS 2 AND 3:</u> CANYON RIM BACKPACK

- **Hiking Zion's East or West Rim**
- **Camping near a canyon overlook**
- **Gas, groceries, showers, and laundry available in Springdale**

The low-mileage, overnight backpacking alternatives presented below both start on high plateaus and work their way to the edge of Zion's unexcelled canyon. Either is excellent preparation for more ambitious trips to come. You can day-hike portions of these trails starting from the canyon floor, but be warned that the substantial elevation gains make this quite demanding physically. An advantage of the backpack routes is that they are almost all downhill. Backpackers should take about 1.5 gallons of water each in the summer months. Since water availability from springs varies both annually and seasonally, make the appropriate inquiries at the visitor center when you obtain your required camping permit. Arrange for a shuttle, if necessary, at Zion Lodge. Plan to camp in one of the park campgrounds at the conclusion of your hike.

Backpack 1: West Rim Trail

> **Distance: 15.25 miles, one way, including side trip to Angels Landing**
> **Time: 2 days**
> **Map: USGS topo for Zion National Park**
> **Difficulty: moderate, with strenuous climb to Angels Landing**

This magnificent and varied hike to the rim and then floor of Zion Canyon (involving a 3000-foot descent) begins near the Lava Point fire lookout, about an hour's drive north of the Zion Lodge (see map, p. 219). If you are shuttling cars, leave one at the Grotto Picnic Area, where the hike concludes.

To reach the trailhead, drive west through Springdale on UT-9 to the town of Virgin. Turn right (north) onto a spectacularly scenic road, which

White sandstone labyrinth beckons from West Rim Trail, Zion National Park, Utah

climbs into heavy timber toward Kolob Reservoir. At mile 21, turn right onto a dirt road in the direction of the Lava Point Campground and fire tower. Within a mile, three roads intersect. At the junction take the middle road, immediately left of the road to Lava Point. The trailhead, situated just where this bumpy road bends sharply to the left in 1.25 miles, is marked by a register box and a vehicle barrier. In the summer, except after a rainstorm, this road should be passable to most cars.

Follow the jeep road on the other side of the barrier, passing a signed junction with the Wildcat Trail, for several miles through the cool, semi-wooded uplands of **Horse Pasture Plateau.** This is fast, easy walking over level terrain, and before too long the trail veers to the edge of the plateau for a tantalizing preview of Wildcat Canyon. Next the trail descends into Potato Hollow at mile 5, a rather humid, boggy valley that teems with aspens, flowers and wildlife. Then it climbs several hundred feet, heading once again toward the rim of the plateau, which it hugs for the next few miles. Peering into **Great West Canyon** is unforgettable, especially at dawn and sunset. Camp here, at least 0.25 mile off the trail, to wake up to that view: enormous mesas of muscular pink and white rock, often cross-hatched, separated by deep canyons and blanketed on top with tall conifers.

At the loop trail near the end of the plateau, bear right and continue skirting the rim. Where the trail begins its long descent to the floor of the main canyon, at mile 9.5, look for a pit toilet and a sign indicating a spring. From the overlook to the Grotto Picnic Area is 4.75 miles, all downhill (except for the highly recommended side trip to Angels Landing—see below). But because it offers little shade and no water, you should begin this stretch in the morning hours. The scenery is breathtaking, especially after you cross a low slickrock pass into Zion Canyon itself.

Only 2 miles from the conclusion of the trail, Scout Lookout supplies a commanding vantage point on the whole area. But nothing rivals the vistas from **Angels Landing** (elevation 5785 feet). A rather hair-raising trail—1 mile round-trip and very strenuous—climbs steeply to the top of a tall fin that juts out into the middle of the canyon, nearly 1400 feet above the river. You can see the entire canyon at a glance. Although the spur trail has guard rails, its 500-foot climb can be frightening; children must be very closely supervised. Drop your pack before climbing to Angels Landing, bringing only your valuables, camera, water, and a snack.

Returning to the main trail, descend quickly on twenty-one switchbacks (called "Walters Wiggles" after the park's first superintendent) into cool, shady Refrigerator Canyon. At the base of the canyon, about 1500 feet below Angels Landing, the trail emerges into hotter, more open country. Turning right, it parallels the Virgin River the rest of the way. Eventually it crosses a bridge and ends at a parking lot opposite the Grotto Picnic Area.

Backpack 2: East Rim

Distance: 10.5 miles, one way, plus side trips
Time: 2 days
Map: USGS topo for Zion National Park
Difficulty: moderate

This excellent hike, starting high above the deep gorge of the Virgin River and ending at Weeping Rock parking area (see map, p. 219), winds through forested country to the canyon rim and then drops to its floor far below. With an early start, it could be done as a long day trip. When you obtain your permit, check with rangers about water availability.

Drive around to the east entrance station to the start of the **East Entrance Trail.** Just before the entrance station, turn left onto an unpaved road to reach the trailhead. On foot, follow the road up Clear Creek in the

The breathtaking Kolob Canyons section of Zion National Park, Utah

White Cliffs region for a few miles, passing a series of huge pink and white domes. The road climbs through woodlands, eventually turning into a regular foot path. At mile 5.5 is Stave Spring (usually the only water around, and sometimes just a trickle); from here, a level, clearly designated spur trail veers left to **Cable Mountain** (6 extra miles, round-trip) and **Deertrap Mountain** (6.5 extra miles). Camping is prohibited within 0.25 mile of the rim. At Cable Mountain, the remains of a cableworks operation built by a lumber company early in the century are still evident.

Back at the fork where the spur trail originated, turn right. From here it is 5 miles to the bottom of the canyon, 2100 feet below. Pick up the **Echo Canyon Trail** to your left in about 0.25 mile and head northwest through timber in the direction of the rim. Expect some gradual ups and downs. Before reaching the rim, descend rapidly alongside a neatly eroded wash. The view from the rim is panoramic, dominated by Angels Landing and the Organ on the far side of a big U-turn by the river.

The trail now plummets to the canyon floor. Along the way are three spur trails. The first is a 3.5-mile round-trip detour up 850 feet of switchbacks to **Observation Point.** At this first junction, the Echo Canyon Trail merges with the **East Rim Trail.** The second goes to narrow **Hidden Canyon,** suspended almost 1000 feet above the valley. This exhilarating route, up to 3 miles round-trip, clings to a cliff face initially and can therefore be scary in spots, despite protective guard rails. The final spur leads to Weeping Rock, discussed earlier. Water and rest rooms await you at the bottom.

DAYS 4 AND 5: KOLOB CANYONS

- **Eyeballing the Finger Canyons**
- **Journeying to the world's largest arch**
- **Camping along luxuriant La Verkin Creek**
- **Gas, groceries, showers, and laundry available in Springdale and Cedar City**

The dazzling Kolob section of Zion National Park rivals the main Virgin River canyon for natural beauty, yet attracts far fewer visitors. After reprovisioning for two days in Springdale, take UT-9 west to its junction with UT-17. Turn north on UT-17 and follow that road through the small towns of La Verkin and Toquerville until it intersects I-15 in about 27 miles. Go north for about 13 miles to the **Kolob Canyons** exit. A delightful two-day hike to Kolob Arch begins at the Lee Pass trailhead, 4 miles up the Kolob Canyons Road. Obtain a camping permit at the Kolob visitor center. Only about 2 quarts of water per person need to be carried, since supplies are plentiful en route, but must be purified.

On the evening of Day 5, plan to camp in the Dixie National Forest east of Cedar City, where you can resupply, or even at Cedar Breaks Na-

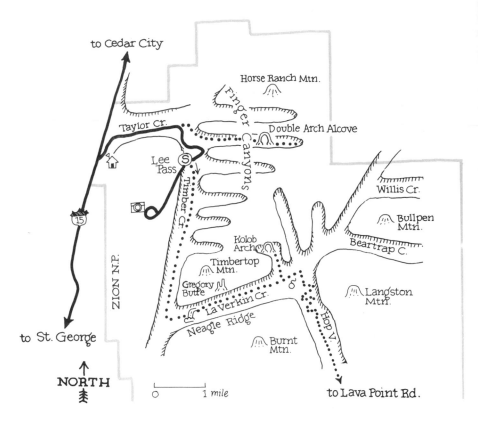

to Cedar City

Horse Ranch Mtn.

Finger Canyons

Taylor Cr.

Double Arch Alcove

Lee Pass

S

Timber Cr.

Willis Cr.

Bullpen Mtn.

Beartrap C.

15

ZION N.P.

Kolob Arch

Timbertop Mtn.

Gregory Butte

La Verkin Cr.

Langston Mtn.

Neagle Ridge

Hop V.

to St. George

Burnt Mtn.

NORTH

0   1 mile

to Lava Point Rd.

tional Monument, since your trip should end fairly early. Drive north on
I-15, then turn right on UT-14 toward the uplands of the national forest.
Cedar Breaks is to the north on UT-148.

Backpack: Kolob Arch

> **Distance: 14 miles, round-trip**
> **Time: 2 days**
> **Map: USGS topo for Zion National Park**
> **Difficulty: moderate**

The trail offers outstanding views of Taylor Creek's **Finger Canyons**
on the rapid 500-foot, 1.25-mile descent to cottonwood-lined Timber
Creek (see map, p. 226). After following the creek for a distance, the trail
climbs to a low saddle above the La Verkin Creek drainage. Met at 4.75
miles, **La Verkin Creek,** a couple hundred feet below, is a rushing stream

with a waterfall and many shallow pools. Purify this water before drinking it. An excellent campsite is at the point where the trail meets the creek. The prominent Navajo sandstone cliffs of Gregory Butte and Neagle Ridge loom on either side; they sit atop the Kayenta formation, through which the stream cuts its channel.

The trail gradually ascends the creek, crossing it several times in the next 1.75 miles. A cool, small grotto to the left of the trail provides spring water. Inaccessible **Kolob Arch** is perched in a cliff at the head of the first side-canyon to the left. At 310 feet across, it is by some measurements the biggest arch in the world. A viewpoint is 0.5 mile up the 2-mile-long side-canyon.

Return to La Verkin Creek and either retrace your steps to the parking lot or take a side trip to Hop Valley overlook or Beartrap Canyon. By continuing through **Hop Valley,** you could hook up via a jeep road to the West Rim Trail and ultimately end up in the main section of Zion Park, for a wonderful five-day hike.

One final word: The well-watered Kolòb region attracts not only hikers but also rattlers, black widow spiders, deerflies, porcupines, red ants, and other creatures you might rather avoid. Long pants will protect you from insect pests, caution and common sense from the others. Wear heavy boots if you have them.

Before you leave the area, drive the short distance from Lee Pass to the end of the paved road, for an outstanding view of the territory you've just traveled.

DAY 6: CEDAR BREAKS TO BRYCE CANYON

- **A car and foot tour of majestic Cedar Breaks**
- **A drive through the national forest**
- **Camping at Bryce Canyon National Park**
- **Gas, groceries, showers, and laundry available in Rubys Inn**

Begin this day in **Cedar Breaks National Monument,** located east off UT-14, 23 miles from Cedar City. Once called "the circle of painted cliffs" by local Indians, Cedar Breaks sits high in the evergreens of the Markagunt Plateau at 10,000 feet, so you'll need a sweater here even in summer. The scenic road through the monument stays close to the lip of a 2500-foot-deep amphitheater, providing extravagant views of the pastel badlands (or "breaks") below. Very similar to lower-lying Bryce Canyon, Cedar Breaks features rows of tall Claron formation spires marching down a limestone cliff.

Overlooks and short trails enable you to explore at closer range the national monument's orange, pink, and white spires, alpine glades blanketed

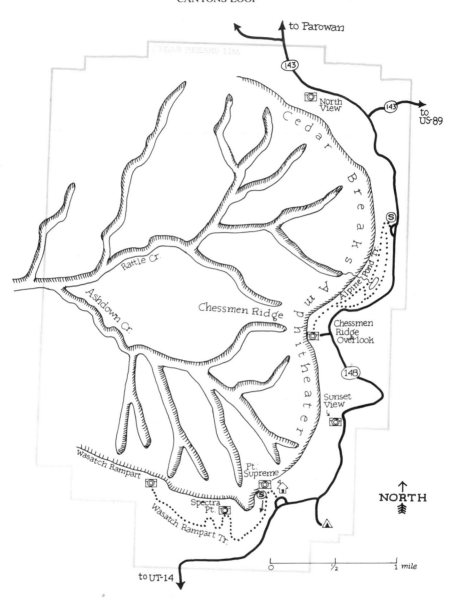

with wildflowers, and bristlecone pine trees, the oldest living things (see map, p. 228). The very short and very easy **Bristlecone Pine Trail** extends from Chessmen Ridge Overlook to the canyon rim. The 2-mile round-trip (1.5-hour) **Alpine Pond Trail,** beginning at Chessmen Ridge Overlook, parallels the highway, looping past a pond on upper Rattle Creek and back through forested country. The more scenic **Wasatch Rampart Trail** from the visitor center (4 miles, round-trip; allow 2 hours) follows the edge of the amphitheater to Spectra Point and beyond, with a 600-foot elevation change. These last two trails are rated easy and moderate, respectively.

For further information, write to the Superintendent, Zion National Park, Springdale, UT 84767.

Continue north on UT-148 to its junction with UT-143. Turn right (east) and proceed 26 miles, passing a fishing lake to the small town of Panguitch. Turn south on US-89 and continue driving for 7 miles until UT-12 comes in on the left. Take UT-12 east past incredible **Red Canyon,** another Bryce look-alike, where three short trails wind past limestone spires and hoodoos. At Rubys Inn, 13 miles past Red Canyon, go south on UT-63 to arrive at the entrance station to **Bryce Canyon National Park.**

After securing a campsite, take the 17-mile scenic drive or hike the Navajo/Queens Garden Loop that begins at Sunset Point overlook. This 3-mile trail is described under Day 8 of Chapter 2, Desert Rivers Loop.

DAYS 7 AND 8: DAY HIKER'S SPECIAL

- **Trails—your pick**
- **Camping at Bryce Canyon**
- **Gas, groceries, showers, and laundry available in Rubys Inn**

For these two days, follow the itinerary and various options given for Days 8 and 9 of Chapter 2, the Desert Rivers Loop.

DAY 9: BRYCE CANYON TO PARIA RIVER

- **Sand pipes and a double arch**
- **Practical hassles**
- **Camping at Paria Canyon trailhead**
- **Gas, groceries, showers, and laundry available in Page**

Today will be schizophrenic, with the morning devoted to sightseeing and the afternoon to finalizing plans for a multiday hike in Paria Canyon. An early start is advisable, since car shuttling or some equivalent will probably be necessary. From Bryce Canyon, go right (southeast) on UT-12 to Cannonville. Turn south on the 46.5-mile Cottonwood Canyon Road, which crosses the Paria River and extends to US-89. Inquire locally about the condition of this road, paved only as far as the turnoff for Kodachrome Basin State Park; if it is not in good shape, detour back to Red Canyon to pick up US-89 south, which eventually gets you to the Paria entrance station.

About 4.5 miles past the Paria River crossing is a spur road on the left to **Kodachrome Basin State Park.** Don't forgo a side trip to this area, with its wonderful "sand pipes." (See Day 10 of Chapter 2, the Desert Rivers Loop.) Another 10 miles south of here on the Cottonwood Canyon Road is a 1-mile spur road to **Grosvenor Arch,** to the left. This heavenly white arch, with its unusual double opening, derives its name from the founder of the National Geographic Society.

Continue on the main road in a southerly direction, entering even more beautiful country as you approach the **Cockscomb,** a long monocline. At the junction with US-89, turn right, descending a grade, and look for a sign for **Paria Canyon–Vermilion Cliffs Wilderness Area,** about 3 miles down on the left. After deciding which backpacking trip to take in Paria Canyon (the alternatives are described under Days 10 through 13, below), go to the ranger station and get a hiking permit and information about shuttling cars or arranging rides.

Whichever hiking option you select, buy supplies in Page (population 4900) today, fill canteens, take care of car shuttles, and camp at your trailhead (either White House, two miles past the ranger station, or Wire Pass, near the head of Buckskin Gulch). Where you camp at the end of your trip (and where you leave a car if you need to set up a shuttle) will depend on where you exit Paria Canyon, Lees Ferry or White House. Convenient campgrounds exist at Lees Ferry and Wahweap Marina (which has showers and laundry facilities).

Because of the potentially life-endangering flash flood threat, visitors must register at the Paria Ranger Station or the Kanab BLM office, from which up-to-date weather information can be obtained. For the same reason, you can hike Paria Canyon only in the downstream (northwest to southeast) direction. To see the entire canyon, you must leave cars at both ends of the trip, White House and Lees Ferry, or arrange for a shuttle. Contact the BLM office in Kanab for a current list of shuttle operators. An alternative is to hike past the narrows, spend a night in the canyon, and double back. Or, you can take the Buckskin Gulch route, starting at Wire Pass, walking down Buckskin Gulch, and either turning up Paria toward the White House trailhead or going down Paria to Lees Ferry.

To shuttle a car to Lees Ferry (a 145-mile round-trip drive from White House), cross the Colorado River just outside Page at Glen Canyon Dam. Pick up US-89A and recross the river on the Navajo Bridge over **Marble Canyon.** Look for the turnoff to Lees Ferry on the right. A small outpost on the river, Lees Ferry is where Grand Canyon float trips originate. A pioneer named John Doyle Lee began a ferry service across the Colorado River here in the late nineteenth century. The town, located 6 miles off the main highway under the Vermilion Cliffs, has a gas station as well as a primitive campground. You can leave your car at the long-term parking lot between the Paria River bridge and the boat launch ramp.

If you decide on the Buckskin Gulch option, leave one car where your trip will end (either White House Campground or Lees Ferry). Then drive to the Wire Pass Trailhead, traveling west on US-89 past the Paria ranger station for 5 miles, until the road cuts through the Cockscomb. Immediately on the other side of this formation, the highway crosses a dry wash and bends to the right. On the far side of the wash, turn left onto House Rock Valley Road. Continue on this somewhat bumpy dirt road for 8 miles, paralleling the Cockscomb, which is to your left. A sign marks the small parking area on the right, opposite a point of entry into the Buckskin drainage called Wire Pass.

DAYS 10 THROUGH 13: PARIA RIVER

- **Splashing through 1600-foot-deep canyons**
- **Experiencing unrivaled narrows**
- **Visiting major arches**
- **Camping along the riverbank**

The wild and spectacular canyon of the Paria (puh-REE-uh) River, a tributary of the Colorado, represents the ultimate in desert hiking. Except in its lower reaches, the canyon, whose name means "muddy water" in Paiute, is relatively shady and well watered. The terrain is either level or downhill. And the scenery is splendid: enormous sandstone alcoves streaked with desert varnish, hanging gardens of orchids and ferns, deep

Hikers rest in the "windows" of Paria Canyon, Utah

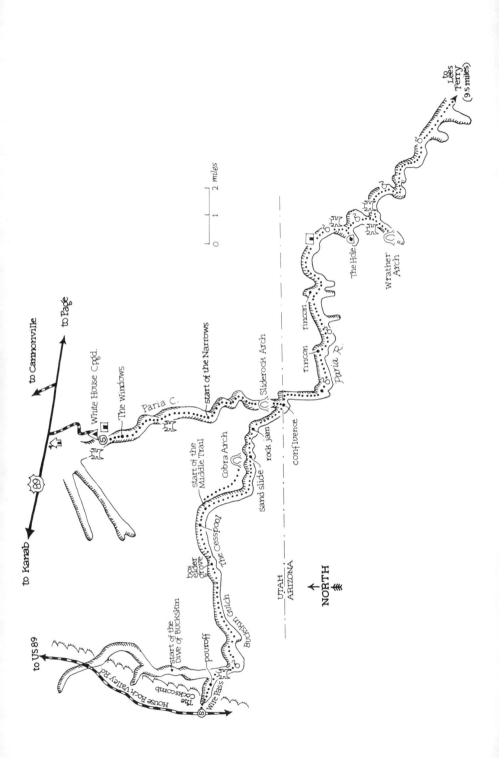

to Cannonville

to Page

to Kanab

to US 89

89

The Cockscomb

House Rock Valley Rd.

White House Cpgd.

The Windows

Paria C.

start of the Narrows

start of the Middle Trail

Cobra Arch

Sliderock Arch

sand slide

rock jam

confluence

Paria R.

rincon

rincon

The Hole

Wrather Arch

to Lees Ferry (9.5 miles)

0   1   2 miles

UTAH
ARIZONA

NORTH

start of the Dive of Buckskin

pouroff

Wire Pass

Buckskin Gulch

box elder grove

The Cesspool

pools, and impressive Sliderock and Wrather arches. Be advised, however, that the canyon is very busy, with some competition for campsites, during May and June and over the Easter holiday.

Paria owes much of its renown to its narrows section, where canyon walls hundreds of feet high close in—and where it would be extremely hazardous to get caught in a flash flood. Late spring and early summer are the best times for undertaking the hike. Since you will be splashing around in ankle-deep water, wear old sneakers or boots and bring several pairs of socks.

For additional information, contact the Bureau of Land Management, Kanab Resource Area Office, 318 North 1st East, Kanab, UT 84741.

Backpack 1: Paria Canyon

> **Distance: 37.25 miles, one way, plus side trips**
> **Time: 4 days**
> **Maps: USGS quads for Paria, Paria Plateau, and Lees**
> **Ferry**
> **Difficulty: moderate**

From the White House campground, the trail leads immediately into the **Paria Canyon,** remaining in its bed the next 28.25 miles (see map, p. 232). Except in very dry years, there should be ample water most of the way, but make sure you have a 1-gallon carrying capacity for the last 11 miles, where no springs exist.

About 1.5 miles downstream you pass a series of low "windows" in the Navajo sandstone cliff. The canyon walls quickly deepen and close in until you reach the narrows section about 4 miles from the trailhead. **Sliderock Arch** spans the canyon 2.5 miles past this point. The darkest narrows continue for 5 miles; don't camp here because of the flash flood danger. Some good high campsites are to the left, just before you enter the narrows, and as the canyon slowly widens beyond the narrowest sections, you can camp on a sandbar on the left at mile 9.75, opposite a freshwater seep. Another campsite is located on a high bench to your right about 0.25 mile up the lower Paria's only significant tributary, Buckskin Gulch. The confluence of Buckskin and Paria occurs 0.5 mile below Sliderock Arch, at mile 7.

A particularly beautiful portion of the hike in the main canyon begins 10 miles from the White House trailhead. The canyon widens somewhat and becomes lusher. You may find shallow pools to splash around in, and you can fill canteens at several reliable springs (at miles 12.25, 20.5, 22, and 25.5). Noteworthy physical features in this part of the canyon include the Hole, an intimate grotto with a keyhole-like opening at mile 19.25, and

Wrather Arch, 0.75 mile up a short side-canyon to the right at mile 20.5. This enormous arch ranks among the Southwest's ten largest, at approximately 200 feet across.

The last spring is located on the left canyon wall at mile 25.5. Here you should stock up for the waterless 11.75-mile stretch to come. Check with the ranger in advance to make sure this spring is flowing. From here on, the trail touches base only occasionally with the river, which by now has cut through many layers of sandstone in rapid succession: the Navajo, Kayenta (starting below Wrather Canyon), Moenave, and Chinle (uranium-bearing) formations. About 2.5 miles beyond the last spring, you face some tedious boulder-hopping in the streambed. Where the river takes a sharp bend to the left, scramble up the slope on the right to pick up a faint trail that will usually stay fairly high above the river. The canyon becomes very wide for its last 10 miles as it crosses open desert. There's not much shade here, so do this stretch very early in the morning, or else split it in half between evening and morning. But the walking is fast and easy. At mile 35 you cross into **Glen Canyon National Recreation Area,** and before you know it you're within sight of the Colorado River confluence at Lees Ferry.

Backpack 2: Buckskin Gulch

> **Distance: 20.5 miles one way to White House; 43.5 miles
> one way to Lees Ferry**
> **Time: 3 to 5 days**
> **Maps: USGS quads for Paria, Paria Plateau, and Lees
> Ferry**
> **Difficulty: moderate**

To hike **Buckskin Gulch** (see map, p. 232), walk 1.75 miles down Wire Pass through a very narrow slot, doing some scrambling and possibly removing your pack once or twice to negotiate pour-offs. Turn right at the intersection with Buckskin, a canyon gouged out of Navajo sandstone. From here it is 11.75 miles to the confluence with the Paria River.

Buckskin Gulch is very narrow (only 3 feet wide in spots) and gothically spooky, much more so than is Paria Canyon. The gulch's silty water is not recommended for drinking. Near Buckskin's junction with Paria, the 400-foot-high canyon walls come so close together that it is almost possible to touch both sides at the same time. Buckskin's height and extreme narrowness prevent much light from penetrating, creating a sort of natural refrigerator. Repeated flash floods have scoured and sculpted the smooth canyon walls into gargoyle-like shapes and left piles of driftwood jammed between rocks.

Paria Canyon's Sliderock Arch, Utah/Arizona, forms natural tunnel (Lew Hinchman photo)

About 8 miles down Buckskin from the Wire Pass Trail is the **Middle Trail**, a route leading to the canyon's north rim near Cobra Arch. Sometimes there are stagnant pools just upstream from the start of this route. Plan to climb out of the canyon here, camping on top. This will allow you to ascertain that weather conditions are favorable before continuing your exploration of the narrows. You may need to do some careful maneuvering to descend a 30-foot rock jam located 10 miles below the Wire Pass junction; ropes are recommended. In another 1.75 miles Buckskin Gulch converges with the Paria River canyon. You can turn left (north) and hike up Paria to the White House trailhead, or take the main canyon southeast to Lees Ferry. In either case, safety dictates that you exit the narrows before establishing your next camp.

DAY 14: PARIA TO NORTH RIM, GRAND CANYON

- **Swimming in Lake Powell**
- **Sight-seeing and camping on the North Rim**
- **Gas, groceries, showers, and laundry available in Page or North Rim**

After reclaiming any vehicle left at your trailhead, a morning swim in Lake Powell at **Wahweap Marina** might hit the spot. Then leave Wahweap and cross Glen Canyon Dam at the mouth of Lake Powell. Detour into Page to stock up on supplies. Continue south on US-89 to its junction with US-89A and turn right, recrossing the river on the Navajo Bridge. For the next 45 miles or so, the Vermilion Cliffs will be on your right.

Past here, as the road climbs, you enter Kaibab National Forest and continue on for 11.5 miles to Jacob Lake. Here you pick up AZ-67 south, which crosses the Kaibab Plateau to **Grand Canyon National Park** (44 miles). The plateau, most of it in the 8000-foot range, is a heavily wooded region characterized by Ponderosa pines and quaking aspens, small lakes, and lupine-covered meadows. When you arrive at the **North Rim,** look for a campsite; if all sites are occupied, there may still be room in the national forest campgrounds to the north. Better still, to avoid disappointment, reserve a spot in advance in the North Rim campground through the Ticketron Parks Department, P.O. Box 62429, Virginia Beach, VA 23462, (900) 370-5566.

Dedicate the remainder of the day to the scenic overlooks and nature trails (such as the one to Bright Angel Point) around Grand Canyon Lodge at the road's end. A general discussion of Grand Canyon National Park is in Chapter 6, the Painted Desert Loop, Days 13 through 17. The North Rim, however, differs significantly from the South. It receives fewer than a tenth as many visitors; it ranges between 1000 feet and 1500 feet higher in altitude (making it cooler and wetter); it is considerably farther away from the Colorado River; and it remains open only from mid-May to mid-October, closing during the winter months because of substantial snow accumulation.

Sometime today, stop by the backcountry desk and obtain a permit to hike the Thunder River Trail on Days 16 through 19, if you wish to take that trip. The ranger may advise against it, unless you have some prior experience on the Kaibab or Bright Angel trails. In that case, save this hike for your next Southwestern excursion, and day-hike or backpack instead on the North Kaibab Trail. For all Grand Canyon trails, it is prudent to write long in advance for reservations.

DAY 15: NORTH RIM DAY HIKE

- **Hiking and driving to matchless overlooks**
- **Picnicking on the rim**
- **Camping at the North Rim campground or at Monument Point**
- **Gas, groceries, showers, and laundry available in North Rim**

Today's hike should help acclimate you to the higher elevations of the North Rim. Although its mileage is long, the trail is in good shape and can be walked quickly.

Day Hike: Widforss Trail

Distance: 10 miles, round-trip
Time: 5 or 6 hours
Map: USGS topo for Grand Canyon National Park
Difficulty: easy

This popular day hike, mainly through forested country, culminates at Widforss Point. To reach the trailhead from Grand Canyon Lodge (see map, p. 238), drive north about 2.75 miles on AZ-67 to the dirt road across the highway from the head of the North Kaibab Trail. Turn left here and continue 1 mile to the parking lot. The trail begins by ascending a steep slope. In the next 5 miles, it first remains near the rim of the Transept, and then heads west into a more wooded area, where it dips into a couple of shallow drainages. Pack a lunch to eat at the picnic area near **Widforss Point,** the breathtaking perch at the end of the trail, where you'll enjoy

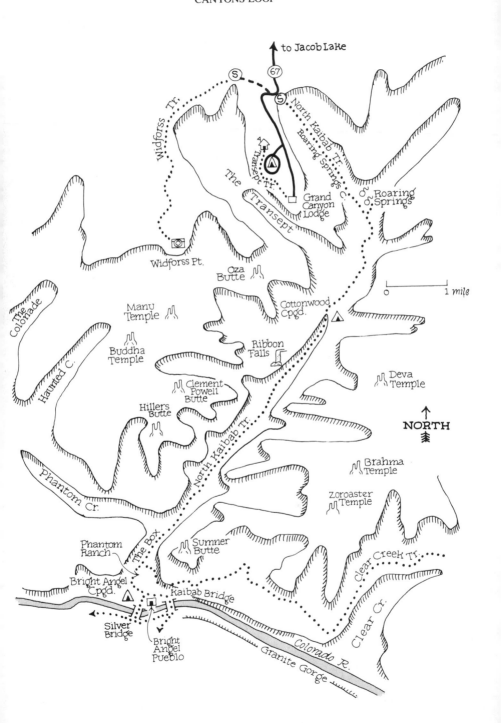

to Jacob Lake

67

S

S

Widforss Tr.

North Kaibab Tr.

Roaring Springs

The Transept

Transept Tr.

Grand Canyon Lodge

Roaring Springs

Widforss Pt.

Oza Butte

Cottonwood Cpgd.

1 mile

Manu Temple

Ribbon Falls

Deva Temple

The Colonade

Haunted C.

Buddha Temple

Clement Powell Butte

Hillers Butte

North Kaibab Tr.

NORTH

Brahma Temple

Zoroaster Temple

Phantom Cr.

The Box

Sumner Butte

Clear Creek Tr.

Phantom Ranch

Bright Angel Cpgd.

Kaibab Bridge

Clear Cr.

Silver Bridge

Bright Angel Pueblo

Colorado R.

Granite Gorge

The forested North Rim overlooks desert lands below

views into Haunted Canyon and The Colonade in the foreground and the South Rim in the distance. A fire some years ago scarred the overlook, but by now little evidence should remain.

At the conclusion of the hike, purchase four days' worth of supplies for the upcoming backpacking adventure. Those who plan to hike the North Kaibab Trail (see below, Days 16 through 19, Backpack 1) can spend the night in the campground and the rest of the day visiting Point Imperial and Cape Royal. The road leading to these overlooks branches off AZ-67 just north of its junction with the Widforss spur. Turn eastward here and continue for 5.5 miles, arriving at a fork. **Point Imperial** (the highest Grand Canyon overlook) is 2.75 miles down the left fork, while a right turn takes you to **Cape Royal,** 14.5 miles distant. Although farther, Cape Royal—considered the supreme Grand Canyon vantage point by some—deserves your attention. A very easy trail, 0.75-mile round-trip, leads to an arch called **Angels Window** and treats you to staggering views of Wotans Throne, Vishnu Temple, and Freya Castle.

Those who have secured permits for the Thunder River backpacking trip (see below, Days 16 through 19, Backpack 2) should fill their water bottles before driving to the trailhead. Water will be needed for tonight's campsite at Monument Point (1 gallon per person), for drinking and caching along the trail (2 gallons apiece), and for storage in the car (0.5 gallon apiece). Autumn and spring hikers will probably not need so large a carrying capacity; the rangers will advise you on this.

From Grand Canyon Lodge, allow about 2 hours to drive to **Monument Point,** where your trail begins. A road map for the Kaibab National Forest (North unit), put out by the Department of Agriculture's Forest Service, proves helpful in locating the trailhead. Drive to the North Rim entrance gate and proceed north for about 4 miles. Just before reaching Kaibab Lodge, turn left on Forest Service (FS) 422, a gravel road. Continue for about 20 miles, then turn left on FS-425, where there should be a sign indicating that this is the way to Monument Point, still about 10 miles distant. When you pass Big Saddle Camp, take FS-292A, a short dirt road that deteriorates markedly in its last mile or so. However, even a regular passenger car should be able to make it all the way to the rim, where other vehicles will doubtless be parked. The view from Monument Point at sunset and sunrise amply repays you for whatever this campsite may lack in privacy and amenities.

DAYS 16 THROUGH 19: INNER CANYON BACKPACK

- **Showering in the spray of a desert waterfall**
- **Watching rafts tackle the Colorado's thrilling rapids**
- **Camping at expansive overlooks or along a cool stream**
- **Gas and groceries available in Kanab; showers available at Coral Pink Sand Dunes State Park**

The above list applies equally to the North Kaibab and Thunder River trips. Whichever you choose, you're in store for the experience of a lifetime.

At the conclusion of your hike, your first priorities probably will be to eat and shower. For this, you can backtrack to North Rim village or else drive north on AZ-67 to Jacob Lake and pick up US-89A north to Fredonia and Kanab, on either side of the state line. Just up the road is **Coral Pink Sand Dunes State Park,** the camping spot for Day 19.

To enter the state park, drive north from Kanab for 15 miles and turn left at a signed junction. The park, in which movies have been filmed, offers beautiful views of the surrounding desert as well as sand of an unusual hue. For obvious reasons, it receives heavy weekend use from all-terrain vehicle aficionados. An interpretive nature trail extends into the dunes on a boardwalk.

Backpack 1: North Kaibab Trail

Distance: 28.5 miles, round-trip
Time: 4 days
Map: USGS topo for Grand Canyon National Park
Difficulty: strenuous

Drive 2.25 miles north of Grand Canyon Lodge to the parking area for the **North Kaibab Trail** (see map, p. 238), one of the two maintained trails that descend into the inner canyon. Shared by hikers and mule trains, it is steep only for its first 4.75 miles, which follow Roaring Springs Canyon to its junction with Bright Angel Creek below the Redwall cliffs. The springs here emerge from caves deep within the earth; to visit them, take a short spur trail to the left (0.5 mile, round-trip). Plan to spend your first and third nights at Cottonwood Campground, 6.75 miles below the rim. Water scarcity does not pose a major problem here, since there is water at both campgrounds and along Bright Angel Creek between miles 5.25 and 8, but be sure to use purifying equipment.

About 1.25 miles past the campground is a cairned spur trail on the right to **Ribbon Falls** (0.5 mile, round-trip). Between here and Bright Angel Campground (mile 14) near Phantom Ranch and the river, the canyon narrows considerably, especially near Phantom Canyon on the right (mile 12.5) and the Clear Creek trailhead (mile 13) on the left. After you establish a campsite, walk down to the footbridge over the Colorado's **Inner Gorge.** Look for Bright Angel Pueblo, an Anasazi site named by John Wesley Powell, just off the trail about 100 yards north of the bridge. On your third day out, you'll have to begin the tedious climb back toward the rim. Get an early start in order to beat the heat.

Backpack 2: Bill Hall and Thunder River Trails

Distance: 25 or more miles, round-trip
Time: 4 days
Map: USGS topo for Grand Canyon National Park
Difficulty: very strenuous

Thunder River—a cold and beautiful waterfall emerging from 3000-foot-deep Thunder Cave, in a limestone formation just below the Redwall—feeds into Tapeats Creek, which can be followed to its junction with the Colorado River. The unmaintained route to this wonder is very scenic but dry and dusty, with little shade and no water for the first 9 miles.

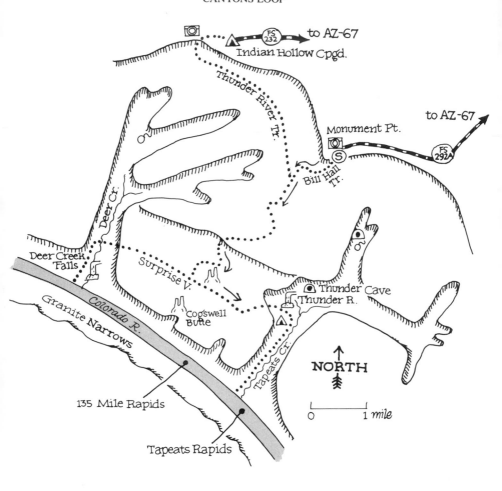

Make a carefully hidden water cache along the way in preparation for the tiring 5800-foot ascent from the river.

The **Bill Hall Trail,** a shortcut into the Thunder River country, starts at the edge of the parking lot (see map, p. 242, and Day 15 for driving directions). The route plunges through the Kaibab limestone, then contours around at the top of the Coconino formation, a prominent band of white sandstone. Heading in a westerly direction, you eventually come to a break in the Coconino, where the trail drops precipitously down a talus slope dotted with pinyons and junipers. After you intersect the **Thunder River Trail** on the Esplanade, coming from Indian Hollow Campground a few miles to the west, things level out. Walk on bare rock for a while, passing a boulder garden to your left, before reaching the notch where the trail, following a rockslide, begins its 1000-foot Redwall descent. At the bottom is

Surprise Valley. Here the trail veers to the right of a large butte, and comes to an important fork. The left fork, which is the one you want, leads to Tapeats Creek; the right goes into the Deer Creek drainage.

At the lip of Surprise Valley, the trail again switchbacks steeply down to **Thunder River**—said to be the world's shortest—where you can pause to enjoy an ice-cold drink (or shower!) from deep within the earth. Many cottonwoods near the spring offer shade. From Surprise Valley to the designated campsites along **Tapeats Creek** is an additional descent of 1000 feet, paralleling Thunder River. Under normal conditions, you should have little trouble continuing all the way to the Colorado along Tapeats Creek, though you may have to ford the cold, fast stream once or twice (a dangerous practice at high water levels). The western bank is generally steeper and more hazardous, though for the last plunge to the river, you will want to locate the established route on that side of the creek.

At the river there's a nice sandy beach where you can watch the float trips run Tapeats Rapids. If the river level permits, turn right at this point and pick your way through the Granite Narrows for about 2 miles to the exquisitely sculpted canyon of **Deer Creek,** a favorite (in fact, overused) stop-over for river runners. For about the first 0.5 mile negotiate a boulder field along the river before ascending a rudimentary trail to some rocky terraces. Once you reach Deer Creek Canyon, you must walk upstream on some hair-raising paths until the route intersects the creek about 0.75 mile above the Colorado. Bring along a lot of water if you attempt this. The safer and surer way to visit Deer Creek is from the trail in Surprise Valley. A large waterfall at Deer Creek's mouth cascades 100 feet down to the river. Beyond the falls lies the creek's much-photographed narrows section; the canyon then becomes less interesting as it opens up.

Split the climb back to the rim into two segments, especially if your visit occurs during the summer months. In the evening after an early dinner, you can hike to the top of the Redwall, finishing the arduous ascent to Monument Point after breaking camp in the cool of the morning.

DAY 20: ON THE ROAD AGAIN?

- **Heading home**
- **Or hiking the Zion Narrows**
- **Gas, groceries, showers, and laundry available in St. George**

For most of you, it's time to head home. You can complete the circuit by driving back to St. George by either of two routes. One of these doubles back through Fredonia to pick up AZ-389 west, which turns into UT-59 across the border. This route goes through the Kaibab Paiute Reservation, allowing a stop at **Pipe Spring National Monument,** a Mormon pioneer historic site. It also passes by Colorado City, where polygamy is practiced even to this day. The alternative is to take US-89 north to UT-9, then east through Zion Park to I-15; if you haven't yet seen the region around the park's East Entrance, you owe it to yourself to select this option!

For hardy hikers with a few more days to spare, a piece of unfinished business remains: the Virgin River Narrows trip. If this prospect intrigues you, check with the rangers to see whether the canyon is open to foot traffic. This decision is generally made on a day-to-day basis.

Optional Backpack: Virgin River Narrows

> **Distance: 16 miles, one way**
> **Time: 1 very long day (12 hours or more) or preferably 2 days**
> **Map: USGS topo for Zion National Park**
> **Difficulty: very strenuous at high water levels**

In the minds of many backpackers, the **Virgin River Narrows** trip (see map, p. 219) offers the ultimate in canyon-stream hiking. The river snakes through unbelievably beautiful country. Awe-inspiring red, black, and gold sandstone cliffs rise 2000 feet above the narrow chasm, which is lined with cottonwoods and box elders for much of the way. This largely trackless wilderness features grottoes, fern gardens, pools, and some incomparable side-canyons. It is one of the most memorable of backcountry trips in all respects, but it should not be underestimated. Especially in high-water periods, the walking can be extremely fatiguing and difficult, since the river gets faster and deeper as it descends. Most of the way the river tends to be fairly shallow, perhaps 6 inches or less, but in a few spots it is sometimes necessary to swim across pools that, at high water, may be up to 50 feet long. Because of the cool water temperatures and minimal sun penetration, hikers can develop hypothermia here even in midsummer. In fact, the canyon is closed to hiking most of the year partly for this very reason, but also because of the threat of flash-flooding. The best times to attempt the Narrows trip are late June, late September, and early October. Old boots are the recommended footwear.

The Park Service requires that all hikers (even day hikers) register at the visitor center the day before starting out. The rangers will provide a list of recommended supplies (a walking stick, for example, is an absolute must) as well as current information about the weather forecast and the swiftness, depth, and temperature of the river. Some people complete the entire hike in one very long day. And this plan does have certain advan-

Backpackers must wade through Virgin Narrows' shadowed gorge, Zion National Park, Utah

tages. It means that you can travel light, carrying only a daypack containing a full canteen (the river water, because of upstream grazing, is not potable without treatment), your lunch, a camera, and extra clothes to change into if you get wet. Moreover, it reduces the danger you will be caught unawares by a flash flood. On the other hand, completing the hike in one day will make you feel rushed and quite likely exhausted.

To get the greatest possible enjoyment from the trip, obtain permission to spend a night in the canyon. Then line each compartment of your backpack with heavy duty plastic garbage bags and put your sleeping bag, also wrapped in plastic, inside the pack's main compartment. A pack lined in this manner will float, should it become necessary for you to swim; you can just push it along in front of you.

Most hikers stay in one of the park campgrounds the night before the trip and arise before dawn in preparation for the 1- or 1.5-hour drive to the trailhead. Because this is a one-way hike, you will need to set up a car shuttle (with one car left in the Temple of Sinawava parking lot), or hire an authorized driver through T. W. Recreational Services, which operates out of Zion Lodge, to take you out to Chamberlain's Ranch, where the hike begins.

On UT-9, drive through the park 2.5 miles past the East Entrance, where an unpaved road will branch off to the left. Take this road for about 18 miles (there will be some very fine views), until you cross a wooden bridge over the North Fork of the Virgin River. Turn left here and proceed 0.5 mile to the gate of the ranch, where you must sign in at the register box. Drive 0.5 mile past the gate (the road has some bad spots) to reach the parking lot.

On foot, follow the dirt road across the river and continue on it for a few miles. The canyon here is wide and shallow, and the walking easy. You pass a small cabin on your left at mile 1.5 as the river winds through hillier country. Where the road crosses the river again and starts to fade out, drop several feet down into the canyon and walk in the streambed. From here, you'll be descending all the way, but the 1300-foot elevation loss to the Temple of Sinawava area is barely perceptible.

For the first half of your hike, from Chamberlain Ranch to Deep Creek at about mile 8, the river should be relatively shallow. The sheer canyon walls grow progressively higher and closer together. About a mile before Deep Creek you reach a very narrow, bankless section where you probably cannot avoid wading, and also a falls which you can skirt on the left side. **Deep Creek,** which comes in at an angle from the right (northwest), serves as a good landmark. It carries a lot of water, making the river considerably colder, deeper, and swifter. From here on you will be in water much if not most of the time, and good campsites on gravel bars above the high water mark become scarce. Within the next 2 miles, two other tributaries—**Kolob** and **Goose creeks**—also join the river on your right, and one good camping spot called the Grotto is not quite halfway between them. These creeks are easy to miss because their mouths are so much smaller than that of Deep Creek.

It is impossible, however, to fail to recognize **Big Spring** on the right at mile 11, an extremely lush and beautiful spot where you can refill your canteens. Below this point, the true narrows begin, and camping is forbidden because of the flash-flood hazard. Here the going may become very rough, since you must cross and recross the deepening river countless times over slippery rocks. These cobbles often aren't visible below the water's surface, so twisted or sprained ankles are a real possibility here. Your walking stick will prove indispensable along this obstacle course.

Between Big Spring and **Orderville Canyon** (a large but often waterless tributary entering from the left at mile 13), there may be a few chest-high pools that require you to swim. Around the mouth of Orderville you start to meet day hikers coming up from the ''Gateway to the Narrows'' trail. At mile 15, pick up this paved, 1-mile trail, which returns you to your car at the Temple of Sinawava parking lot.

FURTHER READING

Edward Abbey, *Desert Solitaire* (Ballantine, 1968). A polemical memoir of the author's seasons as a ranger in Arches National Monument. Indispensable.

Edward Abbey and Philip Hyde, *Slickrock* (Peregrine Smith, 1987). A writer's and photographer's gorgeous love poem to the high desert.

Stewart Aitchison, *A Guide to Exploring Oak Creek and the Sedona Area* (RNM, 1989). With color photos.

Douglas and Barbara Anderson, *Chaco: Center of a Culture* (Southwest Parks and Monuments Association, 1981). Longtime residents of the Navajo Reservation, the authors weave a fascinating account of Chaco's natural and human history.

Douglas and Barbara Anderson and Charles Supplee, *Canyon de Chelly: The Story Behind the Scenery* (KC Publications, 1988). Part of a handsome, inexpensive series of introductions to the national parks and monuments of the region.

Fletcher Anderson and Ann Hopkinson, *Rivers of the Southwest: A Boater's Guide* (Pruett, 1987). A blow-by-blow account of raft, canoe, or kayak travel on the region's major rivers, including the Colorado, Green, Rio Grande, and San Juan.

John Annerino, *Outdoors in Arizona: A Guide to Hiking and Backpacking* (Arizona Highways, 1987). Most of this book, with its lavish color photographs, concerns desert and mountain wilderness areas outside the Colorado Plateau. Will whet your appetite for hiking throughout this magnificent state.

Donald Baars, *The Colorado Plateau: A Geologic History* (University of New Mexico, 1983). The title says it all; one of the authoritative works in its field.

Fran Barnes, *Canyon Country Arches and Bridges* (Canyon Country, 1987). Definitive treatment of the formation, measurement, and discovery of natural spans in the Four Corners region.

Fran Barnes, *Canyon Country Hiking and Natural History* (Wasatch, 1977). A complete and highly informative guide to routes and trails in southeastern Utah. Barnes, based in Moab, has also published a number of excellent books about exploring the area by 4-wheel drive vehicle; these are also replete with hiking ideas.

Fran Barnes and Michaelene Pendelton, *Canyon Country Prehistoric Indians* (Wasatch, 1979). Southwestern archaeology for beginners, with clear discussions of the Anasazi and Fremont cultures.

Joseph Bauman, Jr., *Stone House Lands* (University of Utah, 1987). Geology and history of the San Rafael Swell.

Jack Bickers, *Canyon Country Off-Road Vehicle Trails: Maze Area* (Canyon Country Publications, 1988). A thorough introduction to this remote and fascinating area, written by a born explorer who has pioneered many jeep trails, discovering arches, pools, and other natural wonders.

Jack Bickers, *The Labyrinth Rims* (4-WD Trailguides, 1989). Detailed discussions of sixty accesses to Green River overlooks. Numerous hiking ideas area included.

Eric Bjornstad, *Desert Rock* (Chockstone, 1988). Route and rock information for climbers.

Thomas Brereton and James Dunaway, *Exploring the Backcountry of Zion National Park* (Zion Natural History Association, 1988). Off-trail routes for experienced hikers.

Dee Brown, *Bury My Heart at Wounded Knee* (Washington Square Press, 1984). A sad and shocking account of how several Native American tribes, including the Utes and Navajo, were massacred, expropriated, or dispirited in the nineteenth century. Highly recommended.

Harvey Butchart, *Grand Canyon Treks,* I, II, and III (La Siesta, 1970, 1975, and 1984). The classic works on Grand Canyon hiking and route-finding by a retired professor whose exploits and accomplishments are almost legendary. His estimated times for completing hikes, however, are notoriously optimistic.

Robert Casey, *Journey to the High Southwest* (Globe Pequot, 1988). This half-guidebook, half-memoir is exhaustively researched; besides its historical and geographical material, it includes motel and restaurant recommendations and proves especially useful for car touring.

Natt Dodge, *Flowers of the Southwest Deserts* (Southwest Parks and Monuments Association, 1985). A guide to identification; nicely illustrated.

Natt Dodge, *Poisonous Dwellers of the Desert* (Sundance, 1976). No-nonsense examination of the habits of various creepy crawlers, and the preferred methods for treating bites and stings.

Francis Elmore, *Shrubs and Trees of the Southwest Uplands* (Southwest Parks and Monuments Association, 1976). Plant identification made easy, with beautiful pen-and-ink illustrations.

Colin Fletcher, *The Man Who Walked Through Time* (Vintage, 1971). An account of the author's solo hike from the old westernmost to the old easternmost boundary of Grand Canyon National Park. In a similar trip, Fletcher hiked the length of Death Valley.

Dave Ganci, *Desert Hiking* (Wilderness, 1987). A comprehensive introduction to all the mechanics of preparing for desert excursions.

Dave Ganci, *Hiking the Southwest* (Sierra Club, 1983). Brief descriptions of hundreds of routes and trails in Arizona, New Mexico, and west Texas; a goldmine of trip possibilities.

Paul Geerling, *Down the Grand Staircase* (Westwater, 1981). A primer of Southwestern geology.

Bruce Grubbs and Stewart Aitchison, *The Hiker's Guide to Arizona* (Falcon, 1987). Describes sixty desert and mountain hikes in the Grand Canyon State.

Dave Hall, ed., *The Hiker's Guide to Utah* (Falcon, 1982). Thorough descriptions of sixty hikes from all parts of this incomparable state.

Dorothy Hoard, *A Guide to Bandelier National Monument* (Los Alamos Historical Society, 1983). Complete historical and trail information, with gorgeous maps and illustrations.

FURTHER READING

Michael Kelsey, *Canyon Hiking Guide to the Colorado Plateau* (Kelsey, 1986). Photos, maps, thumbnail trip sketches, and information on rock strata for 117 Southwestern canyons—he's hiked them all! Valuable for experienced backpackers.

Michael Kelsey, *Hiking and Exploring the Paria River* (Kelsey, 1987). Includes Bryce Canyon, which is part of the Paria drainage.

Michael Kelsey and Dee Ann Finken, *Hiking Utah's San Rafael Swell* (Kelsey, 1990). A comprehensive guide to this wonderful but little-known region; incorporates historical material.

Joseph Wood Krutch, *The Desert Year* (W. Sloane, 1952). A naturalist's insights and observations concerning the desert ecosystem.

Joseph Wood Krutch, *The Voice of the Desert* (W. Sloane, 1971). More of the same. Focuses on the Sonoran desert of southern Arizona.

Rudi Lambrechtse, *Hiking the Escalante* (Wasatch, 1985). A useful Baedecker containing information on a beautiful tributary of the Colorado and all its major side-canyons.

Patricia Nelson Limerick, *Desert Passages: Encounters with American Deserts* (University of New Mexico, 1985). Reviews the extraordinary experiences of several articulate desert lovers, including Edward Abbey and Joseph Wood Krutch.

Bob Lineback, compiler, *Hiking in Zion National Park* (Zion Natural History Association, 1988). A guide to all the park's trails.

James MacMahon, *Deserts: Audubon Society Nature Guide* (Knopf, 1985). Field guide to identification of plants and animals, with color photos.

David Mazel, *Arizona Trails: 100 Hikes in Canyons and Sierra* (Wilderness, 1985). Most of this book focuses on desert mountains, but it also includes very careful and detailed descriptions of popular Grand Canyon routes.

Gary Nichols, *River Runners' Guide to Utah and Adjacent Areas* (University of Utah, 1986). Covers all major waterways in its area.

David Noble, *Ancient Ruins of the Southwest* (Northland, 1981). Anasazi, Fremont, Sinagua, and other prehistoric ruins are photographed and discussed in this well-written and handsome volume. Highly recommended.

John Wesley Powell, *The Exploration of the Colorado River and Its Canyons* (Dover, 1961). The classic nineteenth-century journal written by the captain of the first expedition down the Green and Colorado rivers.

Marc Reisner, *Cadillac Desert* (Viking Penguin, 1986). A caustic study of the fiscally irresponsible and environmentally disastrous attempts by government, in conjunction with ranching and agribusiness interests, to "make over the West in the image of Illinois" by subduing its mighty rivers. Mesmerizing reading; essential.

Ward Roylance, *Seeing Capitol Reef* (Wasatch, 1979). A thorough treatment complete with road logs to interpret scenic attractions, written by a long-time environmental activist.

Rob Schultheis, *The Hidden West* (Random House, 1982). A beautifully crafted memoir concerning the author's travels in the deserts of the United States and Mexico. Schultheis has published numerous articles about the Southwest in national magazines.

Sierra Club, *The Sierra Club Guides to the National Parks: Desert Southwest* (Stewart, Tabori Chang, 1984). Lavishly illustrated handbook on the history, geology, trails, and scenic delights of eleven national parks.

Sharon Spangler, *On Foot in the Grand Canyon* (Pruett, 1986). Memoir of the author's backpacking trips throughout the park.

Wallace Stegner, *Beyond the Hundredth Meridian* (Houghton Mifflin, 1954). Outstanding history of Major Powell's expeditions and his subsequent career as a Washington reformer and bureaucratic empire-builder.

William Stokes, *Scenes of the Plateau Lands and How They Came to Be* (Publishers, 1969). Layman's handbook of southwestern topography.

Tully Stroud, *The Bryce Canyon Auto and Hiking Guide* (Bryce Canyon Natural History Association, 1983). A slim volume with capsule trail and overlook descriptions, color photographs, and discussions of park history and geology.

Tom Till, *Utah: Magnificent Wilderness* (Westcliffe, 1989). These desert and mountain images by one of the nation's premier landscape photographers are as magnificent as the state itself.

Bill Weir, *Arizona Traveler's Handbook* (Moon, 1987). Commendably thorough coverage of all corners and aspects of the state.

Bill Weir, *Utah Handbook* (Moon, 1988). An all-inclusive, up-to-date travel guide. Bring us more!

Stephen Whitney, *A Field Guide to the Grand Canyon* (Quill, 1982). Covers flora, fauna, and geology, as well as hiking possibilities.

Terry Tempest Williams and John Telford, *Coyote's Canyon* (Gibbs Smith, 1989). A beautifully crafted appreciation of the Colorado Plateau.

Ann Zwinger, *Run, River, Run: A Naturalist's Journey Down One of the Great Rivers of the American West* (University of Arizona, 1975). The observations of an articulate and perceptive woman who traveled the length of the Green River from its source in Wyoming's Wind River Range to its confluence with the Colorado in the heart of Canyonlands National Park.

Ann Zwinger, *Wind in the Rock* (Harper & Row, 1978). A naturalist's exploration of Grand Gulch and some of the other ruin-studded tributaries of the San Juan River.

INDEX

About the author:

Sandra Hinchman grew up in New York State, and her first experience backpacking in the Southwest ended in blisters, sunburn, heat exhaustion, and muscle cramps. The unusual beauty of the area, however, convinced her to try again, and for over a decade Hinchman has considered the Southwest her true home. She wrote this guide so that others might profit from her experiences. She is currently an associate professor of the Department of Government at St. Lawrence University in New York, but she returns to the Southwest whenever possible.